THE WORLD'S GREAT BATTLESHIPS

THE WORLD'S GREAT BATTLESHIPS

FROM THE MIDDLE AGES TO THE PRESENT

ROBERT JACKSON

BROWN BOOKS

Published by
Brown Books Ltd
Bradley's Close
74–77 White Lion Street
London N1 9PF

ISBN 1-897884-60-5

Editor: *Matthew Tanner*
Design: *www.stylus-design.com*
Picture Research: *Tony Moore*

Printed in The Czech Republic
60329

Picture credits:
Aerospace: 92-93, Imperial War Museum: 60,
National Maritime Museum: 25, Popperfoto:21, Robert Hunt Library: 14, 91, 100,
TRH: 6, 8, 10-11, 16 (Orbis Publishing), 20, 24-25 (US Navy), 30, 33 (US Navy), 36 (US Navy),
37 (US Navy), 39 (US Navy), 40, 45, 46-47 (US Navy), 50-51 (Orbis Publishing), 52 (Orbis Publishing),
54 (Orbis Publishing), 57, 62-63 (Orbis Publishing), 65(t), 65(b), 66(US Navy), 68-69 (Orbis Publishing),
70-71, 76 (t) (US Navy), 76-77 (National Archives), 79, 80(US Navy), 82, 83(Orbis Publishing), 84(US Navy),
86, 90(US Navy), 94 (IWM), 95 (IWM), 96-97 (IWM), 98 (IWM), 104, 105 (IWM), 108 (IWM),
109 (IWM), 110, 112(US Navy), 114 (US Navy), 115 (US Navy), 117 (US Navy),
118 (US Navy), 119 (US Navy), 122-123 (US Navy), 124 (IWM),
126-127 (US National Archive), 128 (US Navy),
130 (US Navy), 133 (b), 136-137 (US Navy),
138-139 (US Navy), 140 (b) (US Navy),
141 (t&b) (US Navy), 142 (US Navy)

Artwork credits
Istituto Geografico de Agostini: 9, 11, 12, 13, 15, 17, 19, 22-23, 26-27, 28, 29, 31, 32, 34-35, 38 (t&b),
41, 42-43, 44, 46 (b), 48-49, 50, 53, 55, 56, 58-59, 62 (t), 67, 71, 72, 73,
74-75, 78, 81, 85, 87, 88-89, 97 (t), 99, 101, 103, 106-107, 111,
113, 116, 120-121, 124-125 (t), 131, 132, 133 (t),
134-135, 135 (b), 140

Contents

CHAPTER ONE

Mighty Wooden Walls

The concept of the battleship was born in the sixteenth century, as European rulers began to appreciate the importance of ships that were able to dominate naval battles with their firepower. But these new ships were more than floating batteries – they were symbols of their country's power and wealth. Elegantly decorated, at full sail they were an awesome sight to behold.

The very word 'battleship' evokes a picture of power, and of grace too, of a mighty warship battling its way through a heavy sea. But the word itself is comparatively modern; in the days of sail a capital ship was referred to as a 'Man of War', or 'Ship of the Line'.

To find out where the evolution of the battleship began we must return to the 16th century, and in particular to the reign of Henry VIII (1509–1547), who arguably was the first naval planner to envisage a purpose-built, heavily-armed warship capable of outfighting all others. Henry's naval planning was spurred by the activities of one of his main rivals, James IV of Scotland, who already had several powerful warships at his disposal when Henry succeeded to the throne in 1509. From his father, Henry inherited a small fleet headed by two large carracks (ocean-going merchantmen distinguished by a high superstructure fore and aft) called the *Regent* and *Sovereign*. Henry ordered the latter to be rebuilt and provided with a strengthened hull, presumably to carry new and heavier guns.

Left: Arguably the most famous British warship of all time, HMS *Victory* was a typical example of a 'first-rater'. Here she is in 1890, decorated for Trafalgar Day.

Above: Henry VIII's *Henri Grâce à Dieu* was huge for her day. Her main innovation was the heavy gun, mounted on the lower deck and fired through ports in the ship's side.

Over the next few years other large ships were built, the foremost of which were the *Mary Rose*, *Peter Pomegranate* and *Henri Grâce à Dieu*. The latter, also known as the 'Great Harry', was the mightiest warship afloat; displacing 1016 tonnes (1000 tons) she was commissioned as a replacement for the *Regent*, lost in action in 1512 during a fight with the French, and was launched in 1514.

GUNPORTS

One thing that Henry VIII inherited from his father was a sound basis of naval gunnery. From the start of his reign Henry VII had employed French and Spanish gun-founders, and by 1496 they were producing wrought iron guns and iron shot. The first attempt to cast iron guns in England was made in 1508, and by 1510 breech loaders with separate chambers were being successfully cast. A year later Henry VIII established a foundry at Hounsditch, London, one of its principal tasks being to produce guns to arm his fleet. The first ship known to have been designed to carry guns on a gun deck above the orlop (the lowest deck of a ship with three or more decks) was the *Mary Rose*. The idea of firing guns through ports cut in the side of the ship was developed sometime between 1505 and 1509. The *Mary Rose* almost certainly had lidded gun ports from the beginning, and so marked a revolution in warship design. The idea, though, was not new; the credit for inventing gun ports probably belongs to a Frenchman called Descharges who had come up with the idea about 10 years earlier.

By June 1514, after a period of war with France that had seen his large warships in action on several occasions, Henry had a fleet of 30 ships, nine of which had been built since 1512. Significantly, the navy was now operating independently of the army, and was supported by new dockyards and storehouses. For the first time, an efficient naval logistics system was in place, and the fleet was maintained in fighting trim, the larger ships being repaired and renovated on a regular basis.

In October 1515 another formidable fighting ship joined the fleet. Known officially as the *Princess Mary* – or sometimes the *Mary Imperial* – she was popularly called the 'Great Galley', and according to contemporary accounts she carried over 200 guns. Main propulsion was provided by 120 oars, but she also had four masts. She remained in service as a galleasse (the term for a hybrid oared warship with sails) until 1536, when she was rebuilt as a pure sailing ship and renamed the *Great Bark*.

A further outbreak of hostilities with France in 1522–5 saw renewed cross-Channel raiding by Henry's warships. For the next few years Henry was more preoccupied with his private life and war against Scotland than with maritime affairs, but in 1545 full-scale war with France again erupted, and in July French warships made a massive incursion into the Solent almost unopposed, the main body of the English fleet being confined to Portsmouth because of adverse winds. During this incident, on 19 July, the *Mary Rose* – which had been rebuilt in 1536 – foundered and sank with the loss of her captain, Sir George Carew, and about 500 soldiers and seamen. The French claimed to have sunk her, but the real reason was overloading, which had brought her gun deck too close to the waterline. A strong gust of wind caused her to heel over and water gushed in through her gun ports, which were open ready for action.

Henry VIII died on 28 January 1547, six months after peace was finally concluded with France. He left behind him a fleet and the means to sustain it, but it had no regular body of officers and men. There was a nucleus of so-called 'standing officers' – gunners, boatswains and carpenters – who maintained the ships

Below: Also known as the 'Great Harry,' the *Henri Grâce à Dieu* was commissioned to replace the *Regent*, lost in action in 1512. She was launched in 1514.

HENRI GRÂCE À DIEU
Armament: 21 heavy bronze cannon, 130 iron cannon
Displacement: 1016 tonnes (1000 tons) (approx)
Length: unknown
Beam: unknown
Propulsion: sail
Speed: 4 knots (approx)
Crew: 350 (approx)

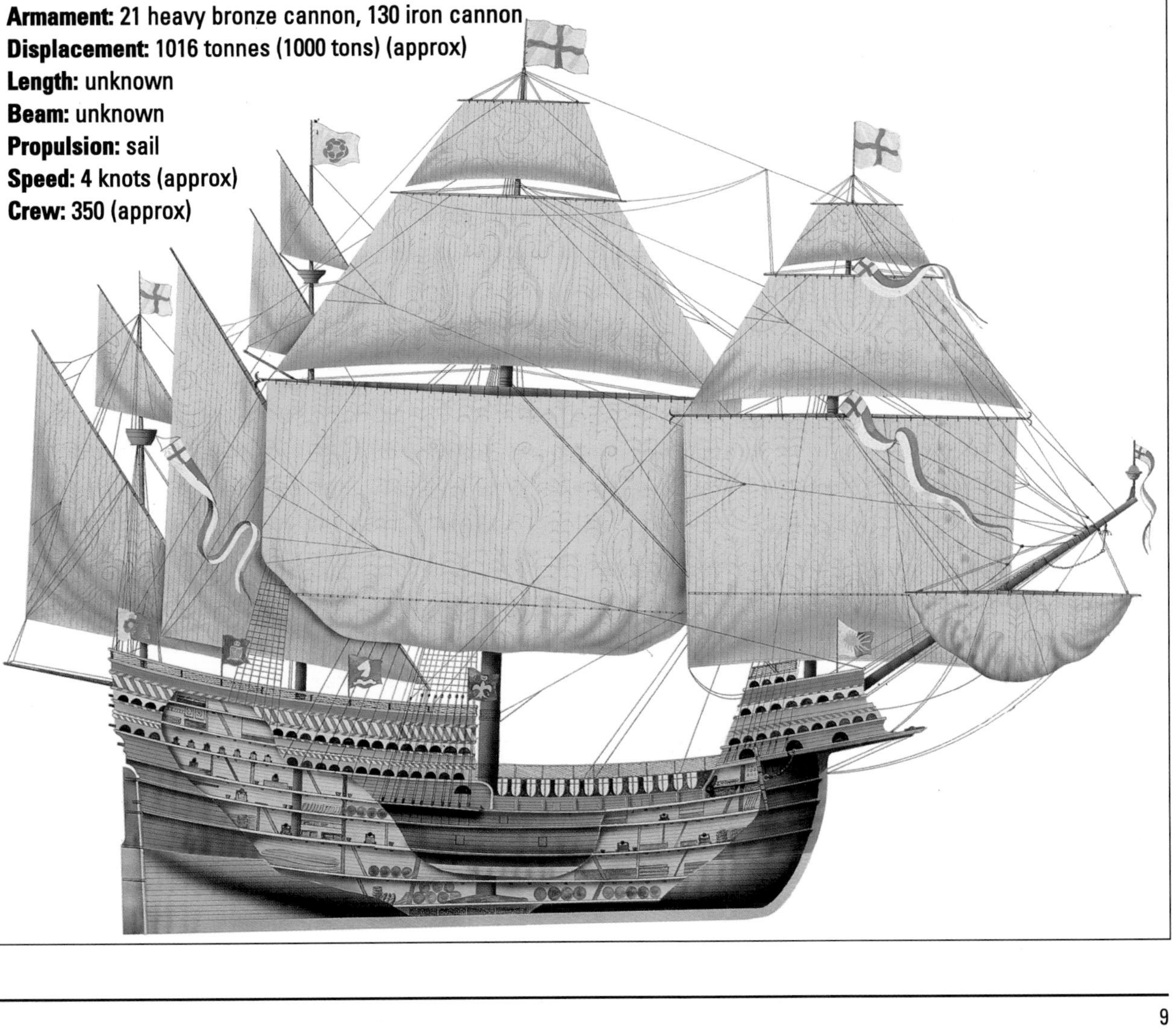

Above: Henry VIII was the true architect of British naval power. He assembled a large war fleet, seen here under review in Portsmouth harbour.

when they were laid up, and they would be joined by the ship's master, sailing master, cook and purser as individual ships were about to be commissioned. The seamen themselves were recruited as the occasion demanded; many, but by no means all, were recruited forcibly.

THE SPANISH ARMADA

It was during the reign of Henry's daughter, Elizabeth I, that England's navy faced its sternest test. In the 1580s Philip II of Spain launched what the Spaniards called the 'Enterprise of England'. First, the English fleet would be destroyed, and then a large expeditionary force, brought partly from Spain by the ships of the Spanish Armada (the name means simply 'fleet') and partly from the Netherlands, would land on the shores of England. The target date for the invasion was set as August 1587.

Elizabeth knew of the invasion plans, and authorised the expansion of her navy. Eleven new ships were completed in 1586 and two more in 1587; they included the *Vanguard*, the *Rainbow* and the *Ark Royal*, each over 406 tonnes (400 tons). She also instructed her 'gentleman adventurer', Sir Francis Drake – already notorious for his piratical activities against Spanish merchant shipping – to launch what amounted to a pre-emptive attack on the Spanish fleet. Assembling a force of 23 ships, Drake accordingly attacked the Spanish harbour of Cadiz on 19 April 1587, destroying or capturing 24 Spanish vessels, together with large quantities of stores and equipment. For several months Spanish warships scoured the ocean for Drake's elusive squadron before returning home in October 1587, their ships weather-beaten, their supplies exhausted and their crews stricken by disease – with Drake long since back in England.

This and other factors delayed the sailing of the Armada for the best part of a year, and had it not been for the energy and efficiency of its commander, the Duke of Medina Sidonia, it would probably never have sailed at all. The Duke eventually had 130 ships at his disposal, but only about 30 were properly armed warships, and only six in the entire fleet carried more than 40 guns, which at that time was the normal level for any English ship of more than 254 tonnes (250 tons). Moreover, many of the guns were old, were not designed for use on board ship, and were manned by soldiers with no experience of sea warfare.

The English, meanwhile, had been mobilising their fleet since the beginning of 1588, having realised that

Drake's attack on Cadiz had merely postponed the planned invasion, not prevented it. All the maritime resources of the nation were mustered, and by mid-summer 1588 the Lord Admiral, Lord Howard of Effingham, had 197 ships at his disposal. Of these, 34 were the queen's own ships; a further 53 smaller vessels were 'taken up' for service and paid for by the queen; and another 23, financed in a similar manner, were under the command of Lord Henry Seymour. The rest of the fleet was provided by private contribution; for example, 30 were provided and paid for by the City of London, and 34 more – commanded by Drake – were furnished by individual nobles and wealthy merchants.

During the early months of 1588 the ships of the fleet were ordered by Lord Howard (on Drake's advice) to concentrate on Plymouth. The assembly took some time, and it was fortunate for the English that the Armada had suffered further misfortune, hav-

Below: The *Ark Royal*, Lord Howard of Effingham's flagship during the Battle of the Spanish Armada. She had originally been commissioned for Sir Walter Raleigh.

ARK ROYAL
Armament: 54 iron cannon (approx)
Displacement: 813 tonnes (800 tons)
Length: 88.7m (291ft)
Beam: 13.1m (43ft)
Propulsion: sail
Speed: 7 knots (approx)
Crew: 300 (approx)

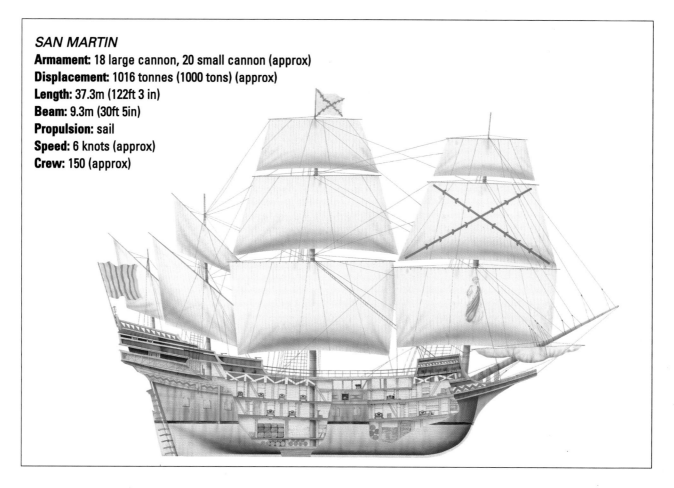

SAN MARTIN
Armament: 18 large cannon, 20 small cannon (approx)
Displacement: 1016 tonnes (1000 tons) (approx)
Length: 37.3m (122ft 3 in)
Beam: 9.3m (30ft 5in)
Propulsion: sail
Speed: 6 knots (approx)
Crew: 150 (approx)

Above: The massive *San Martin*, flagship of the armada that sailed to pave the way for an invasion of England in 1588. Only 67 of the 130 ships returned safely to Spain.

ing been scattered by a southwesterly gale a couple of weeks after it left Lisbon, on 18 May.

Adverse winds also frustrated an attempt by Howard to attack the Armada at Corunna, where its ships had sought shelter. The English fleet returned to Plymouth, its provisions exhausted and many of its ships in need of repair, on 12 July, and it was still there when the Spanish were sighted off the Lizard. Hurriedly preparing for sea, the English captains managed to sail out of Plymouth Sound against the adverse wind, and on 20 July, in thick, drizzly weather, the two fleets made contact.

At this point the Armada was sailing in a formation that had the main fighting strength and the troopships in the centre and two wings trailing to form the characteristic crescent shape of a galley fleet in battle order. To open the battle, Lord Howard sent his pinnace the *Disdain* forward to fire a single shot by way of a challenge, then he led his squadron to attack the seaward wing of the Armada while Drake's squadron attacked the other. Sweeping round the two wings, where the best Spanish fighting ships were positioned, they raked them with continuous fire, and although this did not do a great deal of damage the Spaniards suffered two serious losses. Firstly, the *Nuestra Señora del Rosario* lost her bowsprit and foremast in a collision, and then the *San Salvador* was badly damaged by a powder explosion. The *Rosario* and *San Salvador* were later captured, the former by Francis Drake.

For the next three days, Wednesday to Friday, the two fleets moved slowly up the Channel before very light breezes, and Saturday morning found them off the Isle of Wight, where there was more heavy fighting. The threat of a possible landing on the Solent was averted by an attack on the seaward wing of the Spanish fleet, forcing it to alter course out to sea, but the crisis of the battle was still to come. The Armada, still intact and undefeated, was now approaching the Netherlands, where the Spanish army under the Duke of Parma was waiting for it.

Medina Sidonia now chose to abandon his original orders, which were to embark Parma's army from Flanders – an operation that would have been impossible in any case, as the Spaniards lacked the flat-bottomed craft necessary to cross the shallow waters of the Flanders Banks. Instead, the Spanish admiral anchored off Calais, where he received the unwelcome news that Parma's army would not be ready to embark for another week. This left Medina Sidonia in a dangerous position, with his ships in an exposed anchorage and around 140 English vessels anchored close to windward. Nevertheless, Parma was only 30 miles away at Dunkirk, and the English commanders, unaware of the delay, believed that his army might arrive at any moment. At all costs, the Armada had to be broken, and quickly.

On the night of Sunday 28 July the English launched eight small fireships at the Spaniards. Two were grappled and towed aside, but the rest menaced the Spanish ships, which cut or slipped their cables and stood out to sea. Only Medina Sidonia's flagship and four other vessels retained a semblance of cohesion during the manoeuvre; the rest were scattered, their formation broken.

Howard's ships, upwind and to seaward, now closed in on the Spaniards like terriers, approaching to 'within half a musket shot' – about 45m (150ft) – to pound the enemy with their heavy guns. For nine hours the battle went on, until the English ships ran out of powder and shot. One Spanish ship, the *Maria Juan*, was sunk; two more were driven onto the shoals and taken by the Dutch; and many others were damaged more or less seriously. The damage sustained by the English ships was negligible.

It says much for the courage and discipline of the Spaniards that they succeeded in restoring a fighting formation. But the weather was now worsening, and the Armada was being driven inexorably towards the Zealand Banks. Then, early on Tuesday 30 July, the wind suddenly backed, enabling the fleet to stand out into the North Sea. The English continued to follow close behind, despite their lack of ammunition, speculating as to which friendly port the Spaniards might be making for.

Indeed, Medina Sidonia might easily have decided to head for Hamburg, Denmark, Norway or Scotland; instead, he opted for the long and dangerous route home around the north of Scotland. On 2 August, past the latitude of the Firth of Forth, the English at last abandoned their pursuit of the battered Armada, which struggled on to face the autumn gales of the North Atlantic. Sixty-seven ships reached Spain, with many men dead or dying. Some captains, despite dire warnings, took a gamble and sought refuge on the shores of Ireland, where almost all were drowned or

Below: The *Sovereign of the Seas*, commissioned by King Charles I in 1637, was the biggest fighting vessel ever built in England up to that time. She served for many years.

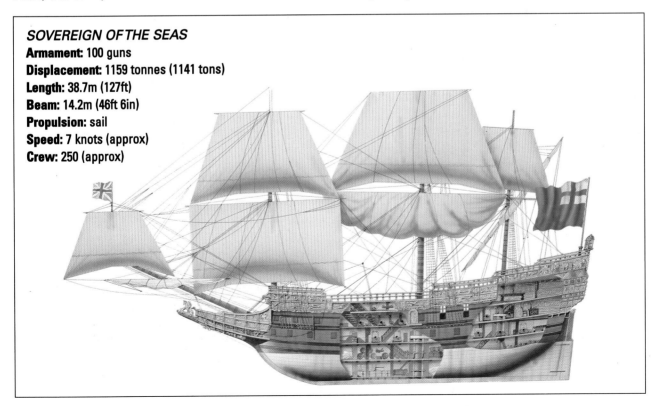

SOVEREIGN OF THE SEAS
Armament: 100 guns
Displacement: 1159 tonnes (1141 tons)
Length: 38.7m (127ft)
Beam: 14.2m (46ft 6in)
Propulsion: sail
Speed: 7 knots (approx)
Crew: 250 (approx)

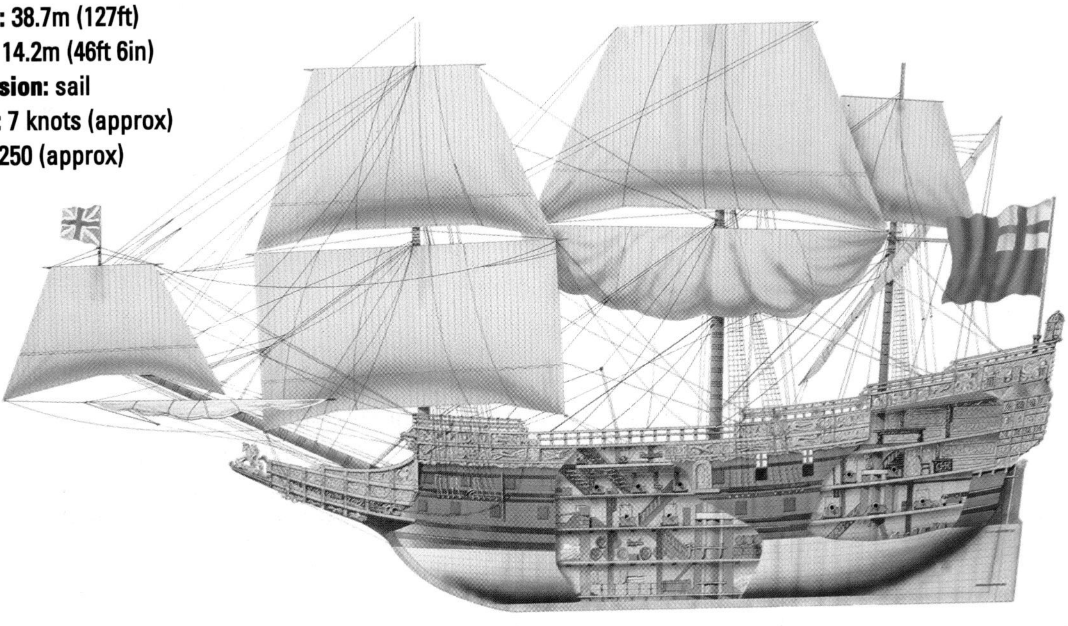

Above: The deck of a ship in battle was a dangerous place to be, as shown in this scene on board the French 80-gun battleship *Tonnant* at the Battle of Aboukir, 1798.

slaughtered and their ships destroyed. At least a third of the Armada's complement of 29,000 seamen and soldiers never returned home. It was a catastrophe that plunged the whole of Spain into mourning.

The Spanish Armada is significant in naval history not only because it saved England from invasion, but also because it marked the first long-range gun duels. Naval gunfire had been used to deadly effect at an earlier date, at the Battle of Lepanto in 1571, when Venetian gunnery pounded the Turkish fleet to destruction; but on that occasion the object had been to kill as many oarsmen as possible in the Turkish galleys. The lesson to be learned from the battle in the English Channel was that ships could be sunk by gunfire, but only with concentrated fire at short range. At a distance of 640m (700yds) or more shot might damage a wooden hull, but it would seldom penetrate. The quest was now a scientific one and aimed at perfecting guns that would penetrate and sink their adversaries at maximum range. After the Armada, naval science was on the first rung of the ladder that would lead to the modern battleship.

During the reign of James I – James VI of Scots, who succeeded Elizabeth on her death in 1603 – the English fleet fell into sorry neglect. Even so, British merchant adventurers continued to further Britain's naval presence and with the union of the crowns of England and Scotland, maritime trade was now a matter of joint enterprise. Nevertheless, James did commission one new warship, the *Prince Royal*, built by Phineas Pett. She was not a particular success; the longest voyage she made was to Spain, and after only 10 years she had to be rebuilt at three-quarters of her original cost.

THE *SOVEREIGN OF THE SEAS*

Although the *Prince Royal*'s design faults brought much scorn down on Pett, in 1637 Charles I commissioned his son, Peter, to build a very large warship of 1663 tonnes (1637 tons). Named *Sovereign of the Seas*, she was the biggest fighting vessel ever built in England up to that time, and she carried over 100 guns mounted in three tiers, making her the first three-decker man-of-war. She was lavishly decked out with ornate carvings and other trappings. Later, her gun decks were reduced to two. She served the nation well for many years. After the restoration of the English monarchy in 1660 she became the *Royal*

Sovereign, and was still a flagship at the Battle of Barfleur against the French in 1692. Five years later she caught fire in the Medway and was destroyed, the consequence of a lighted candle left untended by a careless cook. She was 60 years old. But other nations were also building splendid warships in the seventeenth century; France, for example, produced the magnificent *La Couronne* in 1638.

It was during the reign of Charles I, when the British Navy was mainly involved in hunting down pirates, that the Dutch began to present a serious challenge to Britain's sea trade. It was a curious state of affairs, for although the commercial interests of the two nations clashed everywhere, they were united against their old enemy, Spain, particularly in the West Indies, where both the Dutch and English had begun to settle.

Some of the fiercest sea battles over fought occurred during the Anglo-Dutch war of 1665–7, in the 100 miles of North Sea that lay between the two countries. Apart from a brief period when the British fleet was led by the Duke of York, later James II, who won an early victory off Lowestoft and destroyed the Dutch flagship, joint command was exercised by General Monck and by Prince Rupert, who fought ably at sea as well as on land during the Civil War.

At the end of May 1666 the British received a (false) report that the French fleet had sailed to join the Dutch, and Prince Rupert took half the British fleet to intercept it. Monck was left to face a greatly superior Dutch fleet – 44 ships against 80 – under the command of the brilliant Admiral de Ruyter. Battle was joined on 1 June 1666, and at the end of the second day the British faced even greater odds when de Ruyter was reinforced by 16 more ships.

Monck detached his most damaged ships and sent them home, protecting them in a fighting retreat that lasted throughout the whole of the third day. This tactic proved successful, although there was one major casualty for the fleet. The veteran three-decker *Royal Prince* ran aground on the Galloper Shoal, 20 miles off the coast of East Anglia. She was quickly surrounded and set on fire by the Dutch, who took her whole company prisoner, including her captain, Sir George Ayscue.

That evening, another fleet was sighted, approaching from the English Channel. It was Prince Rupert's force, and its timely arrival enabled the British to attack with renewed vigour on the fourth day of battle, until a thick summer fog descended and brought an end to the engagement. The 'Four Days Battle' had been costly for the British, who had lost 17 ships –

Below: HMS *Victory*, in which Admiral Lord Nelson met his death and found everlasting glory at the Battle of Trafalgar (1805). The whole British nation mourned him.

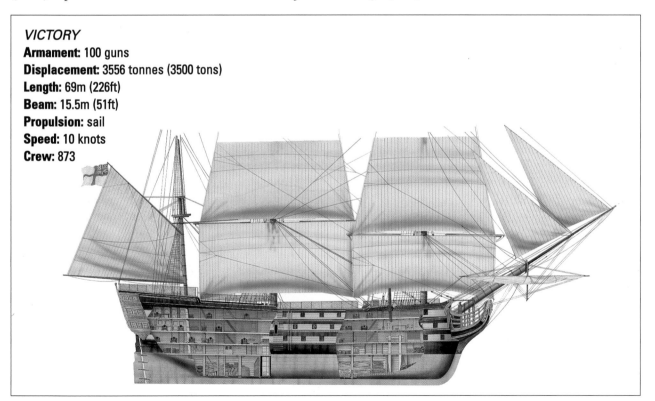

VICTORY
Armament: 100 guns
Displacement: 3556 tonnes (3500 tons)
Length: 69m (226ft)
Beam: 15.5m (51ft)
Propulsion: sail
Speed: 10 knots
Crew: 873

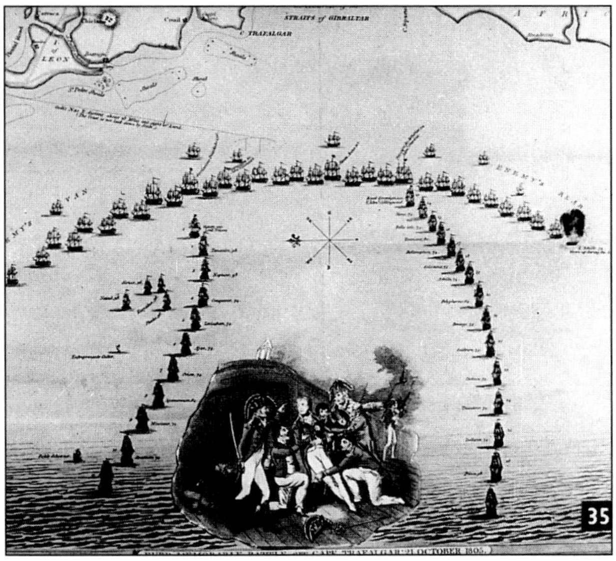

Above: The Battle of Trafalgar in 1805, where the French and Spanish line was disrupted by the two English lines led by Admirals Nelson and Collingwood.

eight sunk or burnt and nine captured – together with 5000 men killed and another 3000 taken prisoner.

Two months later, on 25 July 1666, the fleets met again off the North Foreland, the easternmost point of Kent. On this occasion the British got the upper hand and chased de Ruyter back to Holland, sinking two of his ships and destroying no fewer than 150 merchantmen, as well as burning and pillaging villages and storehouses.

In 1667, following the ravages of the Plague and the disaster of the Fire of London, King Charles, desperately short of money, decided to lay up his fleet in the River Medway. It was a fatal error. In June, de Ruyter blockaded the mouth of the Thames and Medway, sailed boldly into the latter, broke the defensive chain that was stretched across it, bombarded the forts, destroyed many of the ships anchored off Chatham, and sailed home with several prizes – including the *Royal Charles*, the fleet flagship. It was the most daring and skilful sea raid launched on the British Isles since the days of the Vikings.

The wars against the Dutch, who were every bit as skilled as the British in naval tactics and seamanship, forced the rapid development of British naval power. The merchant and war fleets were now separate entities, and the navy was armed with ships built from the outset as fighting vessels. Tactics were evolved whereby ships fought in squadrons, rather than as individual units. Specialised signals were devised, using flags to indicate a commander's intentions and to issue orders. Young men from the leading families of the land began to look to the sea as a career, entering the Naval Service, the King's Service, as boys. And from about 1670, that Service came to be known as the Royal Navy.

While the Royal Navy's operations continued to evolve worldwide in protection of trade during the early part of the 18th century, the ships that conducted them remained virtually unchanged. Only the first-rates of 100 guns could match Charles I's *Sovereign of the Seas* for size, and for most of the century there were only six or seven of them. A first-rater mounted 100 or more cannon ranging from 12-pounders to 32-pounders. They measured over 61m (200ft) on the lower gun deck and were generally crewed by 875 officers and men. Their unit cost was huge for its day – about £100,000 – which accounted for the fact that fewer than a dozen were in service at any one time. A first-rater could loose off half a ton of iron shot in a single broadside.

THE BATTLE OF TRAFALGAR

By the end of the 18th century, the Royal Navy, having won a series of resounding victories over the French, enjoyed undisputed supremacy on the high seas. In 1793, war was declared against the infant French Republic by a powerful consortium of nations led by England. It continued for 22 years, and saw the Royal Navy rise to the peak of its power in the age of sail. The period is remembered for a series of great naval victories over the French, culminating in the Battle of Trafalgar in 1805.

The French component of the combined Franco-Spanish fleet that engaged the Royal Navy off Cape Trafalgar had no first-rate men of war at all; the eight such vessels in service prior to 1793 had all suffered from the ravages of war. Eighteen of the enemy's ships of the line were French (four 80-gunners and the rest 74s) and 15 Spanish. Flagship of the Spanish force was the mighty 130-gun *Santissima Trinidad*; there were also two 112-gunners, one 100, two 80s and one 64, the remainder being 74s. Against this array, Nelson had 27 ships of the line, including three 100-gunners, four 98s, one 80, three 64s and the rest 74s. In an extension of the tactic of cutting the enemy's line, Nelson planned to attack in three columns in line ahead, to overwhelm the enemy's rear and centre before the van could reverse its course and come to their aid. The outcome, Nelson expected, would be a 'pell-mell battle which would surprise and confound the enemy', permitting the superior British gunnery and ship-handling to be exploited to maximum effect. In the event, only two columns were formed. They were to prove enough.

The battle began shortly after noon on 21 October, when the leeward column, led by Admiral Collingwood's 100-gun *Royal Sovereign*, broke the Franco-Spanish line and was soon heavily engaged, Collingwood's flagship battling with five enemy vessels at one point. Within an hour Nelson's windward column was also in action, HMS *Victory*, followed by *Temeraire, Neptune* and *Britannia*, passing astern of the French Admiral Villeneuve's flagship *Bucentaure*, which she battered at point-blank range and caused fearsome casualties among her crew. Then *Victory* was herself engaged by the French *Redoutable* and the two giants poured salvo after salvo into one another, lying entangled, while sharpshooters poured down a rain of musket fire from overhead. At about 1330 hours, a French sharpshooter spotted Nelson on the quarterdeck, clearly identified by the tarnished stars and ribbons on his uniform, and shot him with a ball that entered his shoulder and lodged in his spine.

Below: The mighty 130-gun Spanish flagship *Santissima Trinidad* was Nelson's first objective at Trafalgar, but he switched his attention to the French flagship, *Bucentaure.*

Nelson died at 1630 hours, comforted by the knowledge that victory was his. By the time the leading enemy ships had reversed their course, their centre and rear had been overwhelmed; the shattered *Bucentaure* had surrendered and Villeneuve was a prisoner, and 18 other enemy vessels, including the *Santissima Trinidad*, had struck their colours. Those enemy ships that could, headed for the coast; one was the French ship *Achille*, which caught fire and exploded at about 1730 hours.

The British lost some 450 men killed and 1100 wounded at Trafalgar. The combined Franco-Spanish loss, killed and wounded, was about 14,000, many of these being drowned when their ships were wrecked by fierce storms that swept across Biscay for a week after the battle. No British ships were lost in the terrible weather, but it was a sorry-looking fleet that assembled in Gibraltar; the *Victory*, now minus its mast, had to be towed into harbour by HMS *Neptune*.

To the Lords of the Admiralty, it must have seemed, after Trafalgar, that the men-of-war of England's navy were invincible, and that these stout hulls of oak, crowned with their dazzling white sails, would remain the symbols of British sea power for evermore. But the half-century that followed would see the battleship transformed beyond all recognition.

SANTISSIMA TRINIDAD
Armament: 130 guns
Displacement: 4572 tonnes (4500 tons) (approx)
Length: 61.2m (200ft)
Beam: 19.2m (62ft 9in)
Propulsion: sail
Speed: 7 knots
Crew: 1000 (approx)

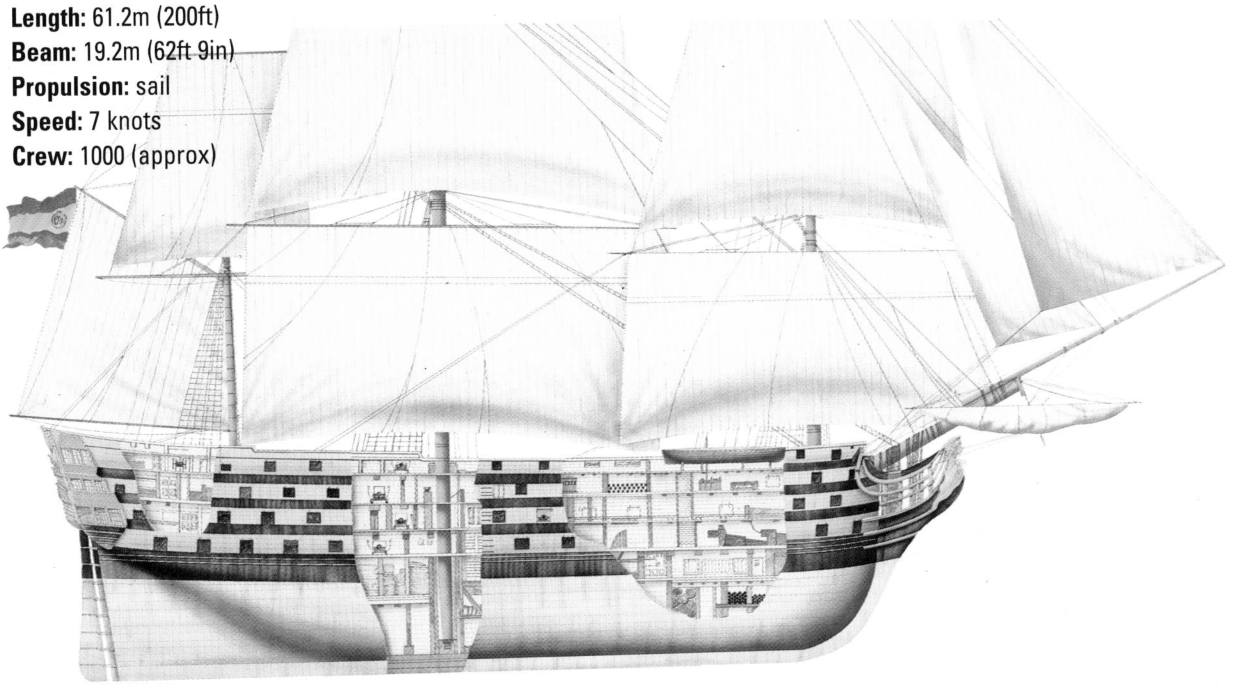

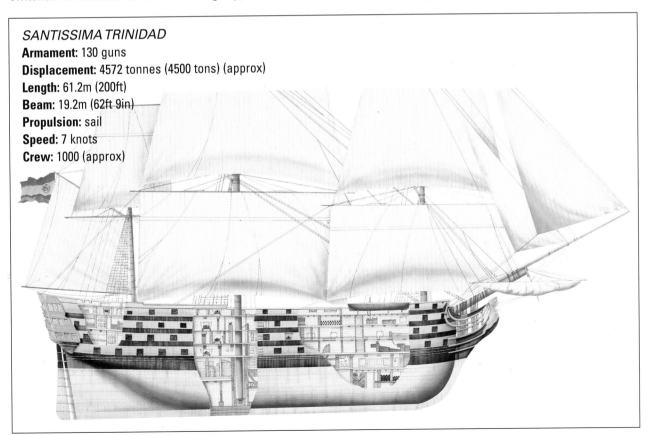

CHAPTER TWO

The Ironclads

The ironclad ships of the nineteenth century were the first to develop the basic principles of modern warship design. Encased in iron plate armour and increasingly powered by steam, they were strange hybrids, mounting fewer guns of larger calibres in traversing turrets. Less glamorous than their wooden predecessors, the ironclads signalled the dawn of a new industrial age of sea warfare.

Two decades of warfare had brought the sailing ship of the line to a high degree of perfection, limited only by scientific knowledge and the construction materials available. In 1808 the Royal Navy launched the 108-gun *Caledonia*, whose 62.5m (205ft) gun deck was thought to be the maximum attainable with a single wooden keel. Then in 1813 the Surveyor of the Royal Navy, Sir Robert Seppings, found a way to preserve longitudinal strength by using diagonal wooden trusses and iron stiffening. All new-build British capital ships would now incorporate a degree of iron in their wooden hulls. Bows and sterns were also redesigned, strengthened and made more rounded.

Left: HMS *Warrior* (1860) was armed with the 68-pounder, capable of firing shells that could smash through armour and burst with devastating effect.

Meanwhile, a quiet revolution had been taking place. At its heart was the *Charlotte Dundas*, a little boat which in 1801 was towing barges on the Forth and Clyde Canal. She was quite unremarkable, except for one thing – she was the first successful steamship in the world.

Steamship development might have progressed at a faster rate had it not been for the war with Napoleon. But in 1812 the *Comet* started a passenger steamship service on the Clyde, and two years later the *Margery*, also built on the Clyde, sailed down the east coast to London, to begin a similar service on the Thames. In 1816 the first Channel crossing was made by a steamboat, the *Elise*, and in 1818 a regular steamship service was inaugurated between Greenock, on the Clyde, and Belfast. After that, progress was swift; in 1825 the 477-tonne (470-ton) *Enterprise* reached Calcutta from England in 113 days, using steam for

Above: Ships like HMS *Caledonia* of the 1850s were hybrids. Their principal power source was still the wind, and they retained their all-sail predecessors' gun ports.

two-thirds of the voyage, and in 1827 the *Curacao*, built in Dover and sold to the Dutch navy, began a series of crossings from Holland to the West Indies.

Apart from hiring steam tugs to tow warships out of harbour in the 1820s when the winds were unfavourable, the Royal Navy showed no interest in steam. For one thing, the argument went, the Royal Navy had commitments worldwide; the use of steamships would mean setting up coaling stations at strategic points, shipping the fuel out to them, and defending them. But there was another factor involved in this lack of interest; in the years after 1815 no new warships were laid down for the simple reason that many partly-completed hulls were already on the stocks. It was not until the late 1820s that a new class of first-rate battleships was begun. They were the *Trafalgar, Prince Regent, Royal George, Neptune, Royal William, Waterloo* and *St George*; they carried an armament of six 60-pounder and 114 32-pounder guns, and their complement was 900 men.

One man, more than any other, was responsible for persuading the Admiralty to change its mind. He was the engineer Isambard Kingdom Brunel, designer of the three great commercial steamships of the mid-19th century: the *Great Western, Great Eastern* and *Great Britain*. The *Great Britain* was the most innovative of the three, and among the innovations was a screw propeller instead of a paddle wheel. The idea was not Brunel's; a screw propeller had already been patented and, in 1838, tested on a small ship called the *Archimedes*, named after the Greek inventor of the screw for raising water in about 200BC. Despite teething troubles that included the break-up of her first propeller, the *Great Britain* – an iron ship 98m (305ft) long, nearly half the length again of any warship afloat – made four trips to New York.

Brunel wrote a lengthy report on the screw propeller while the *Great Britain* was on the stocks. It was examined by Admiralty officials, who realised that the use of a propeller would eliminate one of the principal objections to steam-powered warships, which was that a paddle wheel would get in the way of a ship's broadside gun arrangement. With advice from Brunel, the Admiralty authorised the building of a small screw-driven steam sloop, the *Rattler*, for use as a trials ship. In 1845 she was matched against a paddle steamer of similar size and won easily, ending the test impressively by towing the paddle steamer backwards. In November that year work started on converting the incomplete third-rate *Ajax* to steam

Right: The old sail-and-steam ship-of-the-line *Duke of Wellington* pictured in use as a training vessel, a capacity in which she served from 1863 to 1904.

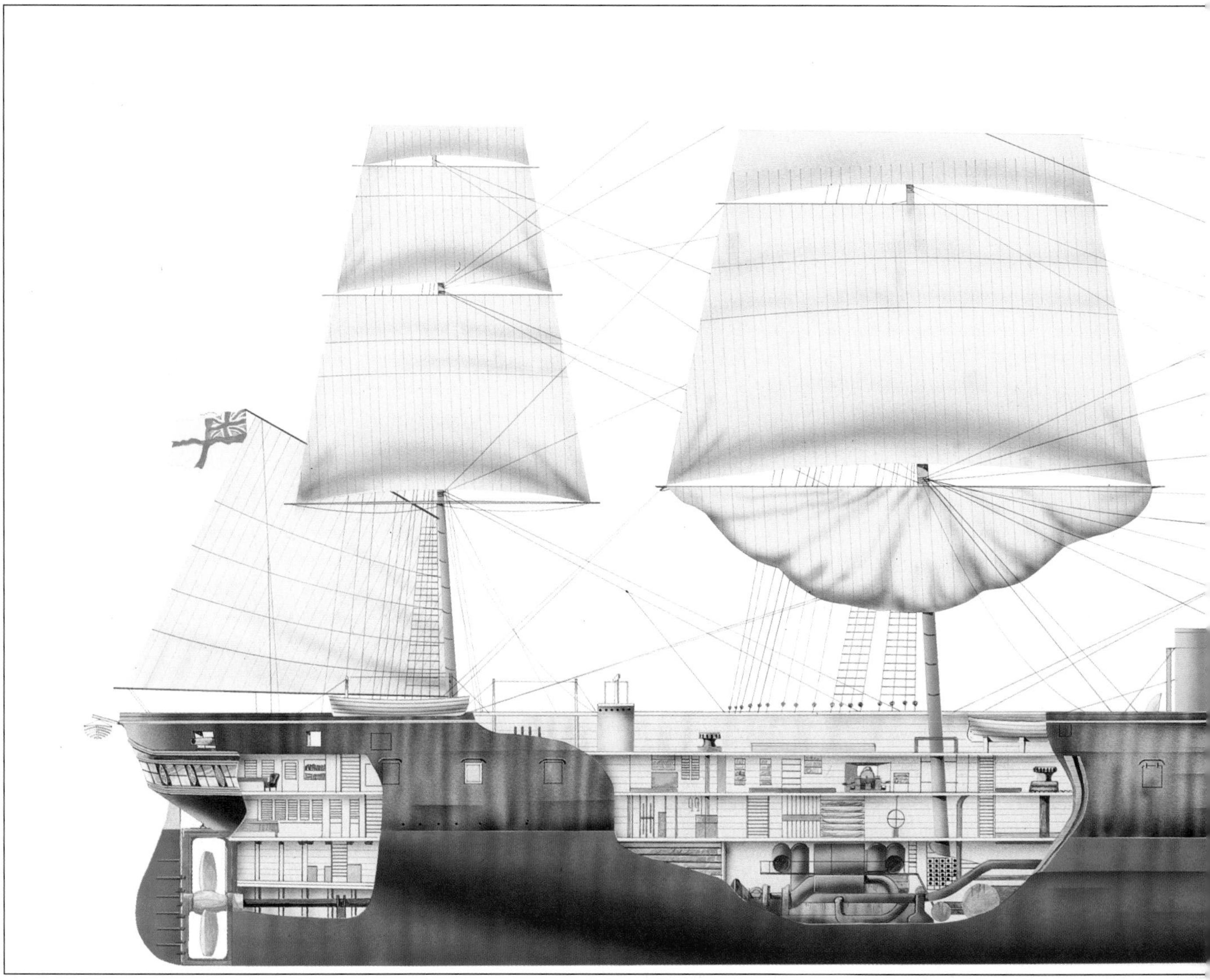

power, and on 23 September 1846 she undertook her maiden voyage as the first seagoing steam battleship in the world. Her sister ship, the *Edinburgh*, joined the fleet shortly afterwards.

THE FIRST STEAM BATTLESHIPS

In 1848 the French launched the *Napoleon*, the first battleship designed to be steam-powered. Two years later Britain made a response of sorts by producing the *Agamemnon*, which, being a sailing ship with an auxiliary engine, was no real comparison; but in 1853 the British launched the *Duke of Wellington*, which resembled the *Napoleon* and had a 2000hp engine. After that, new warships were designed with engines and propellers, and some older vessels were retro-fitted, but the engines were for auxiliary power only; sail remained the main motive force, and many senior naval officers were dead set against change. It was the Crimean War that forced the issue. Although the Russians had no navy capable of confronting the British, the latter quickly discovered, during naval bombardment operations in the Black Sea and the Baltic, that ships with engines were far more useful and manoeuvrable than those with sails only when it came to evading counter-fire from shore batteries.

Naval firepower also underwent a revolution in the first half of the 19th century. It began in 1822, when a French artilleryman called Henri Paixhans published a treatise on how the French Navy, shattered in the long war with Britain, could achieve parity with the Royal Navy without a massive shipbuilding programme. His solution was to adapt the hollow cast-iron mortar bomb, which had been in use for many years, to be fired by naval guns. If such a shell penetrated a ship's timbers, it would explode with enormous force and start uncontrollable fires, leading to a

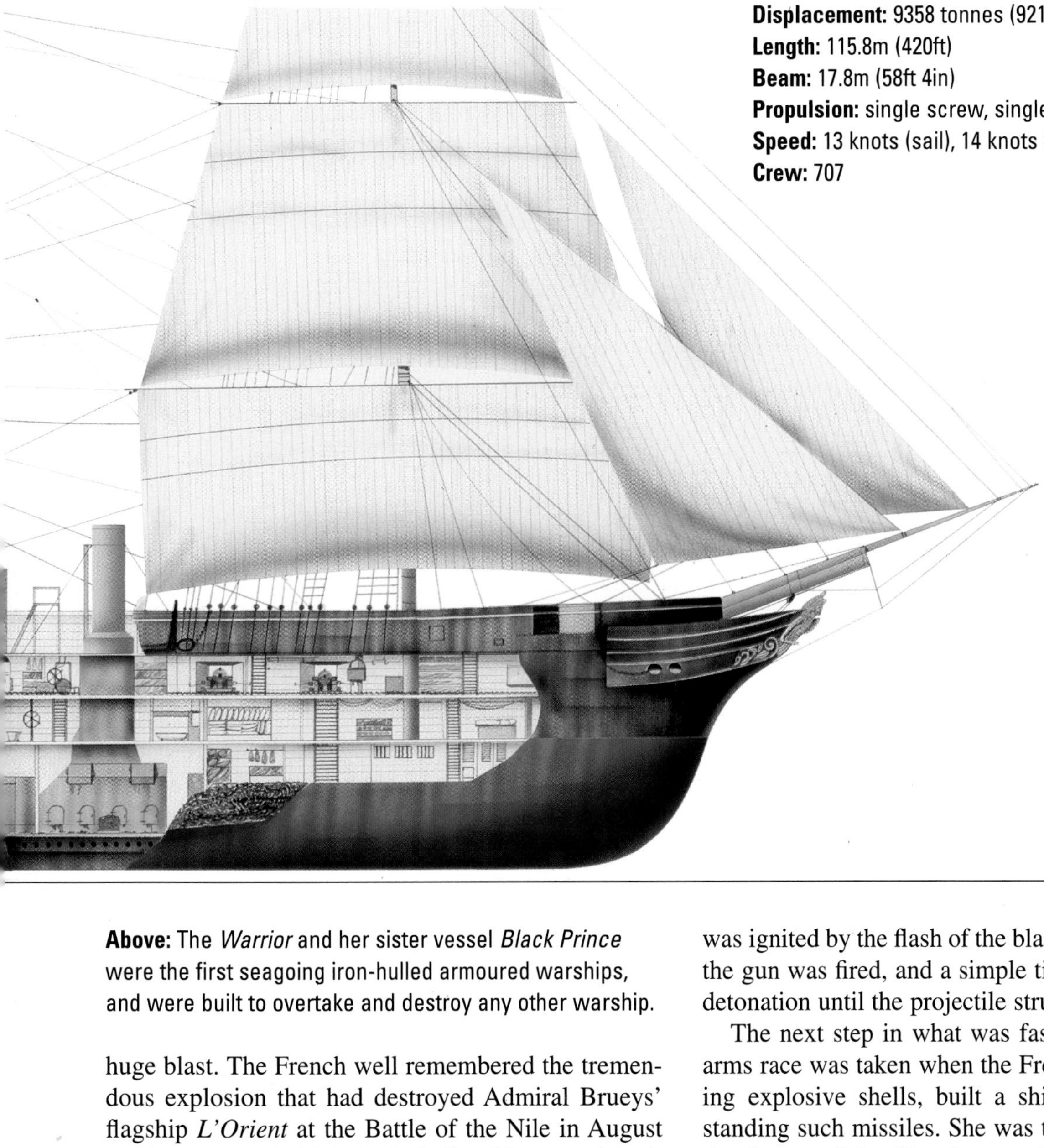

WARRIOR
Armament: 10 100-pounders, 4 70-pounders, 26 68-pounders
Displacement: 9358 tonnes (9210 tons)
Length: 115.8m (420ft)
Beam: 17.8m (58ft 4in)
Propulsion: single screw, single expansion
Speed: 13 knots (sail), 14 knots (steam)
Crew: 707

Above: The *Warrior* and her sister vessel *Black Prince* were the first seagoing iron-hulled armoured warships, and were built to overtake and destroy any other warship.

huge blast. The French well remembered the tremendous explosion that had destroyed Admiral Brueys' flagship *L'Orient* at the Battle of the Nile in August 1798. But the British had similar ideas, and both navies began using the explosive shell at about the same time, the French issuing their new shell in 1824 for use with their 55-pounder guns, and the British issuing their own shell for use with the well-tried 68-pounder some two years later. Both navies continued to use solid shot, however, as the cannon that fired it were more accurate over long ranges, so that by the end of the 1830s most three-deckers carried a mix of 60 per cent solid shot cannon and 40 per cent shell guns. Shells were fitted with a wooden fuse, which was ignited by the flash of the black powder charge as the gun was fired, and a simple time delay prevented detonation until the projectile struck its target.

The next step in what was fast becoming a naval arms race was taken when the French, after introducing explosive shells, built a ship capable of withstanding such missiles. She was the *Gloire*, based on the design of the *Napoleon*, and she carried battery armour of 110-120mm (4.3-4.7in). Begun in 1858, she was the first armoured ship-of-the-line in the world.

Britain's answer was the *Warrior* of 1859, a vessel superior in most respects to the *Gloire*. The was the first seagoing iron-hulled armoured warship, having 114mm (4.5in) of wrought iron on a backing of 457mm (18in) of teak. She started her career with an armament of breech-loading guns of various calibre, but the breech mechanism was prone to failure, with

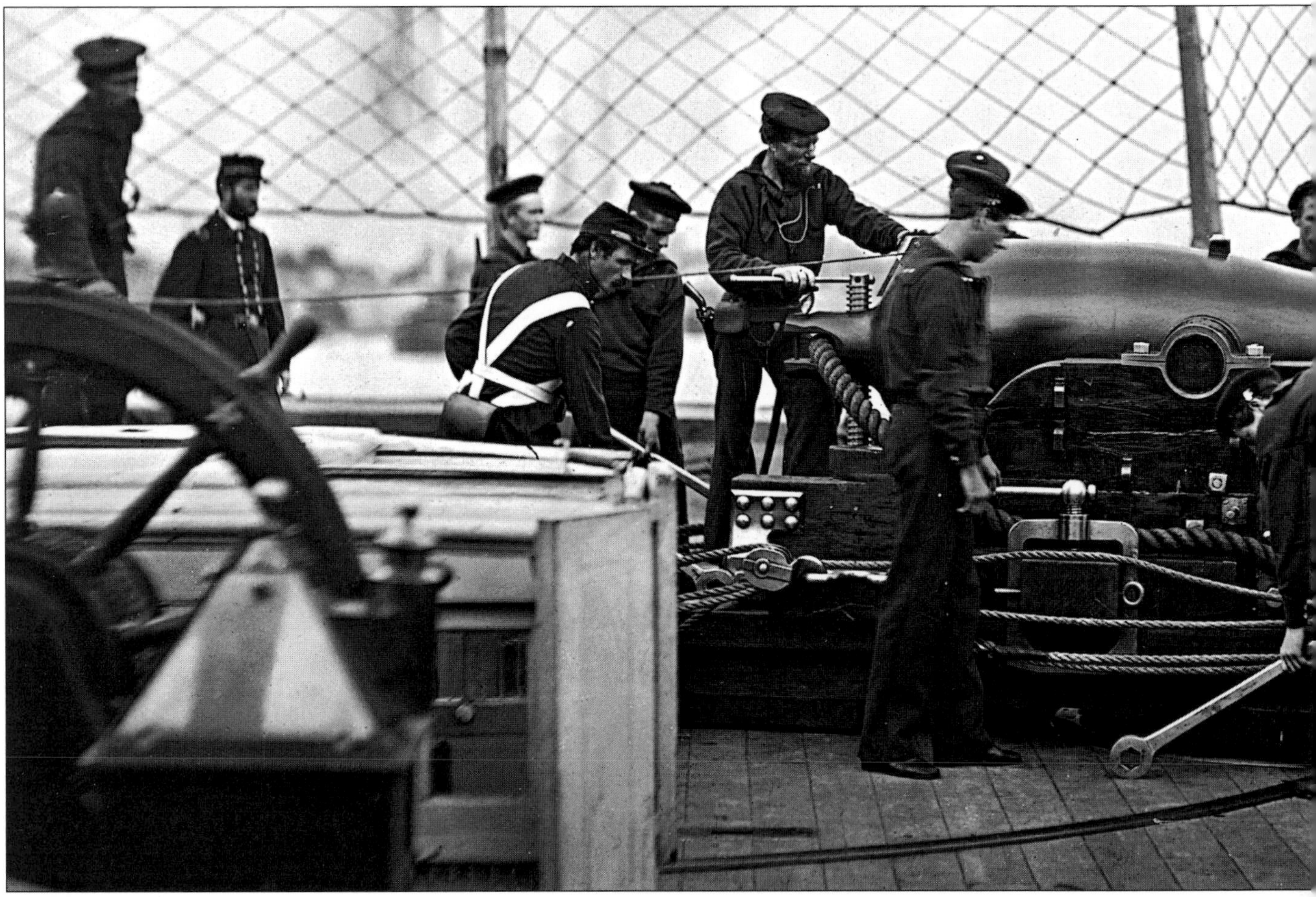

disastrous results for the gun crews, and in 1867 the armament was changed to 28 178mm (7in) and four 203mm (8in) muzzle-loaders. She carried a complement of 707 and had a displacement of 9358 tonnes (9210 tons). She had a sister ship, the *Black Prince*, launched in 1861.

THE 'CHEESEBOX ON A RAFT'

Meanwhile, a new contestant had entered the battleship arena. In 1861, following the outbreak of the American Civil War, the US government ordered the construction of three ironclad designs. One of these, designed by John Ericsson and named the *Monitor*, was a truly revolutionary design, with a single turret mounting two 280mm (11in) guns on a flat deck. The *Monitor*, rather unkindly nicknamed the 'cheesebox on a raft', was the first warship without rigging or sails. On 9 March 1862 she fought a celebrated action in Hampton Roads with the Confederate ironclad *Virginia* (formerly the *Merrimack*), an engagement that rendered all non-armoured warships obsolete at one stroke, the *Monitor* having emerged from it virtually undamaged and in command of the area. The success of the *Monitor* led to other vessels of this type being laid down, some of these fighting actions with Confederate ironclads along the Atlantic coastline and in the Gulf of Mexico, but those incomplete at the end of the war were scrapped or sold abroad.

Above: The 11-inch Dahlgren gun, seen here on a slide-pivot mounting in operation aboard a Union Navy warship in the American Civil War, was a powerful weapon.

Right: Union and Confederate warships in action at Hampton Roads during the Civil War. USS *Monitor* and CSS *Virginia* (ex-*Merrimack*) are in the left foreground.

After the Civil War, interest in the navy waned, and the 'Monitor' class were thought to be the only vessels necessary for the role of coastal defence, the only one envisaged at that time. Not until the 1880s would the United States embark on the design of its first true battleships.

Interest in new warship designs led Britain's principal rival, France, to purchase two American vessels, the *Dunderberg* and *Onondaga*, in 1867. The former, renamed *Rochambeau*, took part in a blockade of

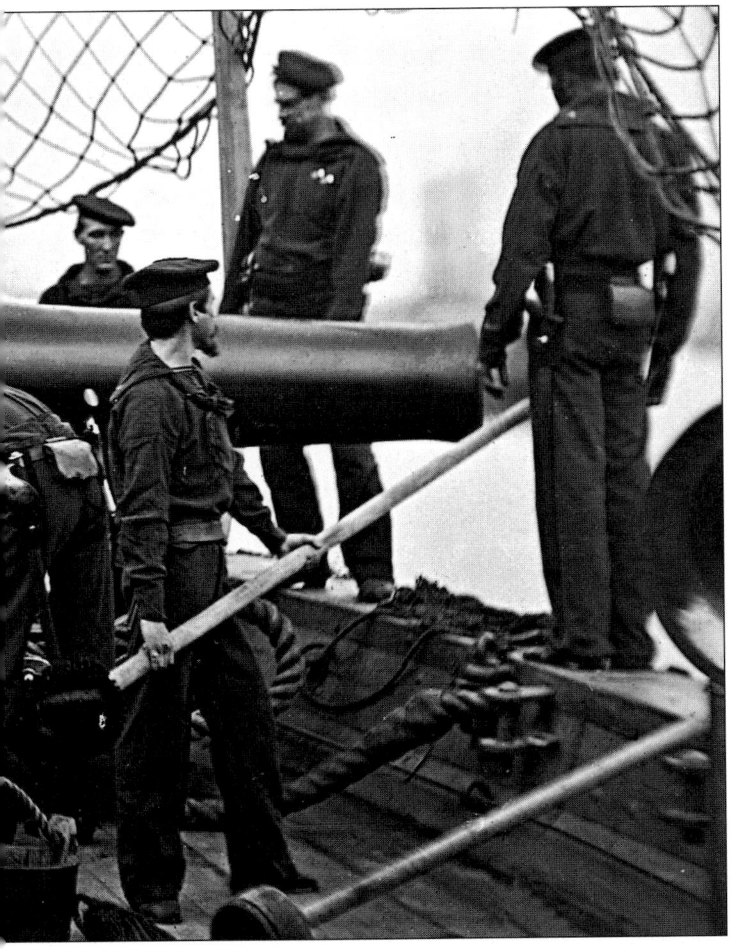

Prussian ports during the Franco-Prussian war of 1870. This conflict and its costs led to major reductions in the French naval budget, placing the emphasis on defence rather than offensive action, which was to have serious implications for the future.

THE BATTLE OF LISSA

Italy founded a navy in 1860, soon after unification, and ordered a number of ironclads from foreign yards. One of the most important vessels in the fleet was the 4446-tonne (4376-ton) turret ship *Affondatore*, mounting two single turrets fore and aft. She was commissioned just in time for the war with Austria in 1866, which culminated on 20 July in the Battle of Lissa, fought off the island of that name in the Adriatic. This action was significant. Not only was it the first major fleet action fought in European waters since Trafalgar; it was also the first battle involving seagoing ironclads.

The Austro-Hungarian fleet, under Rear-Admiral Wilhelm von Tegetthoff, was technically inferior, having only seven armoured ships out of 27; the Italians, commanded by Count Carlo Pellion de Persano, had 12 out of 34. Furthermore, most of the Austrian ships were armed with old muzzle-loaders; they mounted only 74 modern rifled guns against the Italians' 200.

DEVASTATION
Armament: 4 305mm (12in) guns
Displacement: 9480 tonnes (9330 tons)
Length: 87m (285ft)
Beam: 20m (65ft 3in)
Propulsion: twin screw trunk
Speed: 13.8 knots
Crew: 358

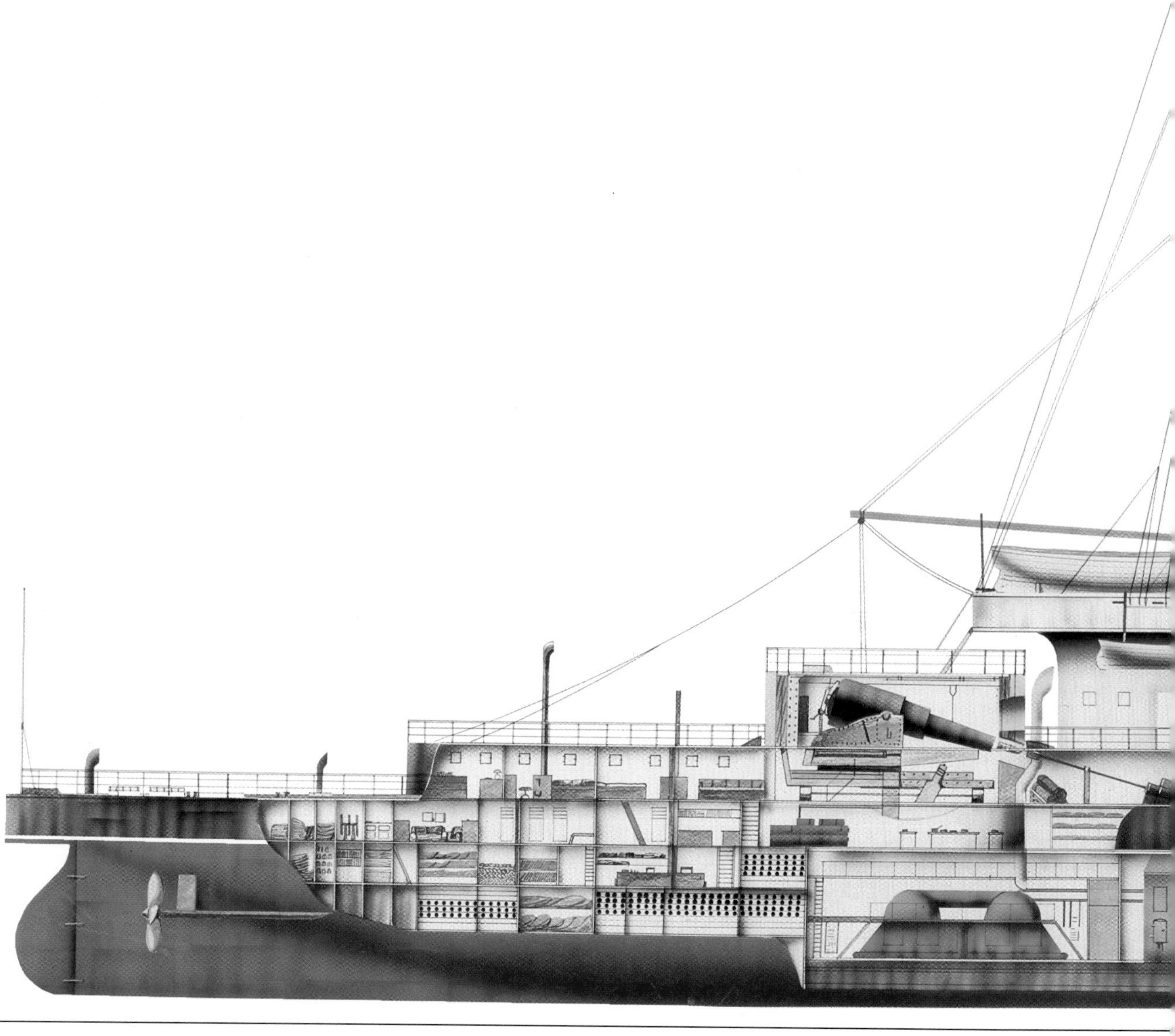

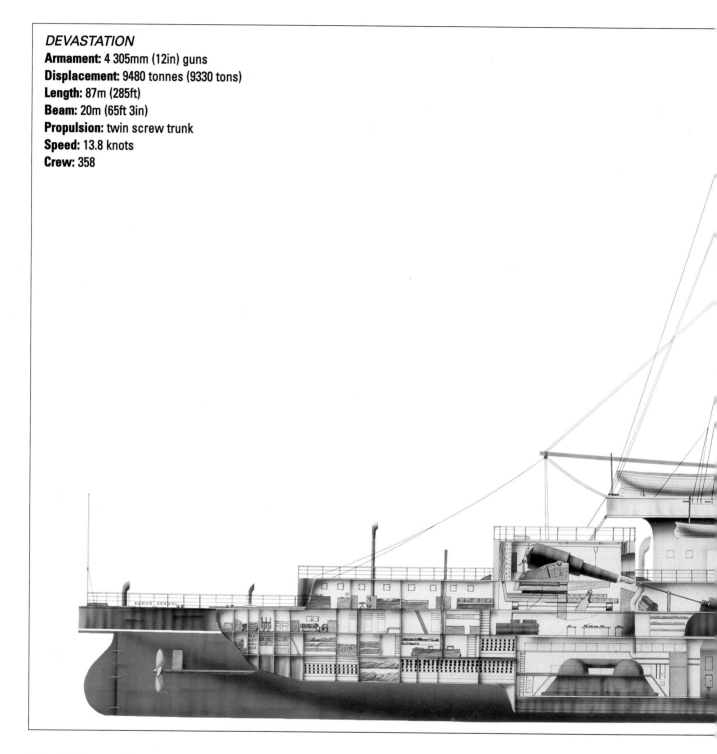

Above: With no sail power, masts or rigging, HMS *Devastation* of 1868 was generally condemned when she was launched, due to her revolutionary design.

Faced with little alternative, Tegetthoff chose to fight using bold tactics. He ordered his captains to close the range so that the old muzzle-loaders on his ships might have a chance of penetrating the enemy's armour, and instructed them to ram the Italian ships wherever possible. His three divisions steamed into the attack in arrowhead formation and succeeded in penetrating the Italian line. A furious mêlée ensued in which the *Affondatore* closed with the Austrian *Kaiser*, a steam two-decker of 90 guns, with a wooden hull and iron upperworks, and riddled the latter with 250mm (10in) shells. Despite the damage, the *Kaiser* tried to ram the Italian ironclad frigate *Re di Portogallo*, losing her bowsprit, foremast and funnel;

she was then hit by several more shells, forcing her to draw clear with 61 casualties.

Shortly afterwards, the 18-gun ironclad frigate *Ferdinand Max* – Tegetthoff's flagship – attacked the Italian frigate *Re d'Italia*, disabled by a shell hit in the rudder. Unable to take evasive action, the *Re d'Italia* was rammed and capsized, taking 383 of her crew to the bottom with her. It was the decisive moment; the Italian commander withdrew, leaving victory to his Austrian adversary. Apart from the *Re d'Italia*, the Italians had lost one other ship, the small ironclad *Palestro*, which exploded after being attacked by the *Ferdinand Max* earlier in the fight. Italian casualties in total were 682 killed and 153 wounded; the Austrians lost 28 killed and 138 wounded.

In one sense, the Battle of Lissa did a disservice to battleship design in the years that followed. The major naval powers, noting how the *Re d'Italia* had

COLLINGWOOD
Armament: 4 305mm (12in), 6 152mm (6in) guns
Displacement: 9652 tonnes (9500 tons)
Length: 99m (324ft 10in)
Beam: 21m (68ft)
Propulsion: twin screw, inverted compound
Speed: 17 knots
Crew: 498

Above: Laid down in 1879, HMS *Collingwood* set the standard for future battleship designs for the next quarter-century.

met her end, decided that ramming was a powerful and effective tactic, ignoring the fact that it had only succeeded in this case because the Italian warship had been unable to manoeuvre. As a result, capital ships were built with reinforced bows for years to come, and navies wasted much time in practising ramming techniques. The real lesson of Lissa was that, although the opposing sides had hurled thousands of shells at one another, not one vessel – not even the *Palestro*, who was destroyed as a result of fire and explosion – was sunk as a direct result of gunfire.

THE FIRST TURRET SHIPS

By 1869, 38 steam-powered capital ships were either in service with, or under construction for, the Royal Navy. The earlier designs were broadside ironclads, but 1864 saw the launch of the 3942-tonne (3880-ton) *Prince Albert*, which had single 230mm (9in) guns mounted in four turrets on the centre-line. Other ships had their guns mounted in a central battery. But all carried sails, and it was not until 1868 that Britain laid down a seagoing vessel designed to be powered by steam alone. She was the *Devastation*, and her concept was much reviled by the traditionalists in navy circles. Completed in 1873, she carried four 305mm (12in) muzzle-loading guns mounted in turrets and was powered by direct-acting trunk engines, with eight rectangular boilers and two screws. She displaced 9480 tonnes (9330 tons) and had a complement of 358. Her sister ship was the *Thunderer*.

Much more satisfying to the orthodox naval mind was the *Captain*, completed in 1870. She was also a turret ship, displacing 7892 tonnes (7767 tons) and her machinery was similar to that of the *Devastation*. But she carried a full rig of sail, and she had a serious flaw. Because overweight material was used in her construction she floated too deeply, having a freeboard of only 2m (6ft 6in) instead of the designed 2.6m (8ft 6in) – already low in itself. On 7 September 1870, only nine months after she was completed, she capsized and sank in a Biscay gale, taking 473 of her crew – including her designer, Captain Cowper Coles – with her. It had taken a major disaster to turn the page on the chapter of naval sailing ships.

Although the naval gun turret was now a fact of life, it was not until the late 1870s that the Royal Navy returned to the breech-loading concept. The first British battleships to feature breech-loading turret-mounted guns were the *Colossus* and *Edinburgh*. Both were laid down in 1879 but took 10 years to complete, the work being held up by delays in the delivery of their armament. They mounted four 305mm (12in) guns in two central turrets amidships, together with a secondary armament of five 152mm (6in) guns. They displaced 9297 tonnes (9150 tons) and had a complement of 396. They were also the first British battleships to have compound armour instead of iron.

But it was the *Collingwood*, laid down in 1880, that set the trend in British battleship design that would endure for a quarter of a century. Her main armament of four 305mm (12in) guns were mounted in twin barbettes fore and aft, a concept originally developed by the French. The barbette consisted of a turntable mounted inside a short, vertical circular tube, the guns firing over a low armoured parapet. Early barbettes lacked overhead protection, but this was added later.

The 'Admiral' class barbette battleships *Anson, Benbow, Camperdown, Howe* and *Rodney*, also constructed during the 1880s, carried a heavy armament of four 343mm (13.5in) and six 152mm (6in) guns, as well as a variety of smaller weapons. The exception was the *Benbow*, whose main armament comprised two 413mm (16.25in) guns. They carried heavy armour, too, their belt being up to 457mm (18in) and the barbettes 355mm (14in), an increase made possible by the growing use of mild steel in place of wrought iron.

The *Camperdown* of this class achieved a certain notoriety on 22 June 1893 when she accidentally rammed and sank the battleship *Victoria*, flagship of Vice-Admiral Sir George Tryon, off the coast of Syria with the loss of 358 lives, including Tryon's, out of a complement of 430. The *Victoria* had only been completed in 1890; she was the first battleship with triple-expansion engines.

ITALY TAKES THE LEAD

Meanwhile, in the 1870s, Italy had shocked the nautical world by producing the largest, fastest and most powerful battleships of their day. Designed by a talented and capable naval engineer, Benedetto Brin, they were the 'Duilio' class, mounting a main armament of four 457mm (18in) guns in twin turrets. The guns were produced by the British company, Armstrongs, and weighed 101.6 tonnes (100 tons). The battleships displaced 11,317 tonnes (11,138 tons). Originally, it had been intended to mount 380mm (15in) guns, also designed by Armstrongs, but the Italian Navy found the bigger gun proposal more attractive and Brin was compelled to modify his design to accommodate the revised armament. The *Duilio* was launched in May 1876 and completed in 1880, suffering an early setback when one of her massive guns burst during firing trials; her sister ship, the *Dandalo*, was launched in July 1878 and completed in April 1882.

Conscious that the 'Duilio' class had many shortcomings, Brin set about improving the design, sacrificing armour for speed. The result was the 'Italia' class of two ships, the second being the *Lepanto*. They carried an armament of four 430mm (17in) breech-loading guns mounted in a heavily-armoured barbette. By the time they were completed however, in 1885 and 1887 respectively, they had been rendered obsolete by new developments – notably high-explosive shells and quick-firing guns – as naval technology continued to advance at a rapid rate.

Below: The *Duilio* and her sister ship *Dandalo*, both laid down in 1873, were the largest, fastest and most powerful battleships of their day.

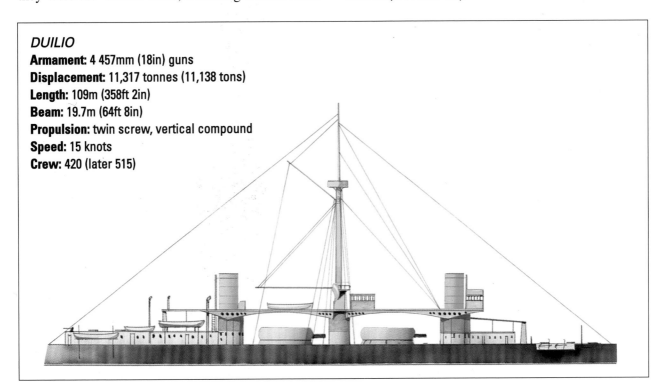

DUILIO
Armament: 4 457mm (18in) guns
Displacement: 11,317 tonnes (11,138 tons)
Length: 109m (358ft 2in)
Beam: 19.7m (64ft 8in)
Propulsion: twin screw, vertical compound
Speed: 15 knots
Crew: 420 (later 515)

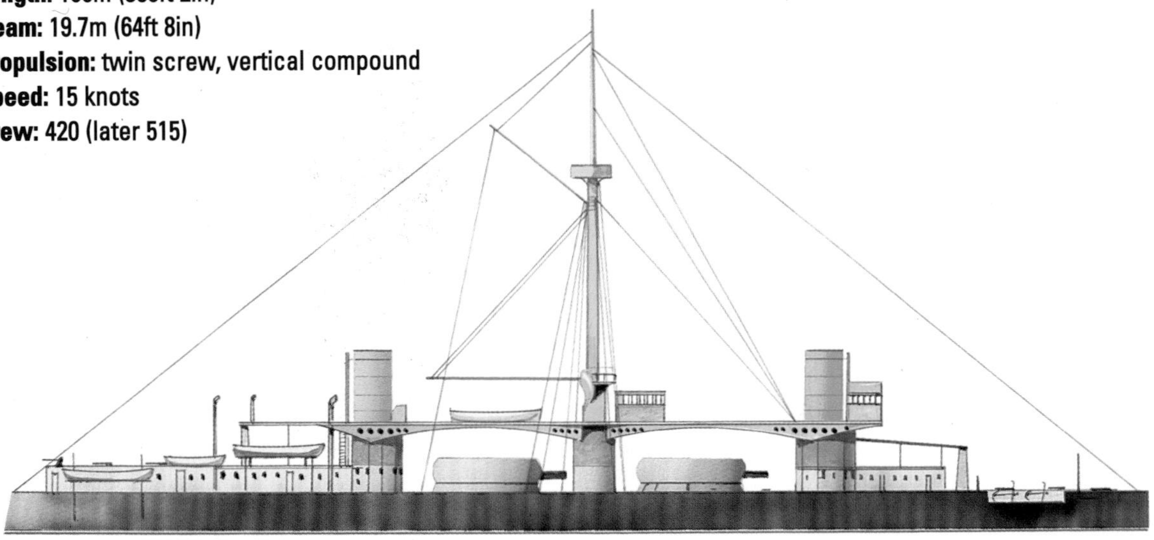

CHAPTER THREE

All-steel Capital Ships

Towards the end of the nineteenth century the British Royal Navy dominated the world's oceans. However, that supremacy was beginning to be challenged by the emergence of new, rapidly expanding rival navies from Germany, America, Japan and Russia. Imperialism was at its height, and newer, faster and better-armoured battleships were needed to safeguard overseas possessions from competitors.

In the last two decades of the 19th century, supremacy on the high seas unquestionably rested with Great Britain. New ideas and inventions were emerging so quickly that a vessel could be obsolete before it was launched. Much of this problem was created by Britain's own naval policy, which was described as a 'two-power standard' and which kept the Royal Navy equal in numbers to any two foreign navies. In simple terms, warships were being built at too fast a rate to incorporate the latest technological advances.

Left: The pre-dreadnought battleship HMS *Formidable* and her seven sister ships were an improved 'Canopus' class, with heavier armour and new 305mm (12in) guns.

In 1889 the two-power standard was modified somewhat when the Naval Defence Act came into force, decreeing that the Royal Navy must be capable of matching the world's second and third largest navies. The result was a new phase of shipbuilding, and at its forefront was the 'Royal Sovereign' class of battleship. Apart from the *Royal Sovereign* herself there were seven vessels in the class: the *Empress of India, Ramillies, Repulse, Resolution, Revenge, Royal Oak* and *Hood*.

A highly successful design, the 'Royal Sovereign' class were faster than any contemporary battleships.

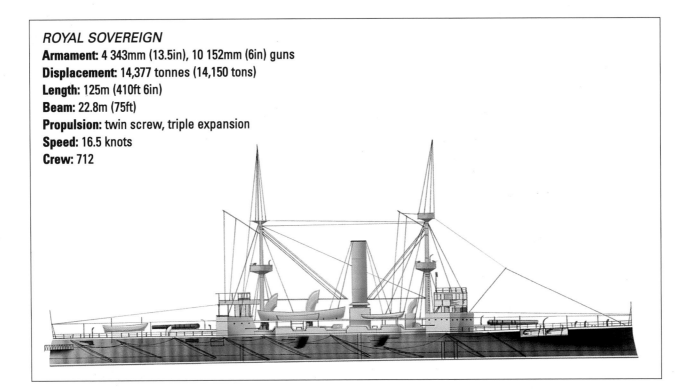

ROYAL SOVEREIGN
Armament: 4 343mm (13.5in), 10 152mm (6in) guns
Displacement: 14,377 tonnes (14,150 tons)
Length: 125m (410ft 6in)
Beam: 22.8m (75ft)
Propulsion: twin screw, triple expansion
Speed: 16.5 knots
Crew: 712

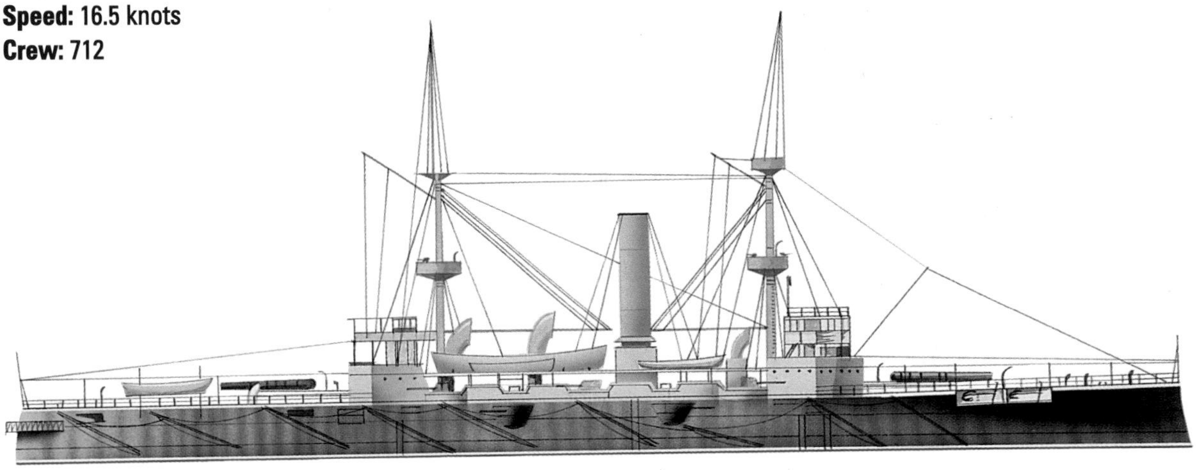

Above: The 'Royal Sovereigns' of the 1880s were a highly successful design, well-armed and faster than any other contemporary battleships.

Their main armament of four 343mm (13.5in) guns was mounted in twin barbettes; they also carried 10 152mm (6in), 16 six-pounder guns and seven 457mm (18in) torpedo tubes. The exception was the *Hood*, whose main armament was mounted in turrets. The barbette arrangement, which saved a great deal of weight, meant that the 'Royal Sovereigns' were a deck higher than contemporary low freeboard battleships, and except for the *Hood* were far better seaboats. They displaced 14,377 tonnes (14,150 tons), carried a complement of 712, had a maximum speed of 16.5 knots and an endurance of 8746km (4720nm).

In the 1890s the Royal Navy, closely followed by other major naval powers, developed a new standard battleship type, later (retrospectively) known as the 'pre-dreadnought'. The first was the 12,548-tonne (12,350-ton) *Renown* of 1892, but it was the excellent 'Majestic' class of 1893-4 that served as the pattern for battleship design for the next decade. Displacing 15,129 tonnes (14,890 tons) they were armed with four 305mm (12in), 12 152mm (6in), 16 76mm (3in) and 12 47mm (1.88in) guns, as well as five 457mm (18in) torpedo tubes. In all, 42 pre-dreadnoughts were built for the Royal Navy up to 1904, and they were to remain an important part of the fleet for many years..

France, whose naval ambitions had been bedevilled throughout the latter half of the 19th century by a succession of changing policies as minister succeeded minister, and whose Admiral Aube, Navy Minister in 1884, had suspended battleship construction altogether, was not a force to be reckoned with on the high seas. Italy was concentrating on armoured cruisers; and the United States was still emerging from the doldrums, legislation authorising the rebuilding of its navy – or rather, the commencement of a new one – having only been passed in 1883. The first two American battleships, the *Texas* and *Maine* of 1888, were both based on foreign designs and in reality were little more than armoured cruisers, carrying a main armament of two 305mm (12in) and four 250mm (10in) guns respectively. The *Maine* was destroyed by an explosion in Havana harbour on 15 February 1898 with the loss of 260 lives, an incident that led to the outbreak of war between the United States and Spain. It was thought at the time that sabotage was the cause, but it was later established, as conclusively as possible, that the ignition of coal gas had been responsible.

THE RISE OF GERMANY

In Europe,the sea power of Germany was rising rapidly, and before long she would assume the position of Britain's main rival. Kaiser Wilhelm II was an admirer of British naval technology, and under the energetic leadership of his naval Chief of Staff, Admiral von Tirpitz, several Navy Acts were passed with the intention of creating a modern naval force. Between 1889 and 1904 Tirpitz ordered the construction of 20 battleships, the first being four ships of the 'Brandenburg' class. These displaced 10,174 tonnes (10,013 tons) and were armed with four 280mm (11in) guns mounted in centre-line turrets. They were followed by five vessels of the 'Kaiser Friedrich III' class (1894–7), five of the 'Mecklenburg' class (1899–1900). five of the 'Braunschweig' class (1900–2) and five of the 'Deutschland' class (1902–4). Tirpitz's simple argument was that the possession of a powerful battle fleet was a matter of national prestige; as Germany was becoming a major industrial nation, she must have a navy to match her economic capability. The fact that he was starting a naval arms race was a matter of little consequence.

Below: HMS *Illustrious* ('Majestic' class), seen here firing her main armament, was an improvement on the 'Renown' class with new 305mm (12in) guns.

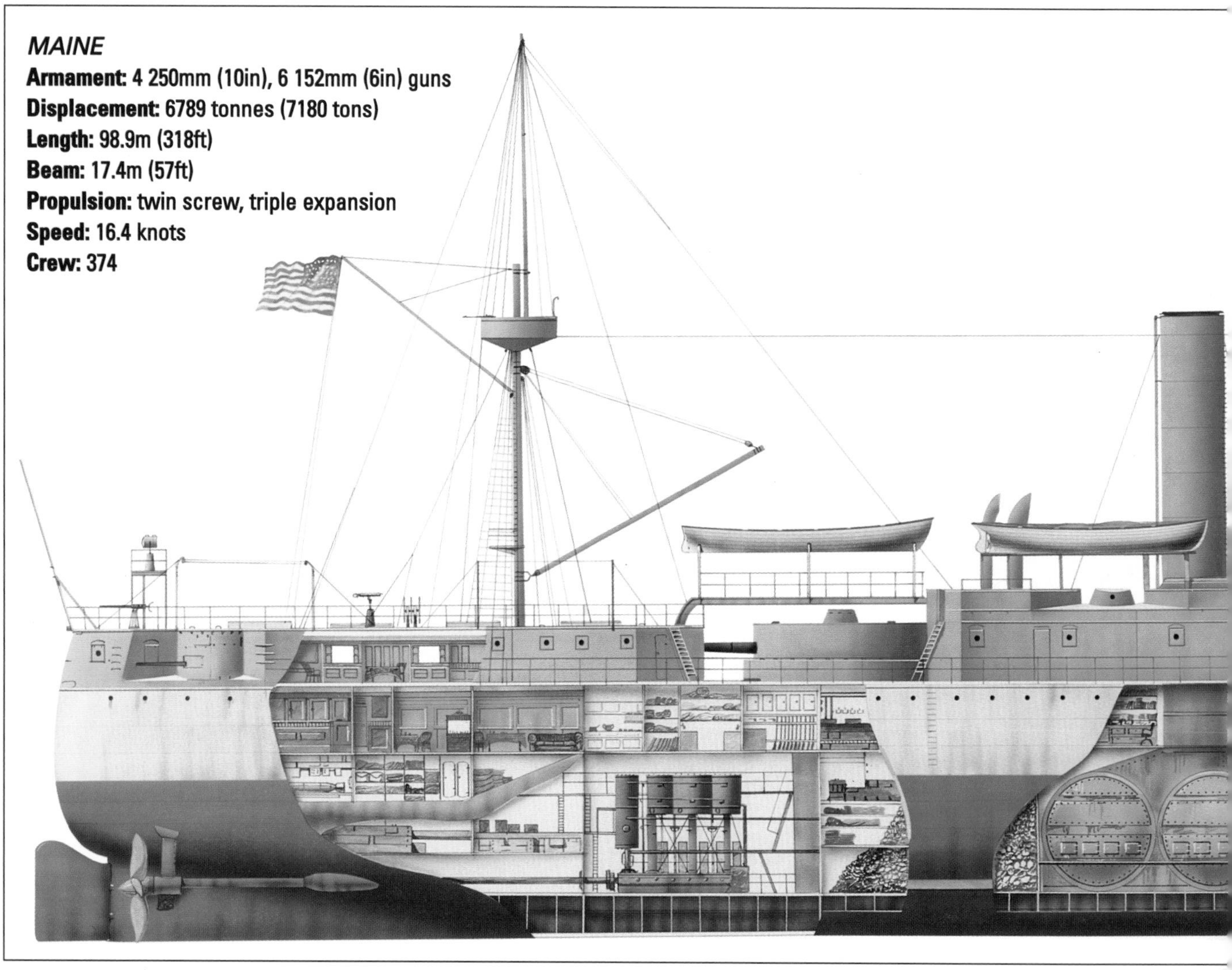
MAINE
Armament: 4 250mm (10in), 6 152mm (6in) guns
Displacement: 6789 tonnes (7180 tons)
Length: 98.9m (318ft)
Beam: 17.4m (57ft)
Propulsion: twin screw, triple expansion
Speed: 16.4 knots
Crew: 374

Above: The US battleship *Maine* was originally authorised as an armoured cruiser. She was laid down in 1888 and completed in September 1895.

Naval affairs in western Europe during this period tended to overshadow events in the Far East, where a great naval drama was soon to be enacted by Russia and Japan. At the turn of the century, Russia's naval assets were divided between the Baltic, the Black Sea and the Far East, where a squadron had been established at Port Arthur in 1895. Early in 1904 the Russians announced that they planned to increase the number of battleships at Port Arthur from 7 to 13 by the end of 1905, and on the night of 8 February the Japanese, aware that their own fleet would be heavily outnumbered by such a reinforcement, attacked the Russian base with a force of 10 destroyers, damaging two battleships and a cruiser. Some time later, the commander of the Port Arthur Squadron, Admiral Makarov, was drowned with 651 others when his flagship, the *Petropavlovsk*, sank after striking a mine as she was making a sortie against the Japanese fleet.

After that, Port Arthur was effectively in a state of siege. The defences, incidentally, proved quite effective, two Japanese battleships (the *Hatsuse* and *Hizen*) being sunk by mines and gunfire during 1904 and others damaged. In December 1904 the surviving Russian warships were sunk at their moorings by Japanese howitzers.

THE STRAITS OF TSUSHIMA

On 27 May 1905 warships of the Russian Baltic Fleet – a force designated the 2nd Pacific Squadron – under Vice-Admiral Rozhdestvensky entered the Straits of Tsushima, at the entrance to the Sea of Japan, having completed an incredible seven-month voyage from its home base. With eight battleships, three armoured cruisers, six light cruisers and 10 destroyers, the

Russians appeared to have a big advantage over the four battleships, seven armoured cruisers and seven light cruisers at the disposal of the Japanese commander, Admiral Heihachiro Togo. But Togo's ships had a three-knot speed advantage over their adversaries, enabling them to manoeuvre and open fire at whatever range they chose; and whereas Russian tactics and training had been influenced by the French, the Japanese had been trained and equipped by the British. There was no comparison.

The Russian fleet was steaming in line ahead, with the four most modern battleships – the *Kniaz Suvorov* (Rozhdestvensky's flagship) the *Imperator Alexander III*, the *Borodino* and the *Orel* – in the van. These were followed by four older battleships, the *Oslyabya*, *Sisoi Veliki*, *Navarin* and *Imperator Nikolai I*, the latter with two cruisers ahead and three coastal defence armour-clad vessels astern. The remaining cruisers brought up the rear.

Togo patiently waited until the whole of the Baltic Fleet was in sight before making his move, turning his ships – which had been following a course that would have 'crossed the Russians' T' – to port so that they were sailing almost parallel to the enemy. The Russians opened up with fierce but inaccurate fire from a range of some 5950m (6500yds), which did not prevent Togo's ships from concentrating their fire on the Russian flagship. The *Suvarov* was soon on fire and she gradually drifted out of line, shrouded in smoke. However she continued to fight on, even after she had sustained a torpedo hit and Rozhdestvensky had been badly wounded. (Rozhdestvensky was taken prisoner by the Japanese after being evacuated from the stricken battleship.) The *Suvorov*'s end came at 1920 hours, when Japanese torpedo boats scored two or three more hits on her. She capsized and sank with the loss of all remaining personnel on board (928 officers and men).

Above: The destruction of the USS *Maine* in Havana harbour, thought to be sabotage but actually a coal gas explosion, precipitated the Spanish-American war of 1898.

Very soon afterwards it was the turn of the *Borodino*, whose captain had been trying to lead the warships out of the trap the Japanese had sprung on them. She was hit, set on fire and blew up, her magazine exploding. She sank with only one survivor from her 830-strong crew. The *Alexander III* had already capsized, having taken numerous hits from 305mm (12in) shells; there were no survivors from her crew of 823. Her demise left the *Orel* as the only modern Russian battleship still afloat. Accompanied by several other survivors, constantly attacked during the night, she surrendered the next morning.

In the second division, one of the older battleships, the *Oslyabya*, had been heavily attacked by Japanese armoured cruisers, taking her first hits only 15 minutes after the start of the battle. After a time she also sank, with the loss of 515 crew. Of the others, the *Navarin* was damaged by gunfire, then sunk by torpedo attack with the loss of 619 lives; the *Sisoi Veliki*, was scuttled by her own crew and went down with 50 dead; and the *Nikolai I* was captured after being damaged by gunfire, being taken into the Japanese Navy and renamed *Iki*. She was sunk as a target ship in 1915.

The only ships to escape destruction or capture were those that sought refuge in neutral ports, where they were interned. The Japanese had gained a victory as great as Nelson's at Trafalgar, a century earlier.

THE TORPEDO

Tsushima was the first major naval battle in which torpedoes were used on a large scale. All the major navies had adopted the self-propelled torpedo by the 1880s, the latest models having a range of about 500m (550yds) at a speed of 18 knots, and the original compressed air method of propulsion was gradually giving way to electric motors. Capital ships and specially-designed torpedo boats – the first of which was the 25m (84ft) HMS *Lightning*, capable of 20 knots – both deployed torpedoes from tubes or launch cradles. As torpedoes had to be launched from close range, torpedo boats were extremely vulnerable to defensive fire, but a Royal Navy exercise conducted in 1885 showed that although all the attacking craft were 'sunk', some of their torpedoes got through. The solution was to counter the torpedo boats with gun-armed 'catchers' that could be deployed from capital ships. By the 1890s these had evolved into larger, independent vessels called 'torpedo boat destroyers' (TBDs) designed to accompany larger units. In 1892–3 the first six ships, now called simply 'destroyers', were ordered for service with the Royal Navy.

By 1895, 36 destroyers, led by HMS *Gossamer* and HMS *Rattlesnake*, had been launched. They were capable of 27 knots, but the torpedo boats then being built could reach 24, so the speed margin was slender. They were succeeded by an improved class, the first of which were HMS *Havoc* and HMS *Hornet*, which could make in excess of 30 knots and were armed with two torpedo tubes mounted on the centre-line, one 12-pounder and five 6-pounder guns. Sixty-eight were built in total.

Torpedo boats and destroyers were not to retain their pre-eminence as torpedo carriers however. By the turn of the century the British Admiralty, which had hitherto shown a complete lack of interest in submarines (a despicable, 'un-English' weapon of war) could no longer afford to ignore the fact that the French and Americans already possessed them in small numbers, and the 1901–2 Naval Estimates made provision for the building of five improved boats of the 'Holland' type (an American design) for evaluation. and they were built under licence by Vickers at Barrow-in-Furness.

The company and the Navy's newly-appointed Inspecting-Captain of Submarines, Captain Reginald Bacon, made a series of improvements, so that when HMS *Submarine No 1* was launched on 2 November 1902 she bore little resemblance to her American progenitor. Displacing 105 tonnes (104 tons) on the surface and 124 tonnes (122 tons) submerged, she was 19.4m (63ft 4in) long and had a maximum beam of

Below: American seamen at work 'coaling ship', a dirty and unpleasant task in which all hands were required to take part.

ASAHI
Armament: 4 305mm (12in), 14 152mm (6in) guns
Displacement: 15,443 tonnes (15,200 tons)
Length: 133.5m (438ft)
Beam: 23m (75ft 6in)
Propulsion: twin screw, triple expansion
Speed: 18 knots
Crew: 836

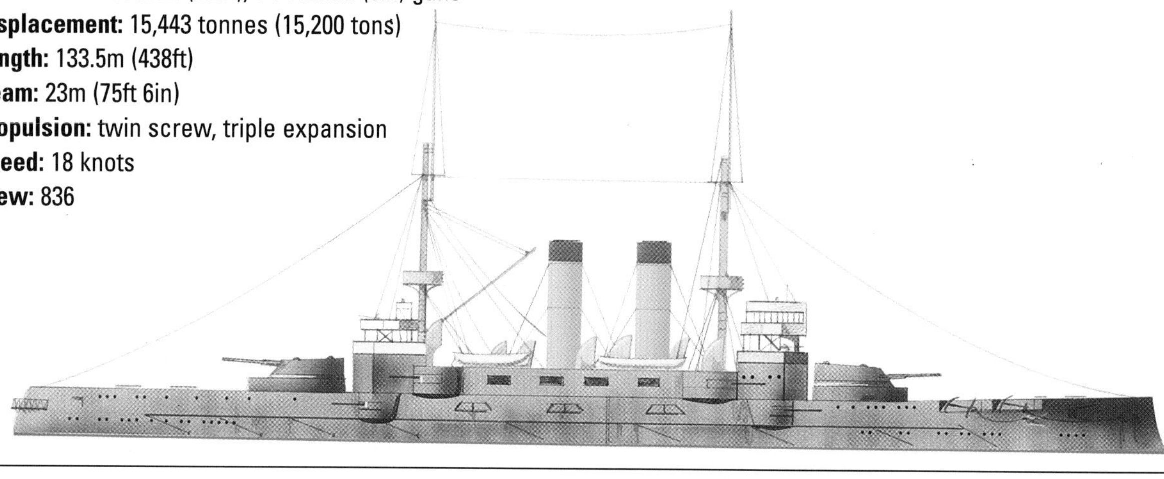

Above: The battleship *Asahi* took part in the Battle of Tsushima. Converted to a repair ship, she was sunk by the US submarine *Salmon* in the South China Sea in 1942.

3.5m (11ft 9in). Her four-cylinder petrol engine developed 160hp, giving a maximum surface speed of about eight knots. Submerged, she was driven by an electric motor powered by a six-cell battery and could make a maximum five knots. Her armament comprised a single 355mm (14in) torpedo tube and she carried a crew of seven. In March 1904 all five boats of the 'A' class, as they were now called, took part in a simulated attack on the cruiser *Juno* off Portsmouth.

Below: Built in France, the Russian pre-dreadnought *Tsessarevitch* was somewhat top-heavy and unstable. She was severely damaged in the Battle of the Yellow Sea.

It was successful, but unfortunately *A.1* was involved in a collision with a passenger liner and sank with the loss of all hands.

In all, 13 'A' class boats were built, followed by 11 'B' class and 38 'C' class. From now on, submarines were to be one of the principal weapons of war in all major navies, and the threat they posed to capital ships would have a profound influence on battleship design and naval tactics. In the Royal Navy, the submarine now had a powerful advocate; an officer appointed First Sea Lord on Trafalgar Day, 1904. His name was Admiral Sir John Fisher, and he would have a significant impact on the navy's development.

Right: The Russian pre-dreadnought *Retvizan*, seen here at the New York Navy Yard in 1901, was sunk by Japanese shore gunfire in Port Arthur harbour on 6 December 1904.

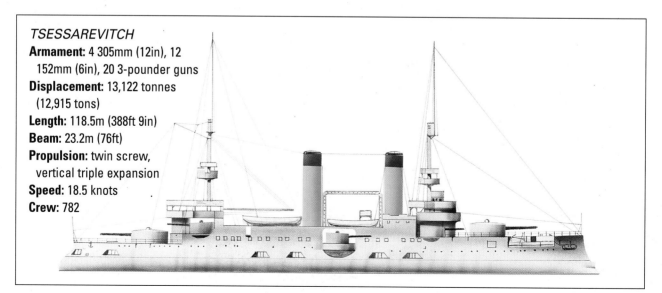

TSESSAREVITCH
Armament: 4 305mm (12in), 12 152mm (6in), 20 3-pounder guns
Displacement: 13,122 tonnes (12,915 tons)
Length: 118.5m (388ft 9in)
Beam: 23.2m (76ft)
Propulsion: twin screw, vertical triple expansion
Speed: 18.5 knots
Crew: 782

CHAPTER FOUR

Dreadnoughts

The new century brought a new type of warship – the dreadnought. Fast and heavily armed at the expense of their secondary armament, this 'super-battleship' was an important factor in the arms race between Britain and Germany before World War I. Designed to engage the enemy at long range, before they could use their torpedoes, the dreadnoughts were the mainstay of the rival fleets during the war.

Jackie Fisher, as he was known throughout the Service, was a comparative rarity in Queen Victoria's navy: a senior officer with a firm grasp of scientific and technological principles. An exponent of gunnery, he harboured a long-standing ambition to improve the fleet's standard of shooting, and during his time in command of the British Mediterranean Fleet he had demonstrated that engagements were feasible at ranges of 5484m (6000yds) and that modern guns could achieve a good hit rate at up to 7312m (8000yds) provided they were deliberately aimed and that full salvoes were fired. It followed that, given such increased accuracy, the chances of success in a long-range naval duel would rise in direct proportion to the number of large-calibre guns that could be brought into action.

Left: The Italian dreadnoughts *Andrea Doria* and her sister *Caio Duilio* were modified 'Cavour' class ships with a 152mm (6in) secondary armament.

By the time he took over as First Sea Lord at the age of 58, Fisher had already put a lot of thought into the concept of a battleship armed with a maximum number of 250mm (10in) guns at the expense of secondary armament, and within weeks of his appointment in 1904 he quickly established a committee to define a battleship armed with the maximum number of 305mm (12in) guns, this calibre being preferred by the Admiralty.

The committee was also to study the concept of a second type of warship, which would carry a battery of 305mm (12in) guns but which would also be able to reach and sustain a speed of 25 knots or thereabouts. This vessel would be in the nature of a hybrid, a cross between a heavy cruiser and a battleship – in other words, a 'battlecruiser'.

DREADNOUGHT
Armament: 10 305mm (12in) guns
Displacement: 18,187 tonnes (17,900 tons)
Length: 160.4m (526ft 3in)
Beam: 25m (82ft)
Propulsion: quadruple screw turbines
Speed: 21.6 knots
Crew: 695–773

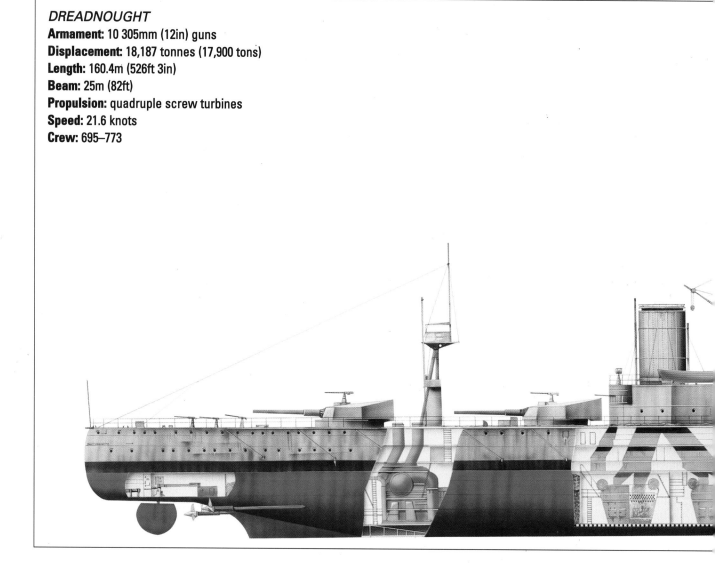

Above: The appearance of *Dreadnought* in 1906 changed the face of naval warfare. She began an arms race with Germany in the years leading up to World War I.

The 'super-battleship' concept took shape rapidly, its development spurred on by the acceleration of the international naval arms race, and a prototype was laid down at Portsmouth in October 1905. It was constructed in great secrecy and in record time, the vessel being ready for initial sea trials a year and a day later. The name given to the formidable new ship was *Dreadnought*.

THE DREADNOUGHT

The *Dreadnought* was revolutionary in that she was armed with 10 305mm (12in) guns, two in each of five turrets centrally placed on the ship. (In fact, only eight guns in the first of these ships could be fully brought to bear, but this was remedied in its successors.) From 1906 onwards a first-class battleship was to be a ship capable of firing 10 heavy guns on either side. Thus a 'dreadnought' could engage one of the older vessels with a superiority of 10 to four, or two of them with a superiority of 10 to eight.

As well as being the first battleship with main armament of a single calibre, *Dreadnought* was also the first with steam turbines and quadruple screws, machinery that gave her a top speed of 21 knots. She carried a crew of 697 and displaced 18,187 tonnes (17,900 tons).

Once the concept of the dreadnought had been proven, construction of this revolutionary type of battleship proceeded rapidly, at the rate of three or four per year. The original *Dreadnought* was followed by the *Bellerophon*, *Superb* and *Temeraire*, all laid down in 1906; the *Collingwood*, *St Vincent* and *Vanguard*,

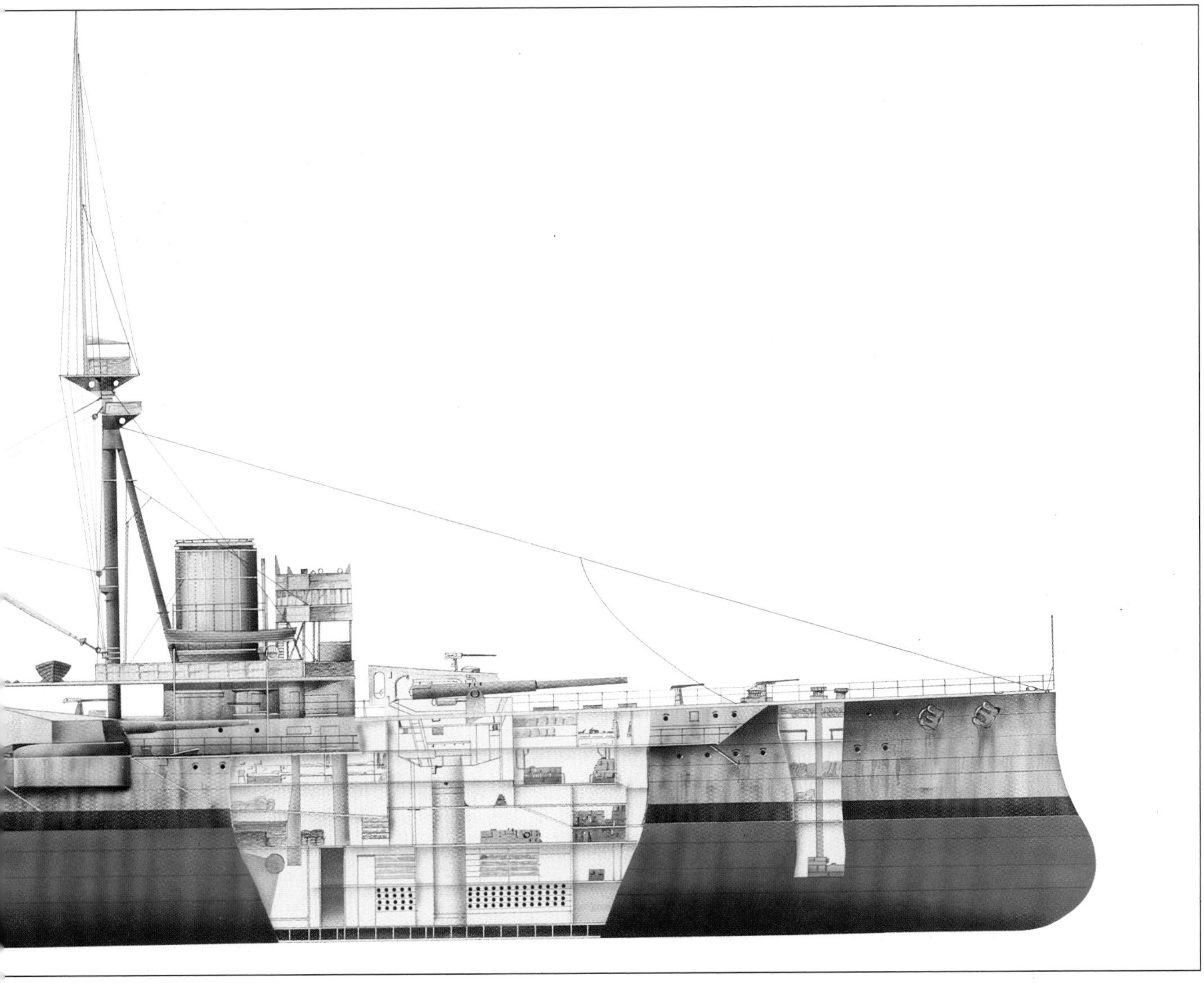

1907; *Colossus*, *Hercules* and *Neptune*, 1908; *Conqueror, Monarch, Orion* and *Thunderer*, 1909; *Ajax, Audacious, Centurion* and *King George V*, 1910; *Benbow, Emperor of India, Iron Duke* and *Marlborough*, 1911; *Barham, Malaya, Queen Elizabeth, Valiant* and *Warspite*, 1912; and *Ramillies, Resolution, Revenge, Royal Oak and Royal Sovereign*, 1913. The 'Queen Elizabeth' class ships of 1912 were designed as fast battleships to replace battlecruisers as the offensive wing of the battle fleet, their task to engage enemy battleships. They were the first battleships to have 380mm (15in) guns and oil-fired engines.

Fisher's critics claimed that his introduction of the dreadnoughts made the great mass of British battleships obsolete and vulnerable, but those who supported him had come to realise that secondary armament was now of minor importance. The increasing range of torpedoes was making close-in actions dangerous. If a battleship could engage its adversary at extremely long range, its 152mm and 230mm (6in and 9in) secondary guns were irrelevant. Gunnery experts realised that at the immense ranges now possible for 305mm (12in) guns – 12,810m (14,000yds) or more – only the biggest guns would count. Effective ranging depended on the firing of salvoes of shells and of a greater number in the salvo, and a full salvo from a dreadnought meant that 3.85 tonnes (3.79 tons) of high explosive was on its way to the enemy over 14km (8nm) away.

BATTLECRUISERS

The other revolutionary warship concept, the battlecruiser, was a vessel nearly equal in armament to the new battleships but very much swifter, a ship that could cruise ahead and scout for the main battle fleet,

INFLEXIBLE
Armament: 8 305mm (12in), 16 102mm (4in) guns
Displacement: 17,527 tonnes (17,250 tons)
Length: 172.8m (567ft)
Beam: 23.9m (78ft 6in)
Propulsion: quadruple screw turbines
Speed: 25.5 knots
Crew: 784

Above: The development of the battlecruiser proceeded in parallel with that of the dreadnought. Pictured here is HMS *Inflexible*, built with her sister ships in great secrecy.

and be capable of overwhelming any conventional cruiser. In fact, the concept arose from the simple fact that existing armoured cruisers had evolved into ships so large and expensive that they had reached the end of their development potential.

The first ship of the new class was the *Inflexible*, completed in 1908. She carried eight 305mm (12in) guns and had a speed of 26 knots. Her firepower was four-fifths that of a dreadnought, but a lot had to be sacrificed in the cause of speed. While the indicated horsepower of the *Dreadnought* was 18,000, that of the *Inflexible* was 41,000, so a large hull was needed to accommodate the necessary 31 boilers. With a reduced armament, and protection sacrificed for speed, the battlecruisers were inevitably more vulnerable, as events at Jutland in 1916 were to show in a tragic manner.

Inflexible's sister ships were the *Indomitable* and *Invincible*. All displaced 17,527 tonnes (17,250 tons) and carried a complement of 784. They were followed by the *Australia, Indefatigable* and *New Zealand*, laid down in 1908–9; *Lion, Princess Royal* and *Queen Mary*, 1909–10; *Tiger*, 1911; *Renown* and *Repulse*, 1914; and finally *Hood*, 1915. Although classed as a battlecruiser, *Hood* was in fact an enlarged 'Queen Elizabeth' -type dreadnought, designed to counter the formidable German 'Mackensen' class battlecruisers laid down at the beginning of 1915. Displacing 41,861 tonnes (41,200 tons), she was completed as the largest warship in the world, and was to remain as such until World War II. Three other ships in this class, *Anson, Howe* and *Rodney*, were also laid down during World War I, but subsequently cancelled; their names were later allocated to a new generation of battleship that would see action in World War II.

GERMAN NAVAL REARMAMENT

In 1908, the Germans had passed yet another of their Navy Acts, making provision for an increase in the number of heavy warships. The 'large cruisers' that were the outcome of an earlier Navy Act, that of 1900, were now reclassified as battlecruisers, so that the planned combined battleship and battlecruiser strength envisaged for the Imperial German Navy over the coming years rose to 58 ships.

Germany's first dreadnoughts were the four vessels of the 'Nassau' class, initiated in 1906. Shorter and wider than the British dreadnought, and less heavily armed, they were nevertheless well protected and well armed: main armament comprised 12 280mm (11in) guns, with a secondary armament of 12 150mm (5.9in). The disposition of the main armament, however, was poor, broadside fire being restricted by the positioning of two turrets on each side amidships and one each fore and aft. Ships in this class were the *Nassau, Posen, Rheinland* and *Westfalen*.

The 'Helgoland' class of 1908 (*Helgoland, Oldenburg, Ostfriesland* and *Thüringen*) were enlarged 'Nassau' types with 305mm (12in) guns. They were the only German dreadnoughts with three funnels. They were marginally faster than the *Nassau* – 20 knots against 19 – and displaced 23,166 tonnes (22,800 tons). Complement was 1100. They were followed by the 'Kaiser' class (*Friedrich der Grosse,*

Kaiser, Kaiserin, König Albert and *Prinzregent Luitpold*) of 1909–10; these were the first German battleships with turbine engines (built, ironically, by Parsons of Tyneside) and with a super-firing turret, mounted aft. The *Friedrich der Grosse*, launched in 1912, was designated flagship of the High Seas Fleet, and was to remain as such until 1917.

German capital ship building continued unabated in the years leading up to the outbreak of war in 1914. After the 'Kaiser' class dreadnoughts came the 'König' class (*Grosser Kurfürst, König, Krönprinz* and *Markgraf*) of 1911, the first German battleships to have all turrets mounted on the centre-line; and the 'Baden' class of 1913 (*Baden, Bayern, Sachsen* and *Württemberg*). The last two were never completed. The 'Baden' class were modified 'Königs' carrying a main armament of eight 380mm (15in) guns.

EUROPEAN DREADNOUGHTS

In 1909 the French Government, realising with a shock that the French Navy had dropped to fifth place worldwide, began a belated attempt to rebuild the fleet. The Navy's already slender resources had suffered another blow in March 1907, when the pre-dreadnought battleship *Ièna* was destroyed by an internal explosion in the after magazine while the ship was in dry dock at Toulon, the result of cordite overheating. An even worse explosion was to destroy another pre-dreadnought, the *Liberté*, in September 1911. The two disasters together claimed 322 lives.

As a result of the reconstruction programme, France embarked on the building of its first four dreadnoughts, the *Courbet, France, Jean Bart* and *Paris*, in 1910–11. These vessels had six turrets, mounting 12 305mm (12in) guns, one turret being on each beam amidships. Only the first two were completed before the outbreak of World War I.

Italy's first dreadnought was the 19,813-tonne (19,500-ton) *Dante Alighieri*, the first battleship with its main armament, in this case 12 305mm (12in) guns, in triple turrets, all mounted on the centre-line to achieve maximum broadside fire. Launched in 1910, the *Dante Alighieri* became the flagship of the Italian fleet in the Adriatic, although it did not see active service.

It was followed in 1909 by the 'Cavour' class (*Conte di Cavour, Giulio Cesare* and *Leonardo da Vinci*), all displacing 23,485 tonnes (23,088 tons) and armed with 13 305mm (12in) guns. Two of these ships, the *Cavour* and *Cesare*, were to be totally reconstructed and uprated in the years between the two world wars.

The last Italian dreadnoughts to be laid down before the outbreak of war were the *Andrea Doria* and *Caio Duilio*, which were modified 'Cavours' with a 152mm (6in) secondary armament. These, too, were

Below: *Ostfriesland*, pictured here in 1921 as a target for American aircraft, belonged to the 'Helgoland' class, the only German dreadnoughts with three funnels.

BADEN

Armament: 8 380mm (15in), 16 150mm (5.9in) guns
Displacement: 32,197 tonnes (31,690 tons)
Length: 179.8m (589ft 10in)
Beam: 8.43m (98ft 5in)
Propulsion: three shaft turbines
Speed: 22 knots
Crew: 1271

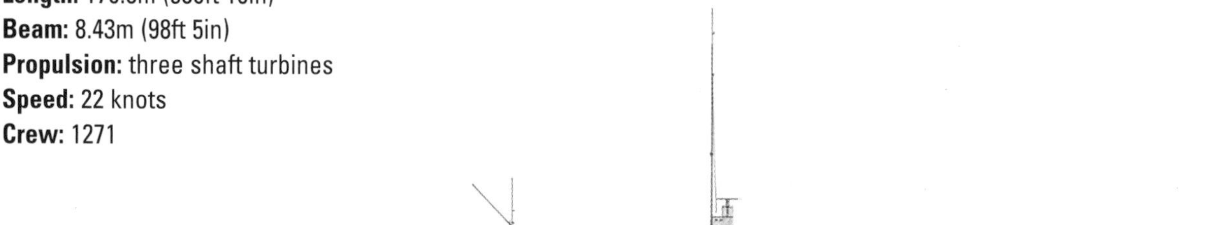

Above: Loading a 152mm (6in) gun during practice aboard an American battleship in 1909. Practice was necessary to speed up the ship's rate-of-fire during combat.

Left: The *Baden* and her sister ship *Bayern* were built as a reply to the British 'Queen Elizabeth' class, and were generally similar.

to be completely reconstructed in the 1930s. Four super-dreadnoughts, the *Cristoforo Colombo, Francesco Caracciola, Francesco Morosini* and *Marcantonio Colonna,* were also planned, but were never completed.

THE GROWTH OF THE AMERICAN NAVY

The first dreadnoughts built in the United States were the *Michigan* and *South Carolina.* Although laid down after HMS *Dreadnought*, they were in fact the first battleships designed with an all-big-gun armament (eight 305mm [12in]) and super-firing turrets, features that were subsequently copied by all other nations. Their propulsion system of two-screw vertical triple-expansion engines left a lot to be desired, producing a maximum speed of barely 17 knots. The *Delaware* and *North Dakota,* suffered similarly, although they were generally a much more successful class with a larger-calibre secondary armament. Other US dreadnoughts laid down before the outbreak of war in Europe were the *Florida, Utah, Arkansas, Wyoming, New York, Texas, Nevada, Oklahoma, Arizona* and *Pennsylvania.*

THE JAPANESE RESPONSE

All the later American dreadnoughts mounted a main armament of 10 or 12 355mm (14in) guns, endowing them with a degree of firepower that the Japanese, on the other side of the Pacific, felt compelled to match. Victory over the Russian fleet at Tsushima had given

LEONARDO DA VINCI
Armament: 13 305mm (12in), 18 120mm (4.7in) guns
Displacement: 23,485 tonnes (23,088 tons)
Length: 176m (577ft 9in)
Beam: 28m (91ft 10in)
Propulsion: quadruple screw turbines
Speed: 21.6 knots
Crew: 1235

Above: The *Leonardo da Vinci* blew up and capsized at Taranto in 1916, possibly due to Austrian sabotage. Refloated but not repaired, she was scrapped in 1923.

the Japanese naval ascendancy in the Pacific, and they were determined to retain it, despite the American challenge. The Japanese Navy's first true dreadnoughts were the *Kawachi* and *Settsu*, laid down in 1910; they carried a main armament of 12 305mm (12in) guns in six twin turrets, one each fore and aft and two on each beam. They were strongly armoured and could make 21 knots. But it was in the design of the 'Kongo' class battlecruisers of 1910–11, the *Haruna*, *Hiei*, *Kirishima* and *Kongo*, that Japan excelled herself.

Designed by Sir G.R. Thurston, the class leader, *Kongo*, was built by Vickers in England (the last Japanese capital ship to be built outside Japan) and was an improved design of the British 'Lion' class battlecruiser, the first of its kind to surpass a battleship in size. The 'Kongo' class, displacing 27,940 tonnes (27,500 tons) mounted eight 355mm (14in) and 16 152mm (6in) guns and could make 30 knots. They carried a complement of 1437 and outclassed all other contemporary ships.

THE FIRST AIRCRAFT AT SEA

In the years before the outbreak of World War I, the mighty dreadnoughts and battlecruisers were visible manifestations of Britain's overwhelming seapower;

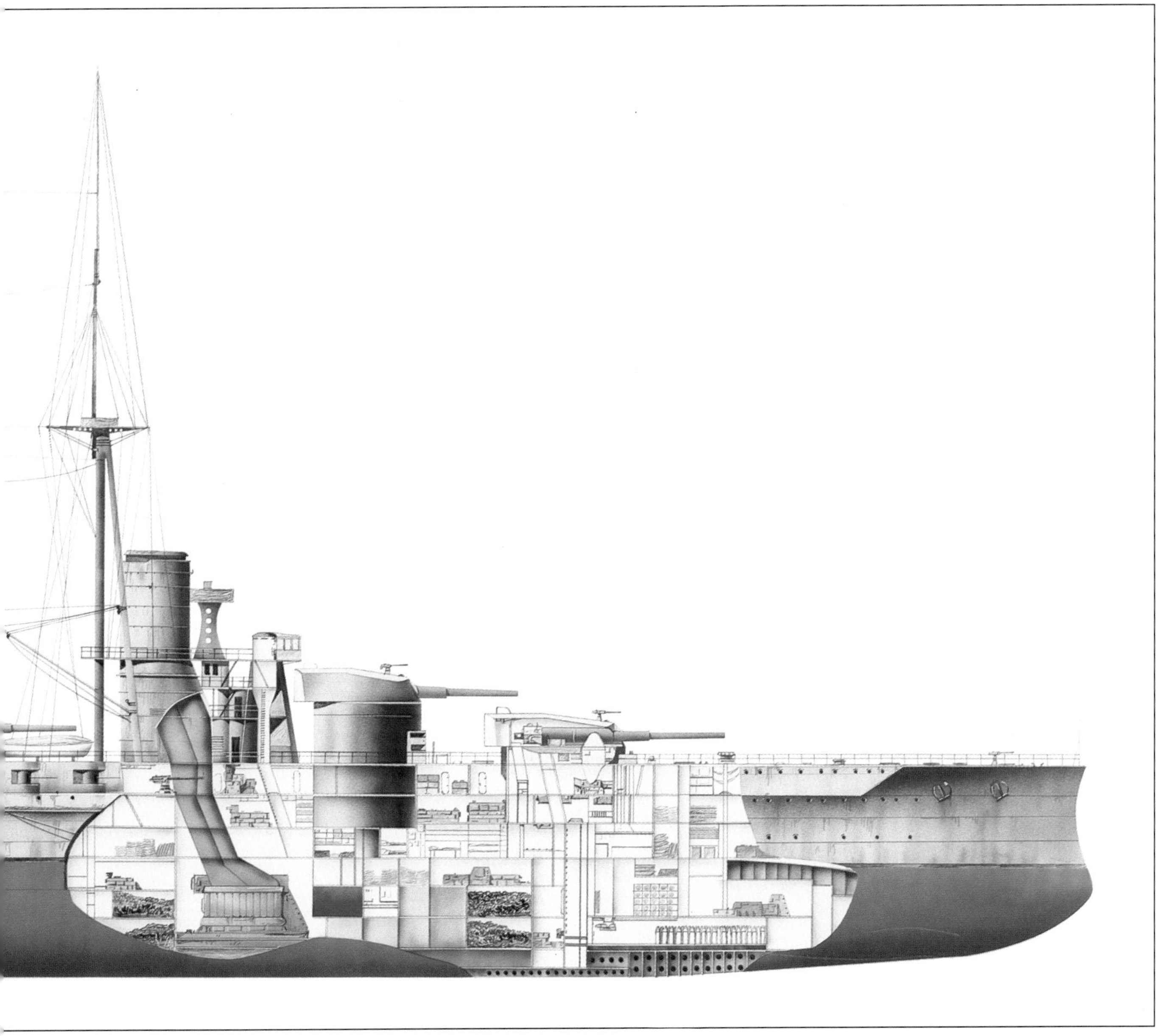

yet behind the scenes, virtually unnoticed, events had been unfolding which would make all of them obsolete within the next half-century.

On 4 May 1912, Commander C.R. Samson, a pilot with the newly formed Naval Wing of the Royal Flying Corps – later to become the Royal Naval Air Service – provided one of the highlights of the Fleet Review at Weymouth by flying a Short S27 biplane from the foredeck of the pre-dreadnought battleship HMS *Hibernia* as she steamed into wind at 10 knots. It was the first time that a British aircraft had taken off from a moving ship. A year later, the old cruiser HMS *Hermes* was commissioned as the headquarters ship of the Naval Wing. She was fitted with a track-way on her forecastle from which a Caudron amphibian made several trial flights during 1913, and was later equipped with three Short S41 floatplanes. In July 1913, for the first time, aircraft were used by the Royal Navy in conjunction with surface vessels during a series of fleet manoeuvres, and aircraft from the *Hermes* experimented with wireless telegraphy.

In the summer of 1913 the Admiralty purchased a second seaplane tender, a 7518-tonne (7400-ton) merchant vessel then under construction at Blyth, Northumberland. She was commissioned in 1914 and honoured with a very famous name: *Ark Royal*. Three more seaplane tenders, the *Empress*, *Engadine* and *Riviera* – all cross-Channel packets – were requisitioned and converted in the summer of 1914, in order to develop this new form of conducting naval warfare.

MICHIGAN
Armament: 8 305mm (12in), 22 76mm (3in) guns
Displacement: 18,186 tonnes (17,900 tons)
Length: 138.2m (453ft 5in)
Beam: 24.5m (80ft 4in)
Propulsion: twin screw, vertical triple expansion
Speed: 18.5 knots
Crew: 869

Above: The USS *Michigan* served with the Atlantic Fleet (1910–16) and performed convoy escort duty in 1917–18. She was decommissioned in 1922 and later broken up.

No one could have envisaged, then, that naval aviation would one day become a potent striking force that would decide the outcome of battles, and hound mighty capital ships to their destruction. The aircraft that were used in the trials were still extremely flimsy creations with very limited endurance times. As the war clouds gathered in 1914, it was the submarine that was seen, rightly, as the principal threat to dominion of the seas.

THE SUBMARINE THREAT

The Royal Navy's submarine fleet had come a long way in the decade since Admiral Fisher's appointment as First Sea Lord. One of his first acts had been to launch a massive submarine construction programme; he had demanded 'more submarines at once – at least 25 in addition to those now building and ordered, and 100 more as soon as practical'. This was an extremely ambitious plan, designed to maintain the Royal Navy's dominance of the seas.

By 1910 the Royal Navy's submarine flotillas had a total of twelve 'A' class boats, eleven 'Bs', and 37 'Cs'. Built by Vickers, all were progressive improvements of the original Holland design; the 'C' class had a length of 43.4m (142ft 3in) and displaced 292 tonnes (287 tons) surfaced. A new class, the 'D', was also laid down. Designed for overseas service, the 'D' class were 50.2m (164ft 6in) long and displaced 503 tonnes (495 tons) on the surface. They were the first British twin-screw submarines and, for surface running, petrol engines were abandoned in favour of heavy oil (diesel) engines. Although beset by teething problems, they were far safer than petrol engines and gave off fewer noxious fumes, significantly improving the crew's working environment. During exercises in 1910, the crew of the prototype submarine *D.1* proved a point when, despite trouble with one engine, they took their boat from Portsmouth to the west coast of Scotland and remained on station off an 'enemy' anchorage for three days, claiming 39 successful dummy torpedo attacks on two cruisers.

The 'E' class, a straightforward development of the 'D', was just beginning to enter service at the outbreak of World War I. Displacing 677 tonnes (667 tons) surfaced, the 'E' class boats carried a crew of 30 and were armed with five torpedo tubes, two in the bow, one in the stern and two amidships, an arrangement which meant that the boat had to turn through no more than 45 degrees to engage any target, giving the commander far greater flexibility. In all, 55 'E' class submarines were built between 1913 and 1916; they were to become the mainstay of the Royal Navy's submarine fleet in World War I, operating in every theatre of war, and their exploits were to become legendary. However it was Germany's submarines that would strike the first blow in the conflict that was to come, and prove how deadly submarines could be to unprotected surface shipping.

Below *Michigan*, seen here firing her guns, and her sister *South Carolina* were the first battleships designed with only big guns, but they were laid down after *Dreadnought*.

CHAPTER FIVE

World War I

The outbreak of war in 1914 brought the expectation of an imminent, decisive battle between the British and German fleets. However, apart from the inconclusive battle of Jutland, the German battleships spent most of the war in port, and it was left to the U-boats to carry the fight to the enemy. Despite this, the German ships remained a threat throughout the war, tying up valuable resources that could have been used elsewhere.

Although the hostilities of World War I were eventually to encompass virtually the whole world, the naval war was decided by the fleets of two nations: Britain and Germany. From the outset, the task facing the Royal Navy was prodigious. Not only had it to protect the shores of Britain from the threat of invasion; it also had to protect the maritime convoys that were vital to the country's survival, and to secure the Channel area so that there was no interference with the constant flow of supplies and personnel to the Western Front.

Above all, the Germans, whose fleet was greatly outnumbered, feared a major attack on their principal naval base of Wilhelmshaven by the British Grand Fleet, based as Scapa Flow in the Orkneys. They would soon be left in no doubt that the Royal Navy intended to follow an aggressive policy; on 28 August 1914 a force of British warships from Harwich swept into the Heligoland Bight and took the enemy completely by surprise. Destroyers of the 1st and 3rd Flotillas, led by the cruisers *Arethusa* and *Fearless*, engaged in a furious battle with German destroyers and cruisers. The *Arethusa* was disabled in the action, but the German cruiser *Mainz* and the destroyer leader *V.187* were sunk. Later, five British battlecruisers under Admiral Sir David Beatty came up in support, sinking the German cruisers *Köln* and *Ariadne*. Two other German light cruisers and three destroyers were damaged.

Left: HMS *Iron Duke*, seen here ploughing through the North Sea. She was the flagship of Admiral Jellicoe at the Battle of Jutland.

Any elation at this British victory soon dissipated when, on 22 September 1914, the British armoured cruisers *Aboukir*, *Crecy* and *Hogue*, each of 12,192

Above: The battlecruiser *Invincible*, which blew up and sank at Jutland with the loss of 1,026 lives, including Rear-Admiral H.L.A. Hood.

tonnes (12,000 tons), were sunk in rapid succession 30 miles southwest of Ijmuiden, Holland, by the German submarine *U.9* (Lt Cdr Otto Weddigen), with the loss of 60 officers and 1400 men. Then, a few weeks later, came news of a major British defeat in the South Atlantic.

THE BATTLE FOR THE SOUTH ATLANTIC

On the outbreak of war, a German naval squadron under Vice-Admiral Graf von Spee, which had been deployed to Tsingtao in China, set out on the long voyage home. It comprised the armoured cruisers *Scharnhorst* and *Gneisenau* and three light cruisers (*Leipzig, Dresden* and *Nürnberg*). By the end of October 1914 it was off the west coast of South America, ready to enter the Atlantic. All that stood between it was a scratch British naval squadron under Admiral Sir Christopher Cradock, comprising the armoured cruisers *Good Hope* and *Monmouth*, a light cruiser, the *Glasgow*, the auxiliary vessel *Otranto* and the old pre-dreadnought battleship *Canopus*.

The 14,224-tonne (14,000-ton) *Good Hope*, completed in 1912, carried one old 233mm (9.2in) gun forward and another aft, as well as 16 152mm (6in) guns of an equally old pattern. The 9144-tonne (9800-ton) *Monmouth*, completed in 1913, had a main armament of 14 152mm (6in) guns, also of an obsolete pattern. The *Glasgow*, launched in 1909, had two 152mm (6in) and 10 100mm (4in) guns of a newer type. The auxiliary vessel, the *Otranto*, was a converted liner of the Orient company, and in no sense did she count as a fighting unit. The old *Canopus*, dating from 1897, had 305mm (12in) guns, but her best speed was barely 15 knots, which was hardly adequate against adversaries that could make 22. In the event, she took no part in the coming action, and was 463km (250nm) away when, on 1 November 1914 *Good Hope, Monmouth, Glasgow* and *Otranto* sighted Admiral von Spee's squadron off Coronel, on the coast of Chile.

Hopelessly outgunned and outranged, *Good Hope* and *Monmouth* were soon on fire, and in the evening *Good Hope* exploded and sank. *Monmouth* went down soon afterwards, whereupon *Glasgow* broke off her own attack and steamed away to join *Canopus*. Both ships headed for the Falkland Islands, where they were ordered to defend the wireless station, coal and oil stores.

The destruction of Admiral Cradock's squadron created a dangerous situation in the South Atlantic. Von Spee was now in a position to paralyse South American shipping; he might even cross the Atlantic to attack the South African mercantile routes. Oddly enough, he failed to exploit this golden opportunity. Instead, after his ships had been replenished and his crews rested off Chile, he planned to attack the Falklands and seize the facilities there.

In London, Admiral Sir John Fisher anticipated von Spee's plan and despatched his Chief of Staff, Vice-Admiral Sir Frederick Doveton Sturdee, southwards with the battlecruisers *Invincible* and *Inflexible*. At the same time, orders were issued to the British warships on station off the Central and Southern American coasts – the cruisers *Cornwall, Kent, Caernarvon* and *Bristol* – to make for the Falklands with all speed and join the *Glasgow* and *Canopus*.

Von Spee's squadron rounded Cape Horn early in December, and on the 8th sighted the Falklands. As the five German warships steamed towards the wireless station they came under fire from the *Canopus*, and just as they were preparing to fire their own first salvoes three British cruisers were sighted coming out of the bay on East Falkland. Von Spee continued to manoeuvre his two principal ships into a position where they could concentrate their heavy guns on *Canopus*, and also ordered the *Leipzig* to come into action and help beat off any possible torpedo attacks by the British light cruisers. At about 0920 hours, von Spee drew his ships up in a new battle line 10 miles from the harbour. It was headed by the *Gneisenau*, with the *Dresden* next, then the *Scharnhorst*, *Nürnberg* and *Leipzig*. The Germans were seeking a running battle in which they would easily be able to out-manoeuvre their opponents.

What von Spee did not know was that, invisible behind the heights surrounding the harbour, were the battlecruisers *Invincible* and *Inflexible*. They had arrived only the day before and had been busily fuelling. Now, at 0945 hours, they emerged under cover of a smokescreen laid by the last British cruiser to leave the anchorage. Too late, von Spee realised that he had fallen into a carefully laid trap.

At 1230 hours Admiral Sturdee increased the speed of his two battlecruisers to 28 knots and, leaving the *Caernarvon, Kent* and *Cornwall* behind, closed in and opened fire on the rearmost German vessel from a range of 15,700m (17,000yds). Von Spee, realising that he could not out-run the British, turned broadside on and engaged the *Invincible*, while the *Gneisenau* took on the *Inflexible*. The three German light cruisers fell out of the battle-line and scattered for the nearest neutral port, pursued by the *Kent, Cornwall* and *Glasgow* while the *Caernarvon* followed the battlecruisers to lend assistance if necessary.

Sturdee used the same tactics against von Spee that the latter had used against Admiral Cradock, using his superior speed and gunnery to good effect. At 1617 hours, after a running fight of some three hours, the *Scharnhorst* went down by the stern and the two British battlecruisers turned their joint fire on the *Gneisenau*, which continued to fight on very gallantly, battered into a blazing wreck, until she too sank at about 1800 hours. About 200 survivors were rescued from her 800-strong crew; all 860 men aboard the *Scharnhorst* perished.

The British cruisers, meanwhile, had caught up with the fleeing enemy ships. In the ensuing battle the *Leipzig* was sunk by *Glasgow* and *Cornwall*, while *Nürnberg* was sunk by HMS *Kent* after a five-hour pursuit. Captain Allen of the *Kent* had exhorted his engineers and stokers to achieve the impossible; the *Kent* was sister ship to the *Monmouth*, which the *Nürnberg* had sunk and left her survivors to drown. The men of the *Kent* were eager for revenge, and they

Below: The battlecruiser *Goeben* took refuge in Constantinople at the outbreak of World War I and entered Turkish service as the *Yavuz Sultan Selim*.

GOEBEN

Armament: 12 150mm (5.9in), 10 280mm (11in) guns
Displacement: 25,704 tonnes (25,300 tons)
Length: 186.5m (611ft 10in)
Beam: 29.5m (96ft 9in)
Propulsion: quadruple screw turbines
Speed: 28 knots
Crew: 1053

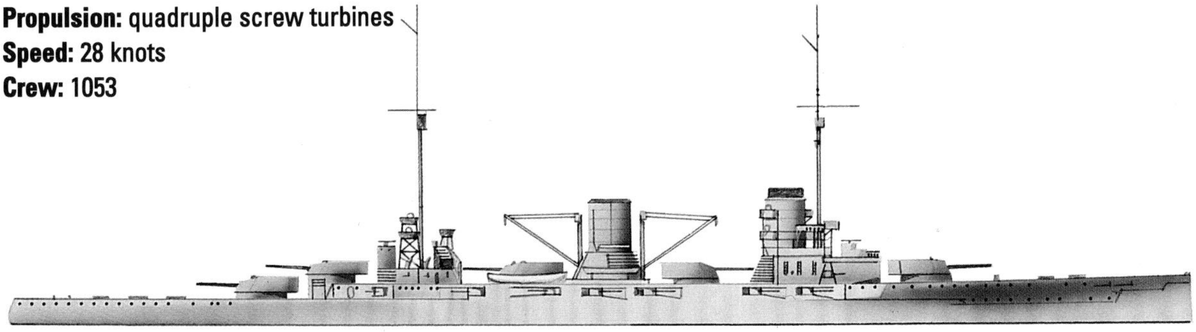

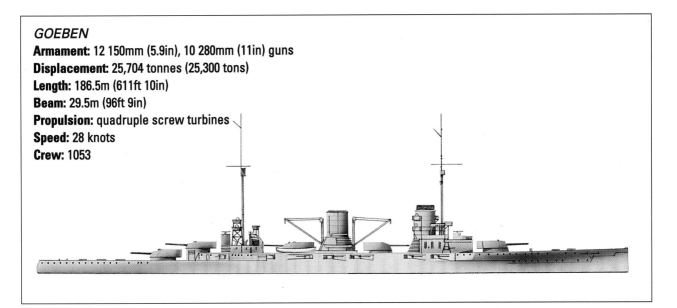

achieved it by feeding their ship's fires with anything that would burn. For a time they actually pushed the old cruiser to go a knot or two faster than she had ever done in the days of her prime, until their efforts brought her guns within range of the enemy.

Of von Spee's Pacific Squadron, only the *Dresden* escaped. But her days, too, were numbered. On 14 March 1915, the cruisers *Kent* and *Glasgow* caught up with her off Juan Fernandez and she was scuttled by her crew after receiving crippling damage.

GERMAN BOMBARDMENTS

The news of Sturdee's victory off the Falklands was soon tempered by the shock of an event that occurred only a week later. The Germans, hoping to lure part of the British fleet into an ambush, decided to carry out a series of hit-and-run attacks on British east-coast towns. The British Admiralty was aware of these plans, because its experts had broken the German naval codes, but it nevertheless came as a surprise when, in the early morning of 16 December 1914, the German battlecruisers *Seydlitz, Moltke* and *Blücher* bombarded West Hartlepool, while the *Derfflinger* and *Von der Tann* shelled Scarborough and Whitby, killing 127 civilians and injuring 567. The *Moltke* and *Blücher* were hit by shore batteries but all the raiders escaped in the mist.

The 1st Battlecruiser Squadron under Admiral Beatty and the 2nd Battle Squadron under Admiral Warrender were already at sea to intercept the attackers, which were sighted on their approach to the coast by British destroyers. At 0445 hours the latter were engaged by the German cruiser *Hamburg* and escorting light forces, which disabled the destroyer HMS *Hardy* and damaged *Ambuscade* and *Lynx*. During the forenoon the German battlecruisers, returning from their attack, passed some miles astern of the 2nd Battle Squadron, which sighted the German ships and turned to close with them – only to be thwarted by deteriorating weather and ambiguous signals from Beatty, which led to the light cruisers breaking off the chase. A golden opportunity had been lost.

Another opportunity was squandered on 24 January 1915, when the Germans set out on an offensive sweep of the southeastern Dogger Bank. Beatty's 1st Battlecruiser Squadron, comprising his flagship HMS *Lion*, together with the *Princess Royal, Tiger, New Zealand* and *Invincible*, sighted the German battlecruisers *Seydlitz, Moltke* and *Derfflinger*, together with the armoured cruiser *Blücher*, six light cruisers and a number of destroyers, steering westward. On sighting the British, the German warships turned and made for home, but were pursued at 28 knots and brought to battle at 0900 hours east of the Dogger Bank. HMS *Lion* led the British line, but dropped out after she was hit, Beatty transferring his flag to the *Princess Royal*. During the action the *Blücher* was sunk and the *Derfflinger* and *Seydlitz* seriously damaged. Greater damage might have been inflicted on the Germans had Beatty, thinking he had spotted a submarine's periscope, not altered course, enabling the enemy to escape.

Below: The dreadnought *Helgoland* was hit by one shell at Jutland. After the battle, the German High Seas Fleet never again contested possession of the North Sea.

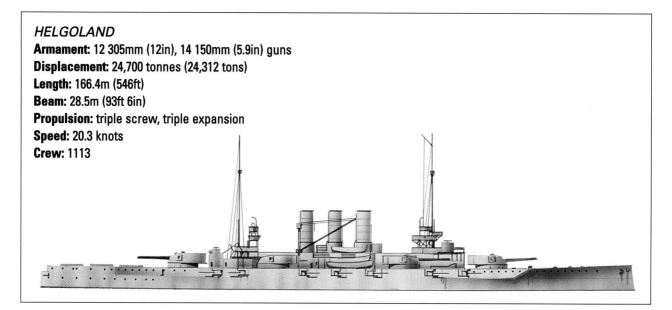

HELGOLAND
Armament: 12 305mm (12in), 14 150mm (5.9in) guns
Displacement: 24,700 tonnes (24,312 tons)
Length: 166.4m (546ft)
Beam: 28.5m (93ft 6in)
Propulsion: triple screw, triple expansion
Speed: 20.3 knots
Crew: 1113

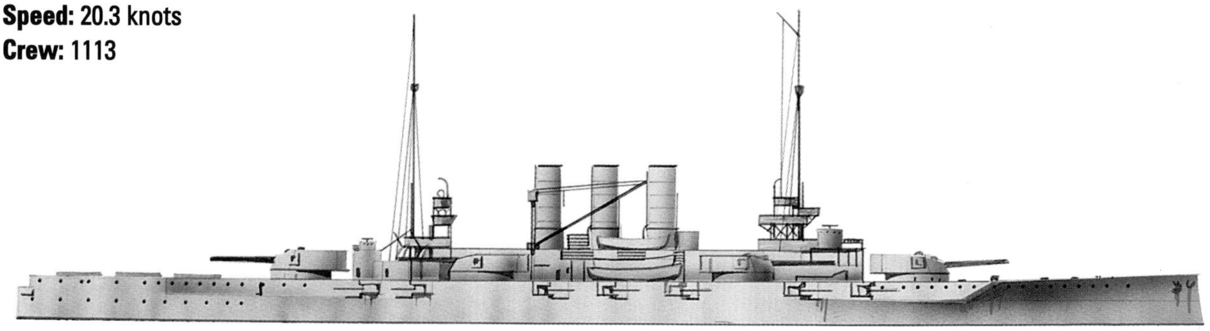

Above: The German battlecruiser *Seydlitz* was severely damaged at Jutland, suffering 23 hits. Her battle scars are clearly visible in the photograph.

JUTLAND

It was not until 31 May 1916 that the British and German Main Battle Fleets met at Jutland. The British forces comprised the Battlecruiser Fleet (1st and 2nd Squadrons), with HMS *Lion* (Adm Beatty), *Princess Royal* (Adm Brock), *Tiger, Queen Mary, New Zealand* (Adm Pakenham) and *Indefatigable*, supported by the 5th Battle Squadron with the battleships HMS *Barham* (Adm Evan-Thomas), *Warspite, Valiant* and *Malaya*, in advance of the Main Battle Fleet under the command of Admiral Lord Jellicoe.

At 1420 hours British Light Forces scouting ahead of the Battlecruiser Fleet sighted German ships to the east-southeast and signalled the information to Admiral Beatty, who turned his ships south-southeast to intercept.

At 1435 hours Beatty altered course again, making for heavy smoke that could be seen to the east-northeast. The seaplane carrier *Engadine* launched a seaplane scout; it was the first time that such a reconnaissance mission was flown in action.

At 1531 hours Admiral Beatty sighted the German Battlecruiser Squadron, comprising HIMSS (His Imperial Majesty's Ships) *Lützow* (Adm Hipper), *Derfflinger, Seydlitz, Moltke* and *Von der Tann*, steering east-northeast. The British battlecruisers closed in on the German squadron from 21,000m (23,000yds) at 25 knots, with the 5th Battle Squadron, 9150m (10,000yds) astern, coming up fast.

At 1548 hours both battlecruiser forces opened fire almost simultaneously at about 17,000m (18,500yds), the range being reduced to 14,600m (16,000yds) over the next 10 minutes or so.

At 1606 hours, HMS *Indefatigable* was hit by a salvo from the *Von der Tann*. The battlecruiser's magazine exploded and a second salvo tore into the wreckage, completing her destruction. She sank in minutes with the loss of 1017 lives.

At 1608 hours the British 5th Battle Squadron joined the action at a range of 17,380-18,300m (19,000-20,000yds), opening accurate fire on the German Light Cruiser Squadron and driving the

DERFFLINGER
Armament: 8 305mm (12in) guns
Displacement: 30,706 tonnes (30,223 tons)
Length: 210m (689ft)
Beam: 29m (95ft 2in)
Propulsion: quadruple screw turbines
Speed: 28 knots
Crew: 1112

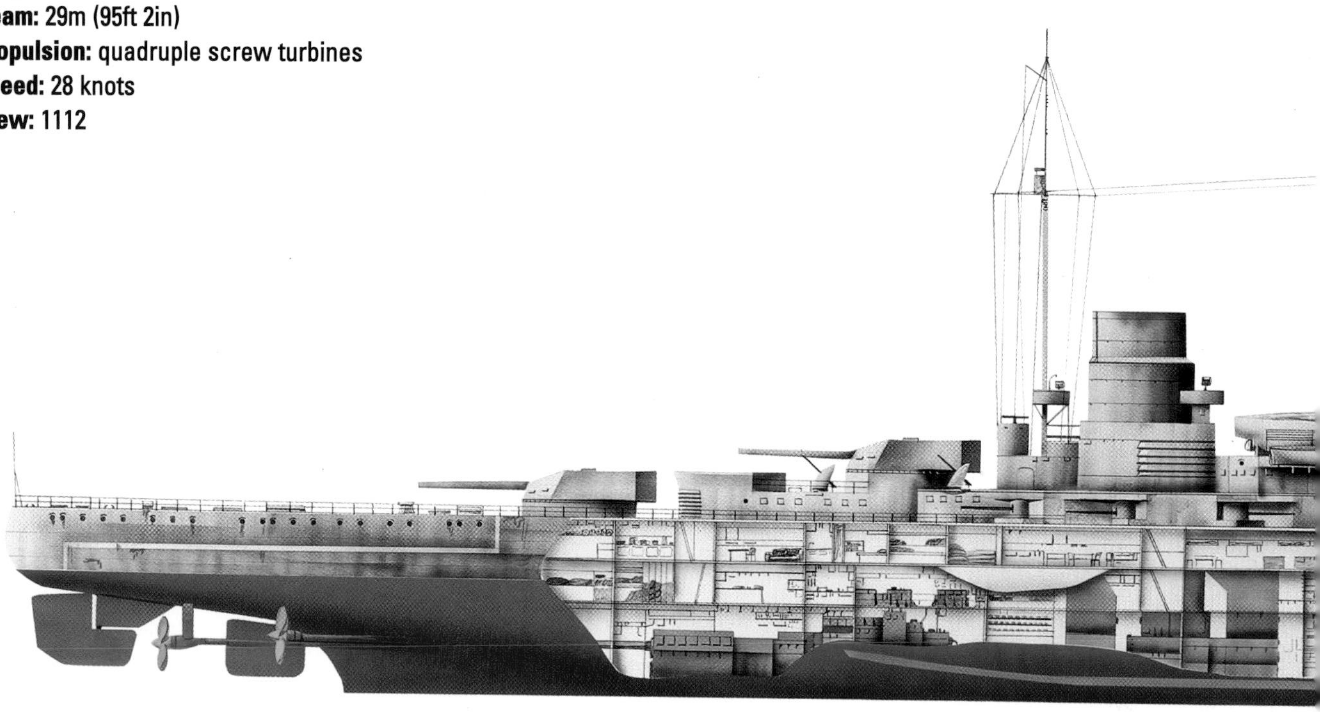

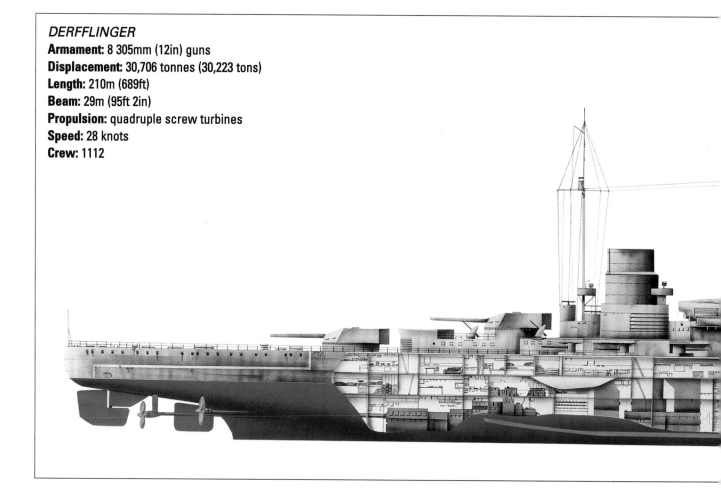

enemy away to the east. Twenty minutes later, there was a repeat of the earlier disaster when the 'Lion' class battlecruiser *Queen Mary* took a direct hit from the German battlecruiser *Derfflinger* and blew up with a tremendous explosion. There were only nine survivors from her crew of 1266.

At 1642 hours Admiral Beatty sighted the German High Seas Fleet under Admiral Scheer (flagship *Friedrich der Grosse*), led by the 3rd Squadron, and steering northwards. In succession the British ships turned 16 points to starboard and the German battlecruisers followed suit, taking station ahead to cover the High Seas Fleet. At the time of this manoeuvre Admiral Beatty's ships and Admiral Jellicoe's Main Battle Fleet were over 80km (43nm) apart and closing at about 20 knots. By 1645 hours the 5th Battle Squadron's 'Queen Elizabeth' class battleships were in a position to engage the enemy, the *Barham* and *Valiant* supporting the Battlecruiser Fleet while the *Warspite* and *Malaya* engaged the German 1st and 3rd High Seas Squadrons at 17,380m (19,000yds). *Barham* was soon scoring hits on the *Seydlitz*, which was further damaged in a torpedo attack by British destroyers, while the *Valiant* was finding the range of the German *Moltke*.

At 1800 hours the Main Fleet under Admiral Jellicoe (flagship *Iron Duke*) arrived, the main force having maintained a 'fleet speed' of 20 knots since 1600 hours on a southeasterly course, with the Battle Fleet in divisions line ahead. Having received Admiral Beatty's report giving the position of the High Seas Fleet, Admiral Jellicoe signalled the Battle Fleet to form line of battle. At this point the Germans inflicted more casualties, the battleship *Friedrich der Grosse* sinking the armoured cruiser *Defence* (Rear-Adm Sir Robert Arbuthnot) with the loss of 893 lives and damaging another armoured cruiser, HMS *Warrior*, which shortly after 1805 hours had crossed *Lion*'s bows from port to starboard in order to finish off *Wiesbaden*, one of the German light cruisers under their fire. The disabled *Warrior* passed astern of 5th Battle Squadron (turning to port to form astern of 6th Division) just as *Warspite*'s helm jammed. This mishap compelled the latter to continue her turn and brought her under heavy fire, but enabled *Warrior* to draw clear. (She foundered under tow the next day.)

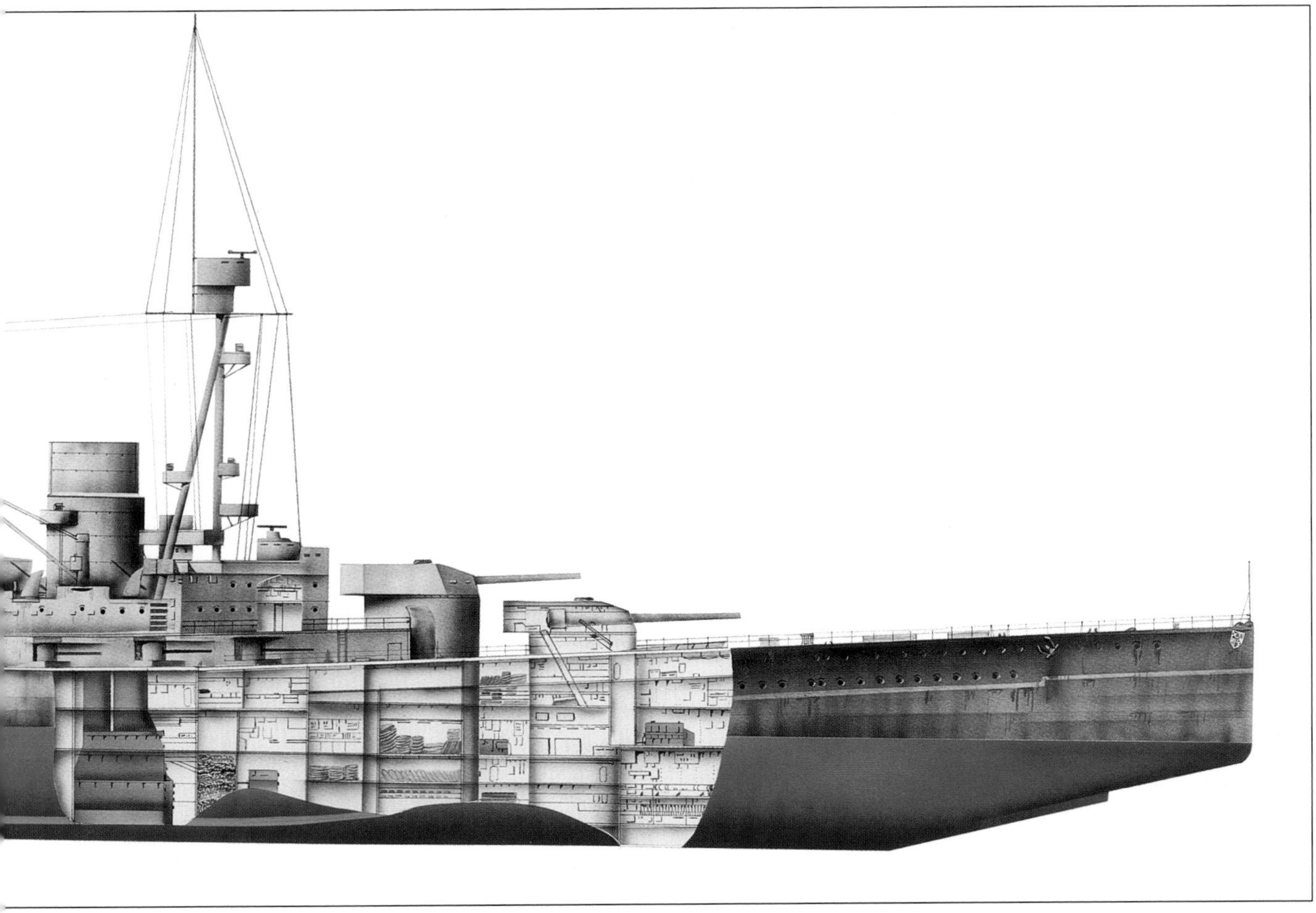

Meanwhile, the 3rd Battlecruiser Squadron, comprising HMS *Invincible* (Rear-Adm Hood), HMS *Inflexible* and HMS *Indomitable*, detached by Admiral Jellicoe at 1600 hours in support of Beatty, had come up from the eastward, where with *Canterbury* and *Chester* it had engaged the German light cruiser screen in a sharp encounter in which the TBD *Shark* was sunk. Upon sighting *Lion*, Admiral Hood at 1816 hours took station ahead of the Battlecruiser Fleet and engaged the German battlecruisers at 7870m (8600yds). Soon after 1830 hours *Invincible*, battered by repeated salvoes, notably from *Derfflinger*, blew up and sank. Even so, Admiral Hood's arrival in a commanding position in relation to the German Fleet caused the latter to make a large turn to starboard, his squadron being probably mistaken for the British Battle Fleet.

At 1831 hours HMS *Iron Duke* engaged the leading ship of König Squadron at 11,000m (12,000yds). On the starboard wing HMS *Marlborough* (Adm Burney) had already opened fire at 1817 hours on a ship of 'Kaiser' class at 11,900m (13,000yds). Within two minutes the Battle Fleet, having increased speed

Above: The *Derfflinger* and her two sister ships, the *Hindenburg* and *Lützow,* all launched in 1913, were arguably the best capital ships of their day.

to 17 knots, was fully committed to the battle, although its gunnery was impeded by mist and smoke. At the head of the German battlecruiser line *Lützow* hauled away badly damaged, and *Derfflinger* ceased firing. A few minutes later the British Fleet altered course to the south by divisions, in order to close the German Fleet. The *Lützow* was now well ablaze and listing heavily. She was later abandoned and sunk by a German destroyer.

At 1900 hours Admiral Jellicoe ordered the 2nd Battle Squadron to take station ahead of *Iron Duke*, and the 1st Battle Squadron to form up astern. During the next half-hour the British ships held their targets under intermittent but effective fire at ranges varying from 13,700m (15,000yds) in the van to 7800m (8500yds) in the rear. Fifteen minutes later Admiral Scheer, drawing off his main force, ordered his already battered battlecruisers to 'close the enemy,' but to all intents and purposes the main battle was

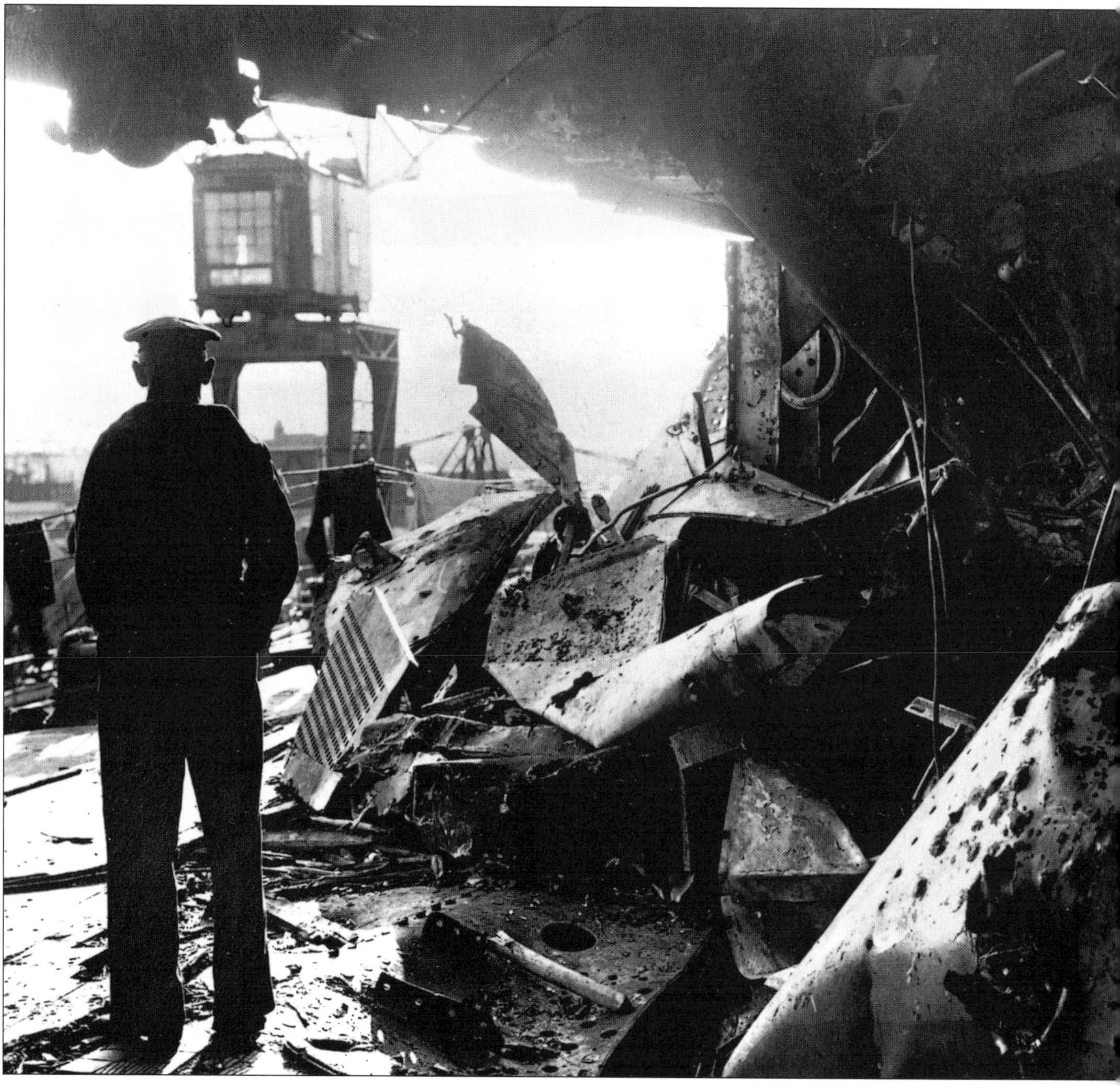

Above: Some of the damage inflicted on the *Derfflinger* at the battle of Jutland. The seaman gives a good sense of scale to the damage caused by a solitary shell.

over. At 1937 hours, with the *Derfflinger* – which had taken over the lead from the stricken *Lützow* – the German battlecruisers broke off the action.

As dawn broke over the North Sea on 1 June, following sporadic night actions in which more ships were lost, the fleets dispersed, and by noon both were returning to their respective bases. Jellicoe had intended to pursue the High Seas Fleet to its destruction; that he failed to do so was due to a combination of circumstances – vague reports, the failure of some of his captains to exercise initiative, the failure of the British Admiralty to relay certain vital intelligence on the movements of the enemy warships. The Germans had meted out far more punishment than they had taken. They had lost one battleship (the *Pommern*, sunk during the night in a torpedo attack), a battlecruiser, four cruisers and five destroyers, but the British had lost three battlecruisers, three cruisers and eight destroyers. British fatal casualties numbered 6097, against the German total of 2551.

Yet the Royal Navy had won a strategic victory. The next time the German High Seas Fleet left Wilhelmshaven in full strength would be in November 1918, after the German surrender, when it sailed into internment at Scapa Flow. There, in 1919, it would be scuttled by its own crews in a final act of defiance.

THE DARDANELLES

In the Mediterranean, the principal area of operations was the Dardanelles. Turkey had come out on the side of the Central Powers (Germany and Austria) and her troops were pressing the Russians hard in the Caucasus. In an attempt to relieve the pressure, an Anglo-French combined operation was mounted, its aim to force a passage of the Dardanelles – the winding, treacherous 64km (40 mile) stretch of water leading from the Aegean to the Sea of Marmara – and land an expeditionary force before Constantinople (Istanbul), the belief being that such a show of strength would quickly force Turkey out of the war.

But the Turks were ready to confront such a plan. With German help they had mined the waters and installed powerful shore batteries to cover the minefields, so that any attempt to sweep them would be met with devastating gunfire. Before the mines could be swept the forts therefore had to be neutralised, and this could only be done by naval gunfire. A powerful Anglo-French naval force was assembled, comprising fourteen pre-dreadnought battleships (four of them French), the battlecruiser *Inflexible* and the new dreadnought *Queen Elizabeth.*

The bombardment of the forts at the entrance to the Dardanelles began on 19 February 1915, with aircraft

Below: The battlecruiser HMS *Invincible* broken in two and sinking at Jutland. The destroyer *Badger* is approaching to pick up the six only survivors.

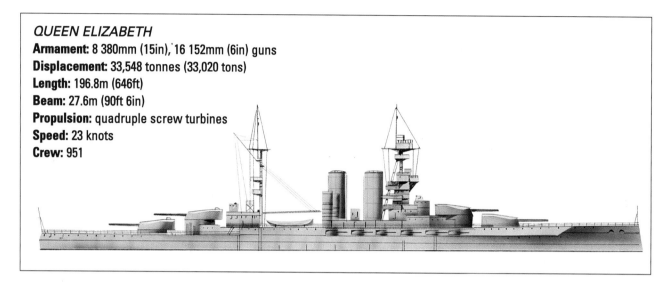

QUEEN ELIZABETH
Armament: 8 380mm (15in), 16 152mm (6in) guns
Displacement: 33,548 tonnes (33,020 tons)
Length: 196.8m (646ft)
Beam: 27.6m (90ft 6in)
Propulsion: quadruple screw turbines
Speed: 23 knots
Crew: 951

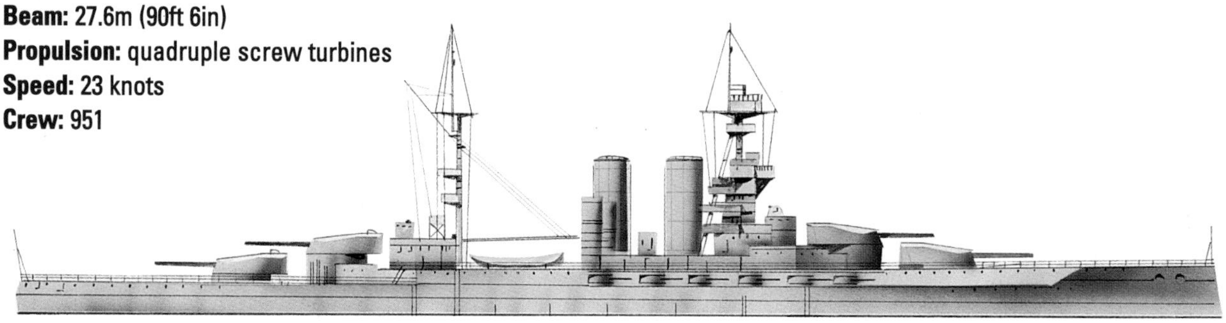

Above: The dreadnought *Queen Elizabeth* saw service in the Dardanelles in 1915 and was later transferred to the Grand Fleet. She saw extensive service in World War II.

from the seaplane carrier *Ark Royal* acting as spotters. The forts were shattered, enabling trawlers to sweep the first four miles of the straits, and on 26 February the pre-dreadnoughts *Albion, Majestic* and *Vengeance* proceeded to the limit of the swept area to bombard fort Dardanus. The bombardments continued throughout March. Other British ships involved including the pre-dreadnoughts *Triumph, Ocean, Canopus, Swiftsure, Cornwallis, Irresistible, Prince George, Agamemnon* and *Lord Nelson*, as well as the *Queen Elizabeth*, whose 380mm (15in) guns were powerful enough to hit the vulnerable reverse faces of the fortifications by shooting right across the peninsula with the help of spotting from the air.

Despite the weight of firepower, progress was slow and minelaying operations were thwarted by powerful searchlights and accurate enemy gunfire. In an attempt to break the deadlock, a maximum effort involving three squadrons of warships was mounted on 18 March 1915. It ended in disaster, the *Irresistible*, *Ocean* and the French *Bouvet* being mined and sunk while *Inflexible* and the French

Gaulois were damaged. The British losses were made good by the pre-dreadnoughts *Queen* and *Implacable*.

It was now becoming increasingly clear that without military support ashore further attempts to force a passage of the Dardanelles would meet with failure, and consequently April 1915 saw the beginning of the disastrous Gallipoli campaign, with Allied forces landing on the peninsula in what was then the largest opposed amphibious invasion in history. Allied warships continued to support the ground forces until they were evacuated in January 1916, having suffered appalling attrition through enemy action and disease. The Royal Navy lost three more pre-dreadnoughts in the course of the campaign, the battleship *Goliath* being torpedoed by the Turkish destroyer *Muavenet* in May 1915 (570 dead) and the *Triumph* and *Majestic* being torpedoed by the German submarine *U.21* in the same month (73 and 40 dead).

BEN-MY-CHREE

One Royal Navy vessel that made an everlasting name for herself in the Dardanelles was the seaplane carrier *Ben-my-Chree*, which arrived on 12 June 1915. She carried two Short Seaplanes, converted to launch torpedoes, and these scored some successes against enemy transports. The *Ben-my-Chree* subsequently operated in the eastern Mediterranean, the Red Sea and the Indian Ocean, until she was sunk by enemy gunfire off Castellorizo in Asia Minor.

Yet the days of hybrid ships like the *Ben-my-Chree* were numbered. By 1917, the Royal Navy was a long way ahead of the rest of the world in the development of vessels that could truly be defined as aircraft carriers. The first was the light battlecruiser HMS *Furious*, laid down shortly after the outbreak of war. Launched on 15 August 1916, she was fitted initially with a flight deck forward of her superstructure, but was eventually completed with a continuous flight deck and hangar accommodation for 16 aircraft. She was also fitted with a primitive form of arrester gear comprising strong rope nets suspended from cross-pieces, a necessary precaution on the narrow decks.

A similarly-equipped vessel, HMS *Cavendish*, was commissioned in October 1918. Renamed HMS *Vindictive*, her operational career was limited to a brief foray in support of the Allied Intervention Force in North Russia and the Baltic in 1919–20. The most important development was centred on three new carriers, all fitted with unbroken flight decks – the 11,024-tonne (10,850-ton) HMS *Hermes*, HMS *Argus* and HMS *Eagle*. Of the three, only HMS *Argus* joined the Fleet before the end of hostilities. Their day would come in a later war, but carriers were soon to dominate the seas, as the battleship once had done.

Below: Launched in October 1913, the dreadnought *Queen Elizabeth* underwent two major reconstructions between the wars, serving latterly in the Eastern Fleet.

BATTLESHIP LOSSES 1914–18

Listed below in date order are the battleship losses of the major combatant nations during World War I.

Austria-Hungary
10 December 1917
WIEN
SECOND CLASS BATTLESHIP
Torpedoed and sunk by Italian MTB *MAS9*, Trieste Harbour.

10 June 1918
SZENT ISTVAN
DREADNOUGHT
Torpedoed and sunk by Italian MTB *MAS15*, Premuda Island.

1 November 1918
VIRIBUS UNITIS
DREADNOUGHT
Sunk by Italian frogmen, Pola.

France
18 March 1915
BOUVET
PRE-DREADNOUGHT
Mined, blew up and sank, Dardanelles.

26 November 1916
SUFFREN
PRE-DREADNOUGHT
Torpedoed and sunk by *U.52*, Lisbon.

27 October 1915
GAULOIS
PRE-DREADNOUGHT
Torpedoed and sunk by *U.47*, Cerigo Island.

19 March 1917
DANTON
PRE-DREADNOUGHT
Torpedoed and sunk by *U.64*, Sardinia.

Germany
1 June1916
POMMERN
PRE-DREADNOUGHT
Sunk by British destroyers, Jutland.

1 June1916
LÜTZOW
BATTLECRUISER
Sunk by German destroyer after battle damage, Jutland.

Great Britain
27 October 1914
AUDACIOUS
DREADNOUGHT
Sunk by mine, Tory Island,

26 November 1914
BULWARK
PRE-DREADNOUGHT
Blew up and sank at anchor, Sheerness.

1 January 1915
FORMIDABLE
PRE-DREADNOUGHT
Sunk by *U.24*, Portland Bill,

18 January 1915
IRRESISTIBLE
PRE-DREADNOUGHT
Sunk by mine, Dardanelles.

18 March 1915
OCEAN
PRE-DREADNOUGHT
Sunk by mine, Dardanelles,

13 May 1915
GOLIATH
PRE-DREADNOUGHT
Torpedoed and sunk by Turkish destroyer *Muavenet*, Cape Helles,

25 May 1915
TRIUMPH
PRE-DREADNOUGHT
Torpedoed and sunk by *U.21*, Dardanelles.

27 May 1915
MAJESTIC
PRE-DREADNOUGHT
Torpedoed and sunk by *U.21*, Dardanelles.

6 January 1916
KING EDWARD VII
PRE-DREADNOUGHT
Capsized and sank under tow after mine damage, Cape Wrath.

27 April 1916
RUSSELL
PRE-DREADNOUGHT
Sunk by mine, Malta.

31 May 1916
INVINCIBLE
BATTLECRUISER
Blew up and sank, Jutland.

31 May 1916
INDEFATIGABLE
BATTLECRUISER
Blew up and sank, Jutland,

31 May 1916
QUEEN MARY
BATTLECRUISER
Blew up and sank, Jutland.

9 January 1917
CORNWALLIS
PRE-DREADNOUGHT
Torpedoed and sunk by *U.32*, Malta.

9 July 1917
VANGUARD
DREADNOUGHT
Destroyed by internal explosion, Scapa Flow.

9 November 1918
BRITANNIA
PRE-DREADNOUGHT
Torpedoed and sunk by *U.50*, Cape Trafalgar.

Italy
27 September 1915
BENEDETTO BRIN
PRE-DREADNOUGHT
Blew up at Brindisi, cause unknown.

2 August 1916
LEONARDO DA VINCI
DREADNOUGHT
Blew up and capsized, Taranto,

11 December 1916
REGINA MARGHERITA
PRE-DREADNOUGHT
Sunk by mines, Valona.

Japan
14 January 1917
TSUKUBA
ARMOURED CRUISER
Destroyed by magazine explosion, Yokosuka.

Russia
20 October 1916
IMPERATRITSA MARIA
DREADNOUGHT
Blew up, Sevastopol.

4 January 1917
PERESVIET
PRE-DREADNOUGHT
Sunk by mines, Port Said.

17 October 1917
SLAVA
PRE-DREADNOUGHT
Scuttled in Moonsund Strait.

18 June 1918
SVOBODNAYA ROSSIA
DREADNOUGHT
Scuttled at Novorossisk,

Turkey
13 December 1914
MESSUDIEH
CENTRAL BATTERY SHIP
Torpedoed and sunk by British sub *B.11*, Chanak,

8 August 1915
HAIRREDIN BARBAROSSA
PRE-DREADNOUGHT
Torpedoed and sunk by British sub *E.11*, Dardanelles.

Above: French gunners in action at the Dardanelles. The French Navy played a considerable part in supporting Allied operations during this campaign.

Below: The battleship HMS *Cornwallis* bombarding Turkish positions in the Dardanelles. The Royal Navy used its elderly pre-dreadnoughts in this theatre.

1號艦

CHAPTER SIX

The Race to Armageddon 1919–39

The scuttling of the German High Seas Fleet at Scapa Flow marked the beginning of a new age of warfare at sea. The war had shown that the battleship faced a new challenge from both the submarine and the aircraft carrier, and battleships became faster and more heavily armed. Although most countries were committed to reducing the strength of their navy after 1918, the growth of the Japanese and later German navies brought a new threat of war.

At the end of World War I the Royal Navy had 44 capital ships, with one building, but by 1920 this was reduced to 29, a figure generally accepted as being the minimum number needed to defend Britain's worldwide interests and maintain parity with the fast-growing naval forces of the United States and Japan. But on 6 February 1922, the number of capital ships available to the Royal Navy was further reduced with the signing of the Washington Naval Treaty.

Left: The Japanese battleship *Yamato*, the mightiest to serve in World War II, undergoing a refit in 1941, only a few months before the attack on Pearl Harbor.

The principal aim of the Washington Treaty, which was engineered by the United States and which in effect was the first disarmament treaty in history, was to limit the size of the navies of the five main maritime powers, which at that time were Britain, the USA, France, Italy and Japan. For Britain, this meant a reduction in capital ship assets to 20 by scrapping existing warships and dropping new projects. However, because her capital ships were older and less heavily armed than those of the United States, she would be permitted to build two new vessels as replacements for existing ones. The other nations would also be permitted to build new capital ships to

WARSPITE
Armament: 8 380mm (15in), 16 152mm (6in) guns
Displacement: 33,548 tonnes (33,020 tons)
Length: 197m (646ft)
Beam: 28m (90ft 6in)
Propulsion: quadruple screw turbines
Speed: 23 knots
Crew: 951

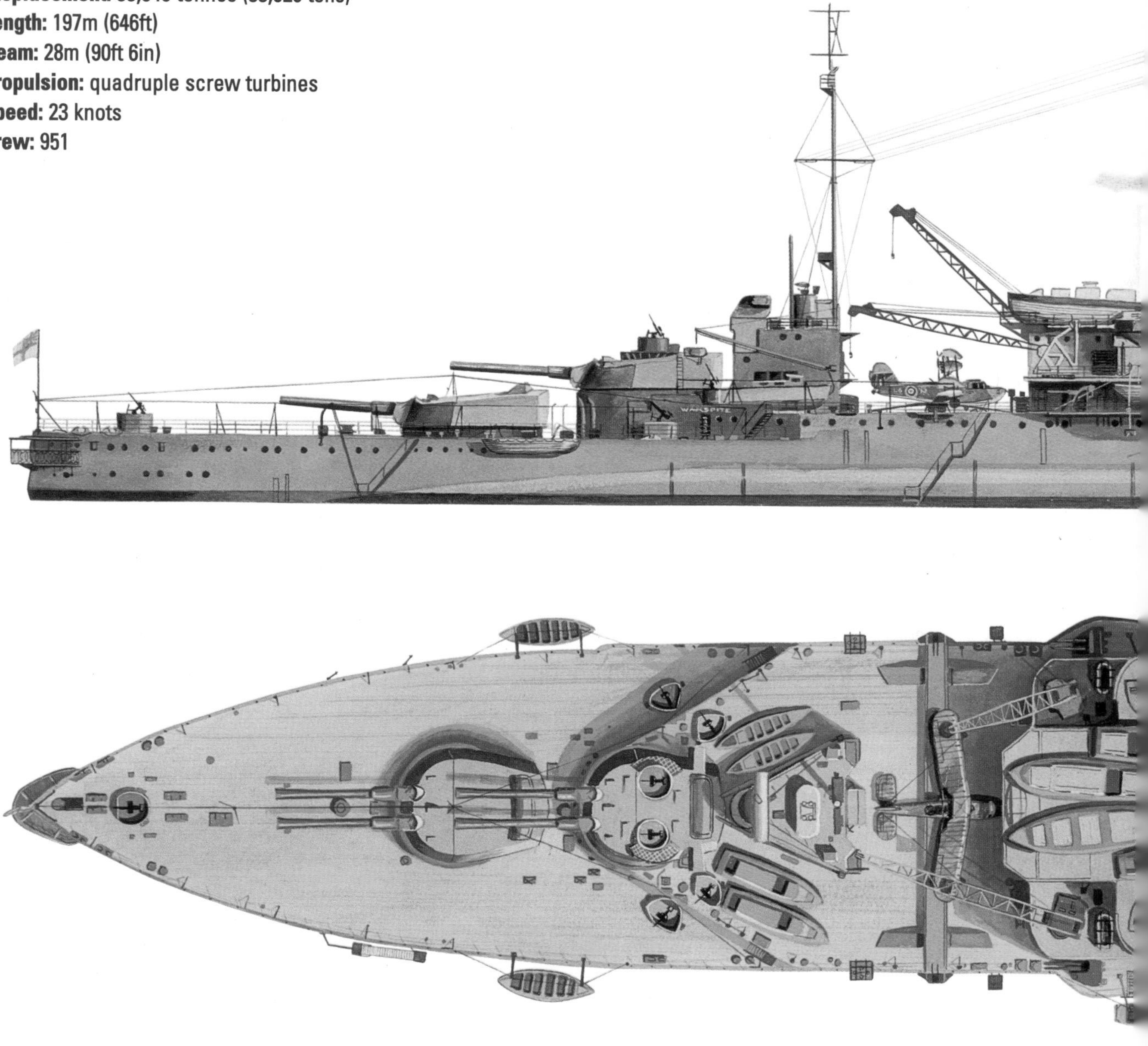

Above: The Dreadnought-class HMS *Warspite* had a long career that took her from Jutland in 1916 to Salerno in September 1943, where she was badly damaged.

replace vessels that were 20 years old. This arrangement would allow France and Italy to lay down new warships in 1927, while Britain, the USA and Japan would not need to do so until 1931, although some of the British ships would be effectively obsolescent by then. No new capital ship was to exceed 35,562 tonnes (35,000 tons), nor mount guns larger than 406mm (16in). No existing capital ship was to be rebuilt, although in recognition of developments in naval warfare, an increase in deck armour against air attack and the addition of anti-torpedo bulges were allowed, provided these modifications did not exceed a total of 3048 tonnes (3000 tons).

The Washington Treaty also limited the tonnage of aircraft carriers. Each signatory nation was allowed to build two vessels of up to 33,530 tonnes (33,000

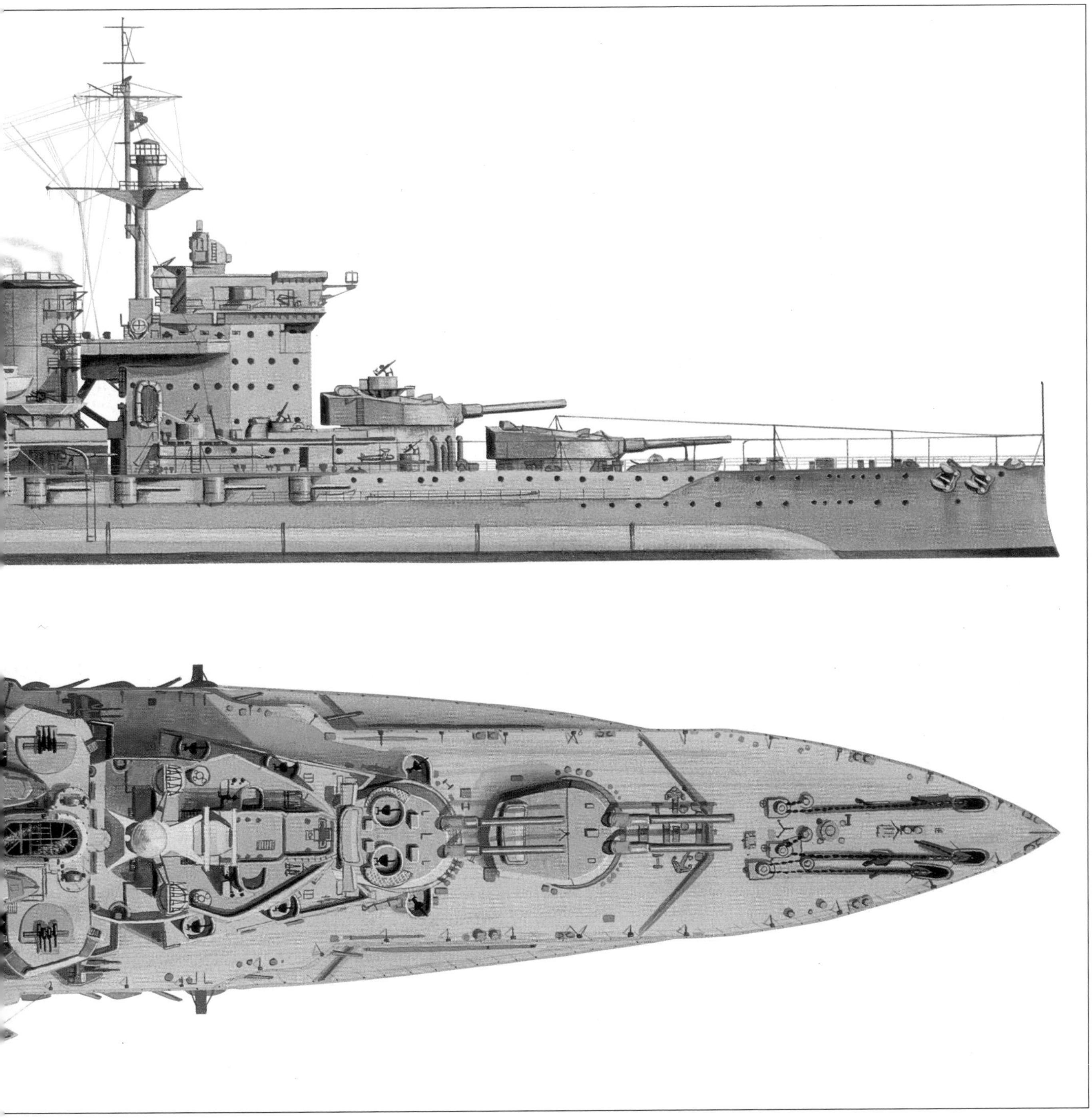

tons); the remainder were limited to 27,433 tonnes (27,000 tons), and the total aircraft carrier tonnage in the case of Britain and the USA was not to exceed 137,167 tonnes (135,000 tons). Japan was allowed 82,300 tonnes (81,000 tons), while France and Italy were permitted 60,963 tonnes (60,000 tons) each. None of the carriers were allowed to be replaced until they were 20 years old. No other warships were to be built in excess of 10,160 tonnes (10,000 tons), nor have guns larger than 203mm (8in).

Naval aviation, in which the Royal Navy had established a commanding lead by the end of World War I, had stagnated in the years since. By 1930, because of the nation's fluctuating political fortunes, with all three Services fighting for survival in the midst of the worst economic crisis in Britain's history and the politicians' fool's paradise of disarmament, nothing at all had been done to authorise even the modest expansion of the Fleet Air Arm that the Admiralty wanted, or indeed, needed.

Above: Sixteen-inch shells being hoisted aboard the battleship HMS *Rodney*, which had a distinguished career in World War II.

The upshot was that of the six aircraft carriers in service at the beginning of 1939, only one, the Ark Royal – in the process of completing her trials – was a modern, purpose-built ship. Four of the others were conversions from battleship or battlecruiser hulls and the fifth, HMS Furious, was too small to be of much use. Five new 23,369-tonne (23,000-ton) fleet carriers were either under construction or planned. Again, it would be 18 months before the first of these was ready for commissioning, leaving a serious gap in the Royal Navy's armoury.

One predictable result of the Washington Treaty was that all five major maritime powers built cruisers right up to the agreed limit of 10,160 tonnes (10,000 tons), and with the heaviest armament allowed. Britain, for example, laid down seven 'Kent' class ships of 10,038 tonnes (9,880 tons), mounting eight 203mm (8in) guns, followed by six similar 'London' class. A destroyer replacement programme of nine vessels a year, each displacing 1371 tonnes (1350 tons) and mounting four 120mm (4.7in) guns and eight torpedo tubes, was also begun in 1929, and in

addition the decision was taken to give Britain's ageing submarine force a shot in the arm by building nine 'O' class vessels and six 'P' class.

By 1930, the strength of the Royal Navy stood at 13 battleships, four battlecruisers, six aircraft carriers, 20 cruisers with 190 or 203mm (7.5 or 8in) armament (with three more building), 40 other cruisers, 146 destroyers (10 more building) and 50 submarines (10 more building).

Of the battleships available to the Royal Navy, the *Iron Duke*, Jellicoe's flagship at Jutland, was now a gunnery and training ship. The *Queen Elizabeth*, leader of her class, had undergone major reconstruction and was on station in the Mediterranean together with her consort, HMS *Barham*, which was due for a refit in 1931. Two more 'Queen Elizabeth' class ships, HMS *Malaya* and HMS *Warspite*, were awaiting reconstruction; and HMS *Valiant* was undergoing reconstruction before returning to the Mediterranean.

HMS *Ramillies* and HMS *Royal Oak* were on station in the Mediterranean in 1930; their sisters HMS *Resolution* and HMS *Revenge* were undergoing a refit; *Royal Sovereign,* recently refitted, was with the Home Fleet, as were the newly-completed *Rodney* and *Nelson*, the latter now Fleet Flagship. Then there were the battlecruisers *Renown*, *Repulse* and *Tiger*, all with the Home Fleet, and finally the mighty *Hood*, then the largest warship afloat, undergoing a refit. It was ironic that a decade later, the *Hood* – designed to counter the uncompleted German 'Mackensen' class battlecruisers of World War I – should spend much of her time trying to hunt down their direct descendants, the battlecruisers *Scharnhorst* and *Gneisenau*.

Below: The battlecruiser HMS *Tiger* was involved in both the Dogger Bank and Jutland battles, being damaged on both occasions. She was broken up in 1932.

TIGER
Armament: 8 343mm (13.5in), 12 152mm (6in) guns
Displacement: 35,723 tonnes (35,160 tons)
Length: 214.6m (704ft)
Beam: 27.6m (90ft 6in)
Propulsion: quadruple screw turbines
Speed: 30 knots
Crew: 1121

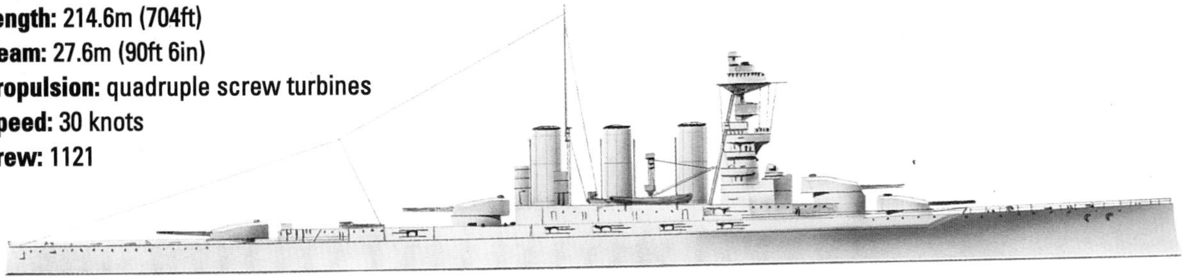

CONTE DI CAVOUR
Armament: 10 320mm (12.6in), 12 120mm (4.7in) guns
Displacement: 29,496 tonnes (29,032 tons)
Length: 186m (611ft 6in)
Beam: 28m (91ft 10in)
Propulsion: twin screw turbines
Speed: 28.2 knots
Crew: 1200

Above: The *Conte di Cavour* was sunk by British air attack in November 1940, refloated and taken to Trieste for repair, only to be sunk again by bombing in February 1945.

THE DEPRESSION

All the construction programmes of the maritime powers during this period were severely affected by economic constraints, the world being in the grip of a savage depression. With the exception of Japan, the maritime nations were eager to escape the cost of building replacement capital ships, as permitted by the Washington Treaty, and on 22 April a new treaty, signed in London by the five principal powers, made fresh provisions. Britain, Japan and the USA agreed that they would lay down no new capital ships before 1936, while France and Italy decided to lay down only the two they were already allowed. Furthermore, the first three countries agreed to make further reductions in existing assets; Britain would reduce her force of capital ships to 15 by scrapping HMS *Tiger* and three 'Iron Duke' class vessels, and relegating the old *Iron Duke* herself to the role of training and depot ship. The United States and Japan also agreed to reduce their capital ship assets to 15 and nine respectively.

Within three years, the Treaties of Washington and London had been trampled by the march of international events. First of all, in 1933, Japan invaded Manchuria, giving notice to the world that she intended to establish domination of the Far East, and then withdrew from the League of Nations. She quickly followed this step with a notice to end her adherence to the Washington and London Treaties, her intention being to establish naval parity with Britain and the USA. France, increasingly alarmed by the growing hostility of fascist Italy, followed suit early in 1935. Also in 1935, and in defiance of the League of Nations, Italy embarked upon a campaign of aggression in Abyssinia; and in 1936 Nazi Germany, having repudiated the Treaty of Versailles, seized the Rhineland.

Faced not only with a potential threat to her possessions in the Far East, but also with one much closer to home from a revitalised and increasingly aggressive Germany and an ambitious Italy, Britain began to rearm. Five 'King George V' class fast battleships of 35,562 tonnes (35,000 tons) were laid down, each armed with 10 355mm (14in) guns and 16 133mm (5.25in) dual-purpose guns. These were followed, after Japan had abandoned the Treaty limits, by four 'Lion' class ships of 40,642 tonnes (40,000 tons) mounting nine 406mm (16in) guns, although the 'Lion' class ships were later cancelled. At the same time, existing British capital ships were modernised with the provision of extra armour and improved armament.

The cruiser force also underwent substantial upgrading. Eight 'Leander' class vessels of 7112 tonnes (7000 tons), armed with eight 152mm (6in) guns were built, followed by four 5304-tonne (5220-ton) 'Arethusa' class ships armed with six. This kept the cruiser tonnage within the limits imposed by the London Treaty, but the subsequent crash rearmament programme produced eight 'Southampton' class ships of 9246 tonnes (9100 tons) mounting 12 152mm (6in) guns, followed by two slightly larger 'Edinburgh' class and 11 'Fiji' class of 8941 tonnes (8800 tons), with the same armament. Eleven 'Dido' class vessels were also laid down; these were 5863-tonne (5770-ton) ships with an armament of 10 133mm (5.25in)

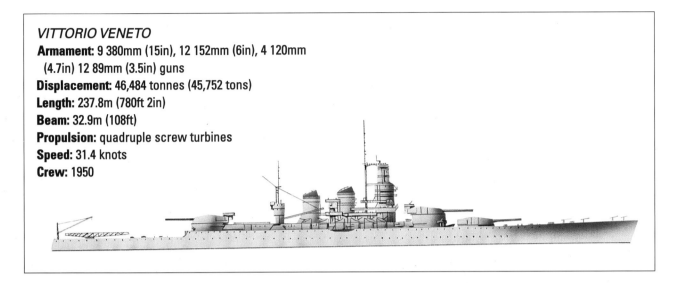

VITTORIO VENETO
Armament: 9 380mm (15in), 12 152mm (6in), 4 120mm (4.7in) 12 89mm (3.5in) guns
Displacement: 46,484 tonnes (45,752 tons)
Length: 237.8m (780ft 2in)
Beam: 32.9m (108ft)
Propulsion: quadruple screw turbines
Speed: 31.4 knots
Crew: 1950

Above The *Vittorio Veneto* was Italy's most modern battleship on the outbreak of World War II. She was torpedoed twice in 1941, but survived the war.

guns, their primary role being to counter air attack. As well as these new warships, the older cruisers of post-war vintage were retained in service, as were 23 'C', 'D' and 'E' class vessels. Six of these were rearmed with eight 100mm (4in) AA guns as anti-aircraft cruisers. There were also three surviving 'Hawkins' class cruisers, one of which, HMS *Effingham*, was rearmed with nine 152mm (6in) guns.

As the New Year of 1939 dawned, it was clear to the British Chiefs of Staff that war with Nazi Germany – and possibly also with Germany's Axis partner, Italy – was inevitable. The signs had been there since 1936, when German troops marched into the Rhineland and set a pattern of aggressive expansion which, faced only with appeasement on the part of the British and French Governments, had resulted two years later in the unopposed annexation of Austria in 1938.

The occupation of the Rhineland had set in motion plans for the expansion of all three of Britain's fighting services. In the case of the Royal Navy, a supplementary naval estimate introduced into the House of Commons in 1936 called for the building of two new battleships, an aircraft carrier and a variety of smaller vessels, and in 1937 a revised estimate included three more battleships, two more aircraft carriers, seven cruisers and a substantial increase in smaller craft, notably destroyers.

Welcome though it was, this increase in Britain's maritime strength could at best be described as modest, and it came too late to provide the Royal Navy with the assets it so badly needed to confront German and Italian fleets which, although a good deal smaller, were in many respects far more modern in terms of equipment. Although four new battleships of the 'King George V' class were building at the start of 1939, none would be ready for at least 18 months; and of the 15 existing capital ships, only two, the *Nelson* and *Rodney*, had been built since 1918.

In the early 1930s, the French Navy's battleship fleet was in a sorry state. Of the older 'Courbet' class dreadnoughts, *Courbet* herself, *Jean Bart* and *Paris* all underwent reconstruction in 1927–31 and were subsequently used as training ships (the fourth ship of this class, the *France*, had foundered in Quiberon Bay in August 1933, after striking a submerged rock). Three more modern dreadnoughts, the *Bretagne*, *Lorraine* and *Provence*, were undergoing a substantial refit in 1932–4; and three modern battleships, the *Richelieu*, *Dunkerque* and *Jean Bart* (the older *Jean Bart* having been renamed *Océan*), were only laid down in 1935–7.

Although it was the Royal Navy which, if war came, would bear the main responsibility for maritime operations in the North Sea and Atlantic, it was envisaged that the French Navy would have an important part to play in convoy protection on the more southerly Atlantic routes and in hunting down enemy commerce raiders. The Mediterranean would be divided between Britain and France, the French being responsible for the western part and the British the eastern, although there were plans for some French warships to operate under the command of the British Mediterranean Fleet.

The Italian Navy, the Regia Marina, was seen as a formidable threat. It possessed modern battleships

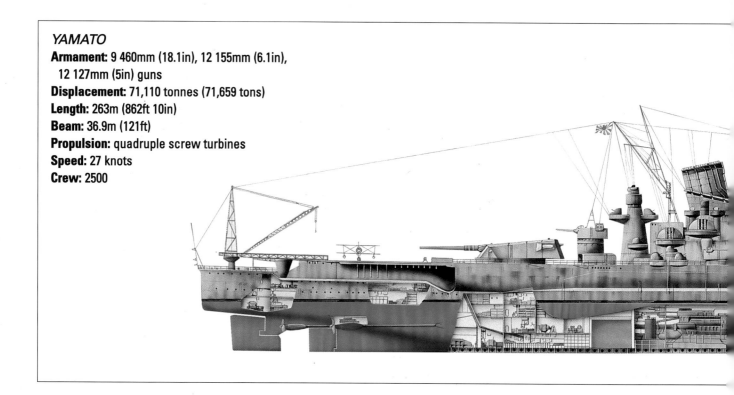

YAMATO
Armament: 9 460mm (18.1in), 12 155mm (6.1in), 12 127mm (5in) guns
Displacement: 71,110 tonnes (71,659 tons)
Length: 263m (862ft 10in)
Beam: 36.9m (121ft)
Propulsion: quadruple screw turbines
Speed: 27 knots
Crew: 2500

Above: The massive battleship *Yamato* and her sister *Musashi* were both sunk by American forces; *Musashi* at Leyte Gulf (1944), *Yamato* off Kagoshima in April 1945.

and cruisers, a force of over 100 submarines, and was backed up by large numbers of bombers belonging to the Regia Aeronautica, the Italian Air Force. In the face of this, the British and French Admiralties took the joint decision that in the event of war the Mediterranean would be closed to all mercantile traffic bound for the Middle East; this would be diverted round the Cape of Good Hope, a 17,700km (11,000-mile) haul necessitating the rapid establishment of shore bases on the east and west coasts of Africa.

The British and French naval planners had little doubt that their combined navies would be more than a match for the Regia Marina, even though its fighting capability was an unknown quantity – for the simple reason that neither the British nor the French had ever fought against it.

Two of Italy's World War I dreadnoughts, the *Conte di Cavour* and *Giulio Cesare*, were completely rebuilt in the early 1930s. In 1937 the *Andrea Doria* and *Caio Duilio* were also rebuilt. In the meantime, in response to the potential threat from France's 'Dunkerque' class, the Italian Admiralty ordered the construction of a new class of battleship, the 'Vittorio Veneto'. The class leader was laid down in 1934, together with a second ship, the *Littorio*; both were completed in 1940. A third vessel, the *Roma*, was not laid down until 1938 and was not completed until 1942. These were excellent, well-designed ships, carrying an armament of nine 380mm (15in), 12 152mm (6in), four 120mm (4.7in) and 12 89mm (3.5in) guns. Displacing 46,484 tonnes (45,752 tons), they were capable of over 31 knots. When France collapsed in June 1940, Italy's battleships were to present a formidable challenge to British naval superiority in the Mediterranean.

Besides Italy's naval potential, another unknown was the true state of the Japanese Navy and its associated maritime air power, on which intelligence was almost completely lacking. In 1915, following disagreements between the USA and Japan over the latter's policies in China, the Japanese Navy had decided to build more battleships to attain parity with the Americans. The plan called for eight battleships and eight battlecruisers to be built by 1922. In the event, as a result of the Washington Treaty, only the first two battleships were built and two more completed as aircraft carriers. The battleships were the *Nagato* and *Mutsu*, each displacing 34,342 tonnes (33,800 tons) and carrying a main armament of eight 406mm (16in) guns. Both were reconstructed in 1934–6.

In 1937, in contravention of the various naval treaties, Japan initiated construction of the Yamato class battleships, the largest and most powerful ever built. One vessel, the *Shinano*, was completed as an

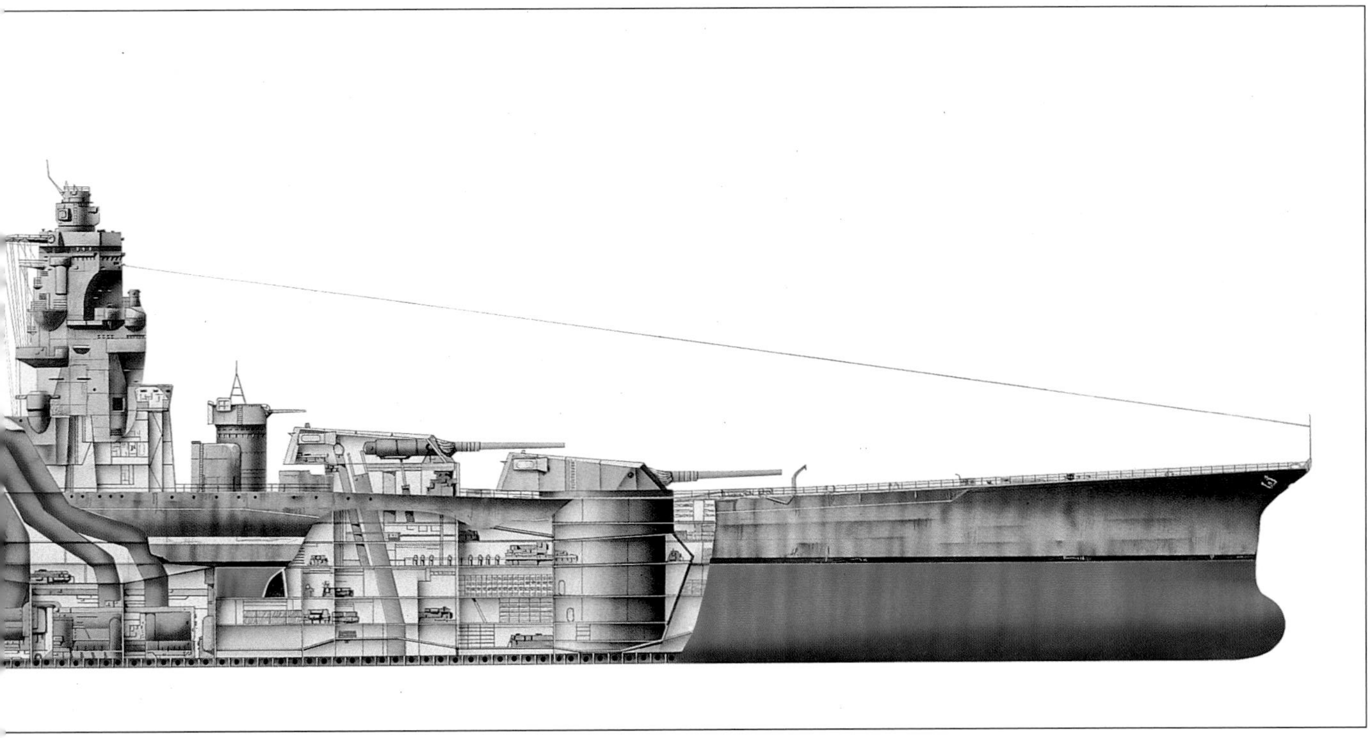

aircraft carrier, and a planned fourth ship was never built. The two remaining ships were the *Yamato* and *Musashi*. Named after Japanese provinces, they were commissioned in 1942. The mighty 68,200-tonne (67,123-ton) warships carried a main armament of nine 457mm (18in) guns, mounted in triple turrets. Built in great secrecy, they were designed to compete on equal terms with any group of enemy battleships. The irony was that both would ultimately be destroyed by the very weapon that would take Japan to her early victories in the Pacific – naval air power.

By 1930, the United States Navy had attained a principal post-war goal, which was to achieve parity in capital ships with the Royal Navy. Fifteen battleships were in commission, all dreadnoughts, and all subject to major reconstruction and refitting programmes. Development continued with the 'North Carolina' and 'South Dakota' classes of 1937-8 (*North Carolina, Washington, Alabama, Indiana, Massachusetts* and *South Dakota*), ships of 35,562 tonnes (35,000 tons) and carrying a main armament of nine 406mm (16in) guns. These in turn were overshadowed by the Iowa class of 1939–40 (*Iowa, Missouri, New Jersey* and *Wisconsin*), displacing 45,000 tons.

As war loomed, Japan was adopting an increasingly belligerent stance towards Britain and the United States, but ships could not be spared to bolster the existing force of mostly elderly cruisers and escort vessels responsible for the defence of British interests in the Far East. Japan had not yet allied herself with Germany and Italy, who had concluded a joint offensive-defensive pact known as the Berlin–Rome Axis on 22 May 1939, but there were indications that she might be persuaded to do so. In that event, a plan existed to reinforce the Eastern Fleet by despatching the bulk of the Mediterranean Fleet to Singapore, leaving operations in the Mediterranean entirely to the French. In reality, it was the US Navy that would have to bear the brunt of any war operations against Imperial Japan.

GERMAN REARMAMENT

There remained Germany, whose increasingly militant activities were clearly the principal threat to the security of the Western Hemisphere.

Under the terms of the 1918 Armistice, the German Fleet, which was then in a state of mutiny, was speedily disbanded. The newest and most powerful units of the Fleet – 11 battleships, five battlecruisers, eight cruisers and 50 destroyers – were seized and sailed to Scapa Flow in the Orkneys, where they were interned and subsequently scuttled by their crews. All the Imperial Navy's submarines were handed over at Harwich.

Of the remaining units of the Fleet, seven cruisers were handed over to the French and Italian Navies; a number of destroyers and submarines were also taken

Above: The American battleship *South Dakota* under attack by Japanese torpedo-bombers during the Second Battle of Santa Cruz, 26 October 1942.

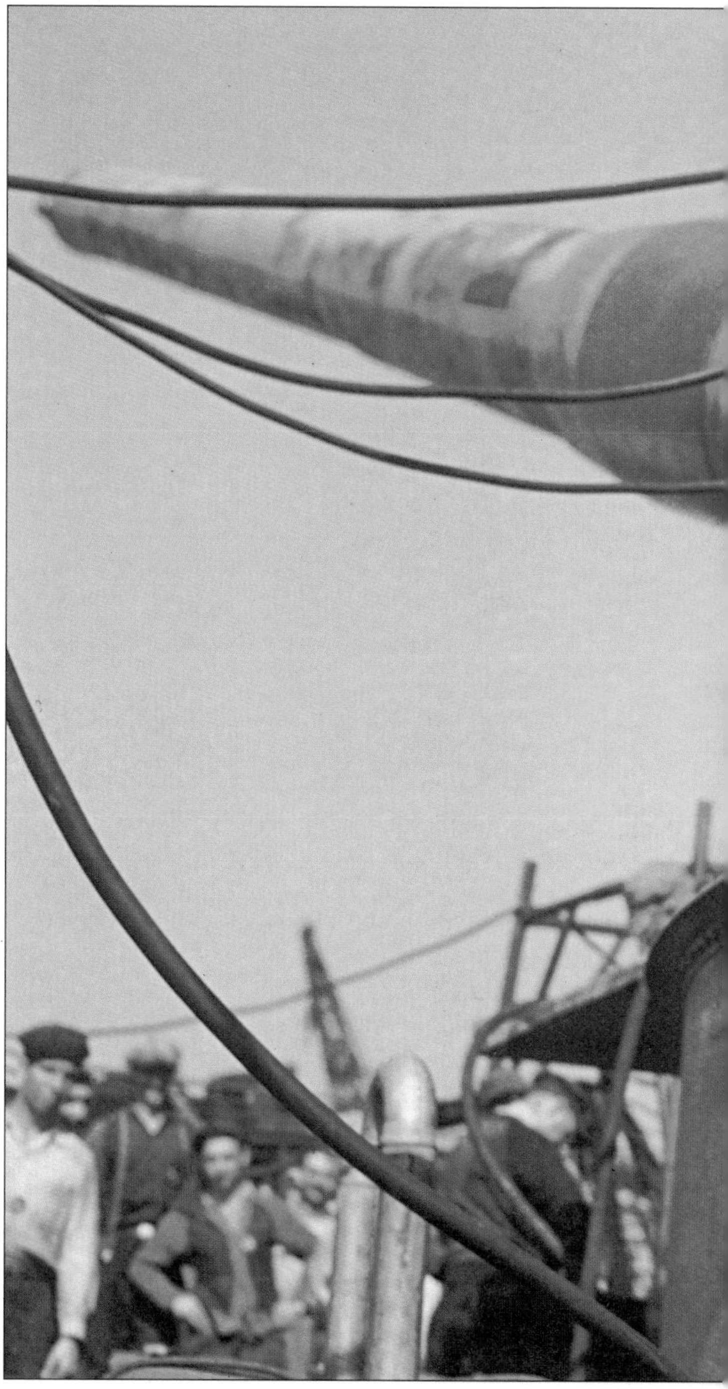

over and commissioned. Almost all the other vessels were scrapped. The ships that were permitted to remain in German service were relegated to a coastal defence role and were already obsolete, comprising eight pre-war battleships, eight light cruisers, 32 destroyers and torpedo boats and some minesweepers and auxiliary craft. The Allies, determined that Germany would never again have warships comparable to those of other navies, stipulated that the size of new-build German capital ships would not exceed 10,160 tonnes (10,000 tons) displacement and cruisers 6096 tonnes (6000 tons).

It was at this juncture, on 6 February 1922, that the Washington Naval Treaty was signed. But outside the orbit of the agreement, a new German Fleet was already being born. The first medium-sized German warship built after World War I was the light cruiser *Emden*, completed in January 1925 at Wilhelmshaven. Originally coal-fired, she converted to oil in 1934. Designed primarily for foreign service, she made nine foreign cruises as a training ship from 1926 and went on to see active service in World War II, carrying out minelaying operations in September 1939 and during the Norwegian campaign of April 1940. She subsequently served with the Fleet Training Squadron in the Baltic and operated in support of the German offensive against Russia. One of her more unusual operations, in January 1945, was to evacuate the coffin of Field Marshal von Hindenburg from Königsberg, East Prussia, after it had been removed from the Tannenberg Memorial during the Russian advance into Germany. In April 1945 she was damaged in a bombing raid on Kiel, and was later scuttled. She was broken up in 1949.

In 1924 the construction of 12 new torpedo boats was also started, six of the ‘Wolf’ class and six of the

'Möwe' (seagull) class, all at the Wilhelmshaven dockyard. With a displacement of around 945 tonnes (930 tons), these vessels were powered by two-shaft geared turbines and were capable of 33 knots. All were armed with six 530mm (21in) torpedo tubes, three 104mm (4.1in) guns and four 20mm (0.79in) AA guns. They carried a complement of 129, and all were completed by 1929.

In that year, a significant step forward was taken with the commencement at the Deutsche Werke, Kiel, of the first of a new class of warship. Designated *Panzerschiffe* (Armoured Ships) by the Germans, they were to become popularly known as 'pocket battleships'. The 11,888-tonne (11,700-ton) *Deutschland* (later renamed *Lützow*) was the first, the others being the *Admiral Scheer* and the *Admiral Graf Spee.*

Below: A welder at work on one of the USS *Iowa*'s 16in gun turrets. *Iowa* was completed in 1943 and served in the US Navy until 1958, when she was mothballed.

Designed from the outset as commerce raiders with a large and economical radius of action (16,677km/9000nm at 19 knots) they were electrically welded to save weight and equipped with diesel engines. They had enough speed – 26 knots – to enable them to escape from any vessel that could not be overwhelmed by their guns. Their armament comprised six 280mm (11in), eight 150mm (5.9in), six 104mm (4.1in) AA, eight 37mm (1.44in) AA, 10 (later 28) 20mm (0.79in) AA and eight 530mm (21in) torpedo tubes. They carried a complement of 1150.

ADMIRAL ERICH RAEDER

Of enormous significance, too, was the appointment in 1929 of Admiral Erich Raeder to command the Reichsmarine. Raeder had served as a staff officer to Admiral Franz von Hipper in World War I, and had later been assigned the task of writing the official German history of the war at sea. In doing so, for the first time, he had become fully aware of the achievements of the handful of German commerce raiders in distant waters. Not only had they sunk a large tonnage of merchant shipping; they had also tied down many Allied capital ships and cruisers, diverted from other operations to search for them.

It was Raeder who authorised the construction of the *Deutschland*'s two sister ships, the *Admiral Scheer* and *Admiral Graf Spee*. He would almost certainly have ordered more, had it not been for Adolf Hitler's rise to power in 1933, with a subsequent change of naval policy dictated by the new political climate in Germany.

Below: The *Admiral Scheer* was the *Graf Spee*'s sister ship. She saw considerable action against Allied convoys in the Atlantic and Arctic, sinking 17 ships in all.

The Nazi Party was now in power in Germany, and one of Hitler's first acts as Chancellor was to initiate a massive rearmament programme. The immediate result for the German Navy was the construction of a new class of *Schlachtkreuzer* (Battlecruiser). Five ships were projected, but only two begun. The first of these, the 32,514-tonne (32,000-ton) *Scharnhorst*, was laid down at Wilhelmshaven in April 1934. She was followed a year later by the *Gneisenau*.

The design of these powerful warships was based on the uncompleted 'Mackensen' class battlecruisers of World War I, which in turn were based on the *Derfflinger* of 1912 – arguably the best battlecruiser of its day. The new ships were fitted with three-shaft geared turbines and their radius of action was 18,530km (10,000nm) at 19 knots. Their armament comprised nine 280mm (11in), 12 150mm (5.9in), 14 105mm (4.1in), 37mm (1.44in) AA, and 10 (later 38) 20mm (0.79in) AA guns, as well as six 530mm (21in) torpedo tubes. Each carried four 'spotter' aircraft and had a complement of 1800. They were capable of a speed of 31 knots. *Scharnhorst* was launched in October 1936 and *Gneisenau* two months later.

In the mid-1930s a new class of *Schwerer Kreuzer* (heavy cruiser) was also laid down. There were five ships in all, named *Lützow, Seydlitz, Prinz Eugen, Blücher* and *Admiral Hipper*. The first, launched in July 1939, was sold in 1940 to the Soviet Navy, in whose service she was successively named *Petropavlovsk* and *Tallinn*. The others were all launched in 1937–9. Capable of 32 knots, their armament comprised eight 203mm (8in), 12 105mm (4.1in) AA, 12 37mm (1.44in) AA, and eight (later 28) 20mm (0.79in) AA guns, in addition to 12 530mm (21in) torpedo tubes. Each carried three spotter aircraft. Complement was 1600.

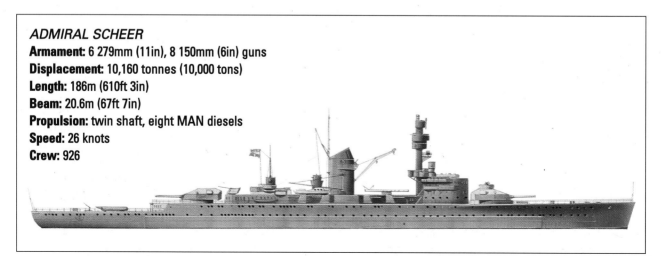

ADMIRAL SCHEER
Armament: 6 279mm (11in), 8 150mm (6in) guns
Displacement: 10,160 tonnes (10,000 tons)
Length: 186m (610ft 3in)
Beam: 20.6m (67ft 7in)
Propulsion: twin shaft, eight MAN diesels
Speed: 26 knots
Crew: 926

Above: The pocket battleship *Deutschland* made a sortie into the Atlantic in late 1939, sinking two merchant ships and capturing a third. She was later renamed the *Lützow*.

In the meantime, Admiral Raeder and his naval staff were putting the final touches to a scheme which was designed to give Germany technological superiority on the high seas. It was based on two super-powerful battleships, the *Bismarck* and *Tirpitz*. Displacing 42,370 tonnes (41,700 tons) in the case of *Bismarck* and 43,589 tonnes (42,900 tons) in the case of *Tirpitz*, they would have a speed of 29 knots and a combat radius of 16,677km (9000nm) at 19 knots. They would carry a formidable armament of eight 380mm (15in), 12 150mm (5.9in), 16 105mm (4.1in) AA, 16 37mm (1.44in) AA and 16 (later 58) 20mm (0.79in) AA guns, together with eight 530mm (21in) torpedo tubes. Their complement would be 2400 officers and men. Both were laid down in 1936, but only the *Bismarck* was actually launched before the outbreak of World War II.

Six even larger (57,100-tonne/56,200-ton) battleships were planned, known simply by the letters *H, J, K, L, M* and *N*. Only *H* and *J* were laid down, in 1938, but these were broken up on the stocks in the summer of 1940, when Germany believed she had won the war. It was speculated that they were to be named *Friedrich der Grosse* and *Gross Deutschland,* although there is no concrete evidence for this.

Finally, there were plans to build a small number of aircraft carriers. In the event there was only one, the 23,370-tonne (23,200-ton) *Graf Zeppelin*, laid down in 1936 and launched in December 1938. It was planned that she should carry an air group comprising 12 Junkers Ju87D dive bombers and 30 Me109F fighters but she was never completed. Construction was suspended in May 1940 when she was 85 per cent complete. In 1942 work on her was restarted but again suspended in 1943. She was scuttled near Stettin in April 1945, raised by the Russians in March 1946, but in September 1947 she struck a mine and either sank or was towed to Leningrad, severely damaged, and was broken up there. The hull of a sister vessel was completed up to the armoured deck but she was never launched, being broken up on the stocks in 1940. It was speculated that this ship was to have been named *Peter Strasser*, after the commander of the German Naval Airship Division in World War I.

In 1942 work was also started to convert the heavy cruiser *Seydlitz* as an aircraft carrier, but very little was carried out and the ship was scuttled at Königsberg in April 1945, later being raised by the Russians. Plans were also laid to convert the liners *Europa, Gneisenau* and *Potsdam* as an emergency measure, but these, too, came to nothing.

When Germany went to war in September 1939, she was at a distinct numerical disadvantage in every respect. Yet during the long years that followed, after the occupation of Europe, she came close to starving Britain into submission. Her principal weapon in the murderous conflict that became known as the Battle of the Atlantic was the U-boat; but in the early months it was the German Navy's surface vessels that were to take the greatest toll of Allied shipping.

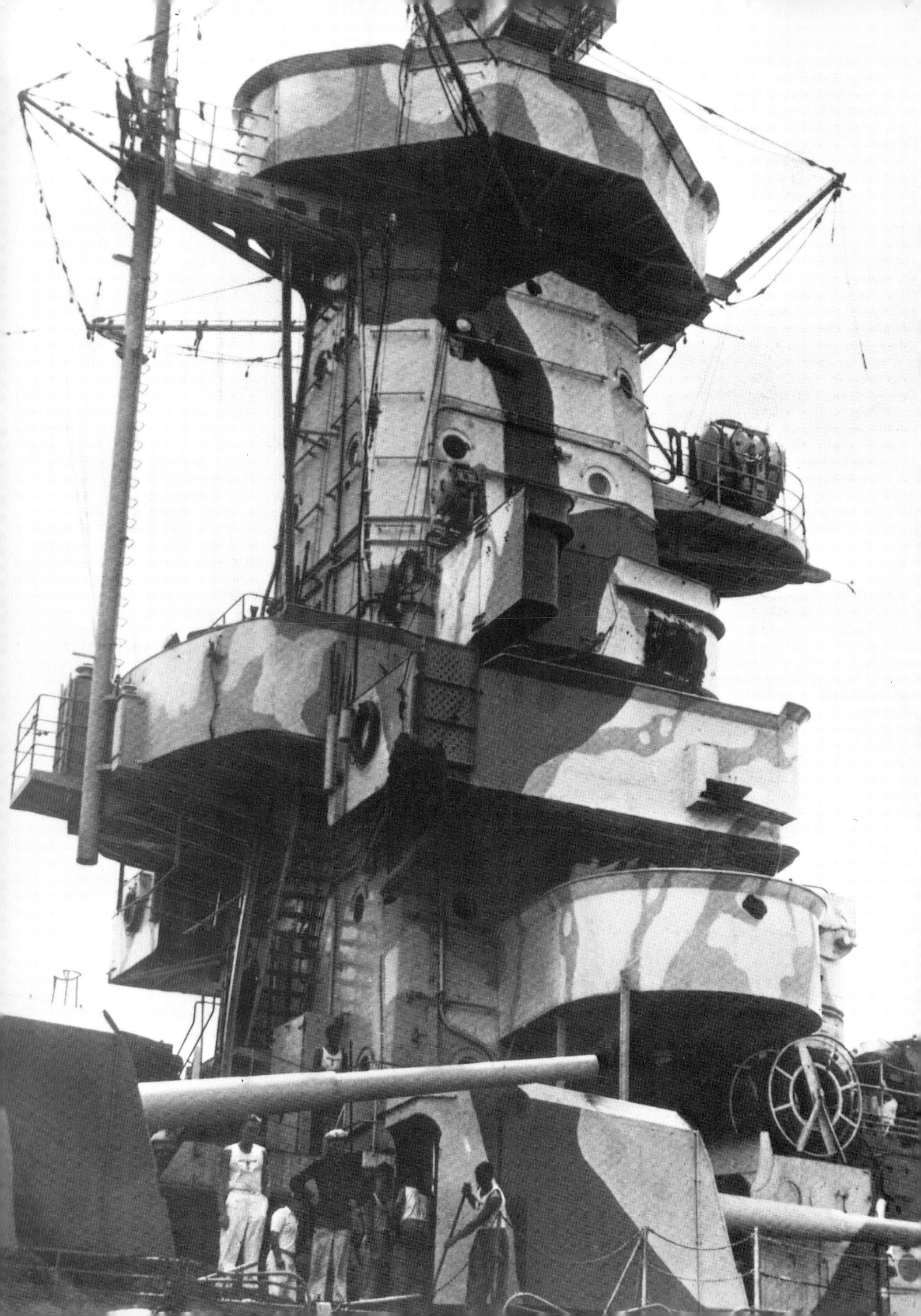

CHAPTER SEVEN

The Naval War in the West 1940–42

The outbreak of war in 1939 saw the Allies quickly trying to establish control of the sea to safeguard their convoys. However, several German ships evaded the blockades and forced the Allies to commit large numbers of ships and aircraft in an attempt to hunt them down. The German battleships proved more than a match for some of their pursuers, and increasingly it became clear that they were to be treated with respect.

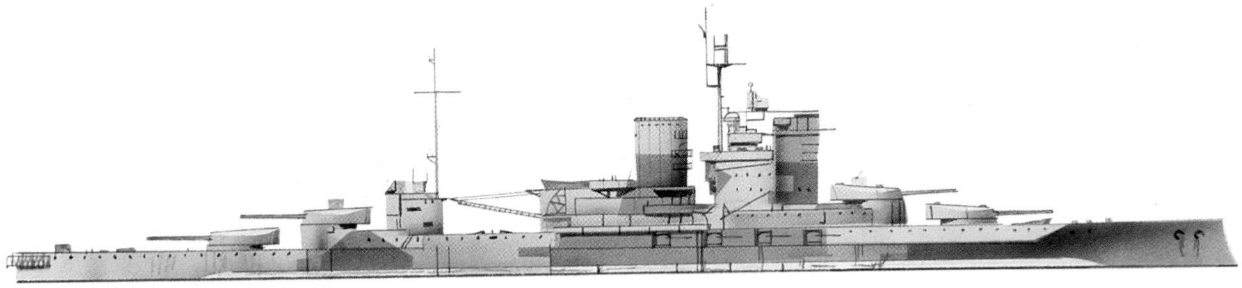

In August 1939, with the invasion of Poland imminent, the German Naval Staff lost no time in deploying units of the Kriegsmarine to their war stations in the Atlantic, ready to begin an immediate offensive against Allied shipping. On 21 August, the 13,209-tonne (13,000-ton) pocket battleship *Admiral Graf Spee* (Capt Langsdorff) sailed from Wilhelmshaven, under cover of darkness and unobserved, to make rendezvous with her supply ship, the fleet tanker *Altmark*, in the South Atlantic. She was followed on 24 August by a second pocket battleship, the *Deutschland* (Capt Wennecker), which sailed for her war station south of Greenland, to be joined later by her own replenishment vessel, the fleet tanker *Westerwald*.

Left: Closeup of the *Graf Spee*'s heavily armoured control tower and gun-laying radar system, taken by a US Navy photographer while the ship lay in Montevideo harbour.

At dawn on 1 September, the old pre-dreadnought battleship *Schleswig-Holstein*, veteran of Jutland, opened fire with her four 280mm (11in) guns on the Polish fortress of Westerplatte, whose garrison was holding out stubbornly against the invading Germans. Together with smaller vessels, she continued to shell the fortress day after day for a week, until the garrison at last surrendered on 7 September under the combined effects of the naval shellfire, air attack and an assault from the ground. The old battleship continued to support the attacking German troops until 13 September, bombarding Polish positions near Hochredlau on the Hela peninsula when she withdrew for replenishment. When she returned, on 25 September, she continued the bombardment with her sister ship, the *Schlesien*, for a further two days.

By 21 September, British Naval Intelligence was aware that the two powerful German commerce raiders, *Graf Spee* and *Deutschland*, were at sea, and the Admiralty was compelled to deploy substantial numbers of ships – including some from the Mediterranean – to search for them. On 7 October, the German Naval Staff, concerned about the mounting pressure on the pocket battleships, ordered units of

Below: Lt Cdr Gunther Prien wearing the Iron Cross awarded for sinking the *Royal Oak*. Prien sank 30 merchant ships before his demise in 1941.

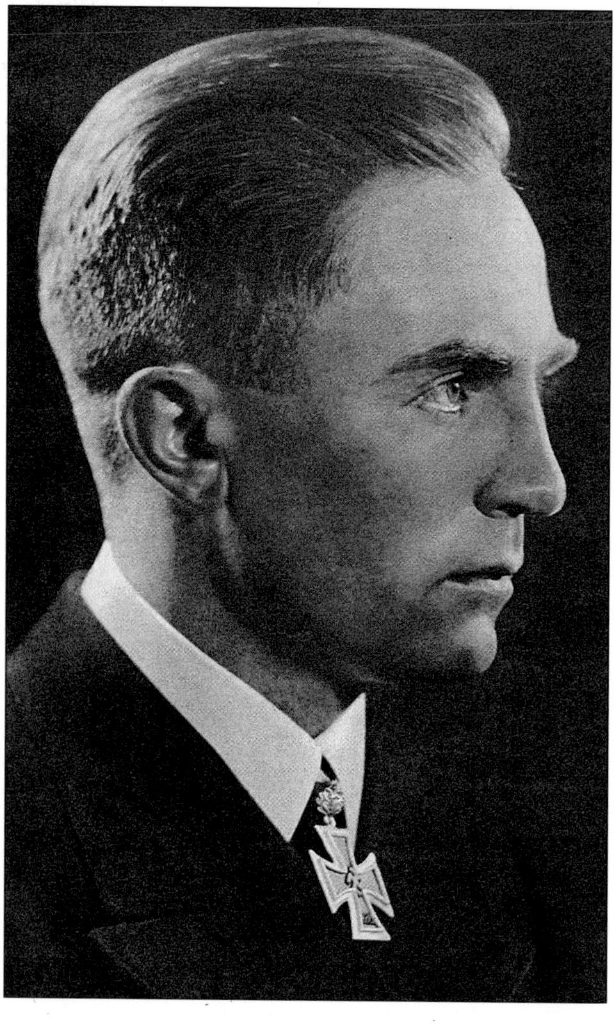

the German Fleet to make a sortie towards the southern coast of Norway. The force comprised the battlecruiser *Scharnhorst*, the light cruiser *Köln* and nine destroyers, the intention being to draw the Home Fleet across a concentration of four U-boats and within range of the Luftwaffe. The German warships were sighted on the following day by a patrolling Lockheed Hudson of RAF Coastal Command.

As soon as Admiral Forbes learned that the enemy was out he stationed his main units – the battleships *Nelson* and *Rodney*, the battlecruisers Hood and *Repulse*, the cruisers *Aurora*, *Sheffield* and *Newcastle* and the carrier *Furious*, accompanied by 12 destroyers – northeast of the Shetlands, where they could cover the exit to the Atlantic. At the same time, he despatched the Humber Force, comprising the light cruisers *Edinburgh, Glasgow* and *Southampton*, to search for the German ships. The operation was fruitless, and bombers despatched by both sides failed to find their targets. On 9 October, after dark, the German force reversed its course and returned to Kiel, and by 11 October the main units of the Home Fleet and the light cruisers were back in port.

There was an exception. One of Forbes' battleships, the *Royal Oak*, had been detached from the main force to guard the Fair Isle Channel, between the Shetland and Orkney Islands, and when the threat receded she made her way to the anchorage at Scapa Flow. On the night of 13/14 October, the German submarine *U.47*, commanded by Lt Cdr Gunther Prien, penetrated the defences of Scapa Flow and sank the *Royal Oak* with three torpedo hits. The attack, which cost 833 lives, was carried out with great skill and daring, and came as a severe shock to Britain.

Later that year, on 21 November, the battlecruisers *Scharnhorst* and *Gneisenau* sailed from Wilhelmshaven for the North Atlantic, the purpose of their sortie being to divert attention away from the operations of the pocket battleship *Admiral Graf Spee* in the South Atlantic. Passing undetected to the north of the Shetlands and Faeroes, the warships were sighted on the 23rd by the Armed Merchant Cruiser *Rawalpindi* (Capt E.C. Kennedy), which engaged them in a gallant but one-sided duel and had time to radio their presence to Scapa Flow before she was sunk by the *Scharnhorst*.

On the 26th the battlecruisers came south once more, passed through the cruiser and destroyer patrol lines which Admiral Forbes had established off Norway, and regained Wilhelmshaven the next day. No fewer than 60 warships – six battleships (three

Above: The pre-dreadnought battleship *Schleswig-Holstein* pictured on 1 September 1939, firing the opening shots of the war against Polish positions on Westerplatte.

French), two battlecruisers, 20 cruisers (two French), 28 destroyers (eight French), three submarines and an aircraft carrier – had been redeployed to various positions in the North Atlantic and North Sea to hunt the *Scharnhorst* and *Gneisenau*, and the Germans had successfully eluded all of them. As a diversionary tactic, it had certainly worked.

The search for the enemy battlecruisers, abortive though it was, illustrated the close co-operation that existed at this time between the Royal and French Navies. On 5 October, the Admiralty, in conjunction with the French Navy, had formed eight Atlantic 'hunting groups' of aircraft carriers and cruisers for the defence of the trade routes against surface raiders. Three were under the orders of the Commander-in-Chief, South Atlantic, whose headquarters were at Freetown, Sierra Leone. One of them, Group G, comprising the heavy cruisers *Exeter* and *Cumberland* and reinforced later by the light cruisers *Ajax* and *Achilles*, the latter belonging to the Royal New Zealand Navy, were responsible for the waters off the east coast of South America – and it was there that the *Admiral Graf Spee*'s rampage at last came to an end.

HUNTING THE GRAF SPEE

The pocket battleship sank her first merchantman off Pernambuco on 30 September, and between 5 and 12 October she sank four more before breaking off to replenish from her supply ship, the *Altmark*. She turned up again on 15 November, when she sank a small tanker in the Mozambique Channel. There was no further news of her until 2 December, when she sank the freighters *Doric Star* and *Tairoa* between St Helena and South Africa.

On receiving intelligence of these sinkings, the C-in-C South Atlantic, Vice-Admiral d'Oyly Lyon, ordered Force H, with the cruisers *Shropshire* and *Sussex*, to proceed to the area between Cape Town

Above: The *Admiral Graf Spee* had only a brief career as a commerce raider before being forced to take refuge in the neutral port of Montevideo, where she was later scuttled.

and St Helena, while Force K, comprising the battlecruiser *Renown*, the aircraft carrier *Ark Royal* and the cruiser *Neptune*, was despatched to search along a line from Freetown to the Central South Atlantic. Force G (as Group G was now designated) meanwhile assembled off the River Plate with the cruisers *Achilles*, *Ajax* and *Exeter*, *Cumberland* having been detached to cover the Falkland Islands. There was plenty of mercantile traffic around the estuary of the River Plate, and Force G's senior officer, Commodore H. Harwood, reasoned that Langsdorff would be attracted there sooner or later. He was right.

After sinking two more ships in mid-ocean, Captain Langsdorff elected to steer directly for the Plate estuary, where he was sighted at 0608 hours on 13 December. The three British cruisers were soon in action, opening fire from different directions. Langsdorff at first divided his armament, but then concentrated his fire on the *Exeter*, his 280mm (11in) shells inflicting heavy damage on the cruiser. Despite this, Captain F.S. Bell continued to engage the enemy throughout the night. By dawn the *Exeter* had only one turret left in action and she was ablaze. Langsdorff could easily have finished her off; instead, he made smoke and turned west, allowing *Exeter* to pull away to the southeast to make repairs, with 61 of her crew dead and 23 wounded.

The *Graf Spee* now steered for the coast of Uruguay, under fire all the while from the light cruisers *Ajax* and *Achilles*. At 0725 hours a 280mm (11in) shell hit *Ajax* and put both her after turrets out of action, but again Langsdorff failed to take the opportunity to finish off one of his adversaries, whose remaining guns were now barely superior to his own secondary armament. The two cruisers continued to shadow the *Graf Spee*, which fired salvoes at them from time to time, until the battleship entered the estuary. Commodore Harwood then called off the pursuit and set up a patrol line, aware that he was in a very parlous position if Langsdorff chose to fight his way out to the open sea.

Langsdorff, his ship damaged – she had taken some 70 hits and 36 of her crew were dead, with another 60 wounded – had decided to make for a neutral port where he could effect temporary repairs before attempting a breakout into the North Atlantic and a run back to Germany. He was also short of ammunition. The *Graf Spee* reached Montevideo on the evening of 14 December, and there now began a prolonged diplomatic effort to remain there beyond the legal limit of 72 hours, since the necessary repairs would take at least two weeks to complete. British propaganda, meanwhile, tried to create the impression that a large British fleet was lying in wait for the *Graf Spee* as soon as she re-emerged from the estuary.

Langsdorff fell for it. On 16 December he signalled Berlin for instructions; the reply that came back was unequivocal. There was to be no question of internment. The authority was given to scuttle the ship, should the German envoy in Montevideo fail to gain an extension of the time limit. By nightfall on 17 December, it was plain that no such extension was to be permitted by the Uruguayan authorities.

On the following morning, watched by a vast crowd of sightseers, *Graf Spee* put to sea. The British warships cleared for action, but before they could engage the enemy, their spotter aircraft reported that the pocket battleship had been scuttled and blown up by her own crew. Within a short time, it was learned that Captain Langsdorff had committed suicide.

While the *Graf Spee* was on the rampage in the South Atlantic, her sister ship, the *Deutschland* (Capt Wenneker), was patrolling the Bermuda–Azores route, and on 5 October 1939 she sank the steamer *Stonegate*. A week later she was operating farther north, on the Halifax (Nova Scotia)–UK route, and between 9–16 October she sank a Norwegian freighter and captured the American freighter *City of Flint,* carrying supplies for Britain, a cargo which the Germans described as 'contraband'. On 17 October the German Naval Staff issued an order permitting the use of all weapons against all enemy merchant ships with the exception of passenger vessels, giving the commerce raiders a much wider scope.

On 5 November, however, the *Deutschland* received a sudden recall order from the German Admiralty. Successfully evading British patrols, she slipped through the Denmark Strait, passed to the east of the Shetland Islands and arrived at Gdynia on 17 November, where she went into dry dock for an overhaul. Shortly before docking her captain received word that his ship had been renamed *Lutzow*, the cruiser of that name having been sold to the Soviet Union, and in February 1940 she was reclassified as a heavy cruiser.

Below: The *Graf Spee* and her sister ships were nicknamed 'pocket battleships' by the Allies, but actually classed as *Panzerschiffe* (Armoured Ships) by the Nazis.

The third pocket battleship, the *Admiral Scheer,* was similarly reclassified. She had taken no part in the early commerce-raiding operations; having survived an attack by RAF Blenheim bombers on 4 September 1939 (three bombs hit her while she lay at anchor in Wilhelmshaven, but all failed to explode). She underwent a refit and did not begin operations until October 1940.

THE INVASION OF NORWAY

On 9 April, 1940, the period that had become known as the 'Phoney War' came to a violent end when German forces invaded Norway and Denmark. The bulk of the enemy invasion force was already at sea on 7 April, steaming northwards through savage weather. This part of the invasion force was divided into three Task Groups. Group One, with Narvik as its objective, had the farthest distance to travel and was escorted by the battlecruisers *Scharnhorst* and *Gneisenau*, together with 10 destroyers. Group Two, bound for Trondheim, was guarded by the cruiser *Admiral Hipper* and four destroyers, while Group Three, heading for Bergen, was protected by the cruisers *Köln* and *Königsberg*, screened by torpedo boats. Groups Four and Five, assigned to Kristiansand and Oslo, did not have to sail so early. The plan was that all five groups would reach their objectives at more or less the same time.

First contact with the German ships was made by the destroyer HMS *Glowworm*, part of a force that

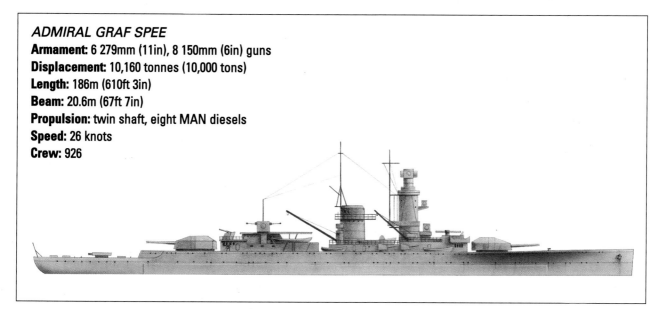

ADMIRAL GRAF SPEE
Armament: 6 279mm (11in), 8 150mm (6in) guns
Displacement: 10,160 tonnes (10,000 tons)
Length: 186m (610ft 3in)
Beam: 20.6m (67ft 7in)
Propulsion: twin shaft, eight MAN diesels
Speed: 26 knots
Crew: 926

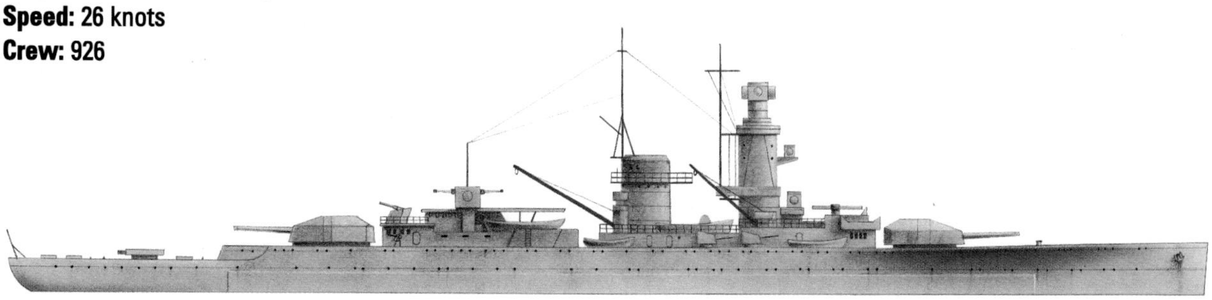

had been covering minelaying operations off Norway. Detached to make a vain search for a seaman swept overboard, she sighted the warships of Task Group Two, bound for Trondheim. *Glowworm* fired two salvoes at an enemy destroyer before the latter was lost to sight in heavy seas and fog; a few minutes later a second destroyer appeared and *Glowworm* gave chase, the two ships exchanging shot for shot. The larger German vessel increased speed in an attempt to shake off her adversary but her bow ploughed under, forcing her to slow down. *Glowworm* closed in, her captain, Lt Cdr G.B. Roope, trying to get into position for a shot with torpedoes.

Some distance ahead, a great, dark shape burst from a fog bank. For a few seconds the men on *Glowworm*'s bridge were elated, believing the ship to be HMS *Renown*. Then a salvo of heavy shells struck the British destroyer, setting her on fire. The newcomer was the *Admiral Hipper*.

Roope sheered off for long enough to radio a report, then turned back towards the German cruiser in the hope of torpedoing her. When this proved impossible he headed his burning ship straight for the *Hipper*, ramming her starboard bow, damaging her armour belt and wrenching away her starboard torpedo tubes. The cruiser's captain, Heinrich Heye, ordered his guns to hold their fire as the *Glowworm* fell away, ablaze and doomed. A few minutes later, at 0900 hours, she blew up. The *Hipper* rescued 38 survivors, Lt Cdr Roope – who was later awarded a posthumous Victoria Cross – was not among them.

On 8 April, having received *Glowworm*'s enemy sighting report and distress signal, Admiral Forbes ordered the ships at Rosyth to put to sea, at the same time detaching the *Repulse*, *Penelope* and four destroyers to join *Renown*. That evening, the Admiralty instructed Forbes that his primary objective was the interception of the *Scharnhorst* and *Gneisenau*, still in the belief that a major breakout into the Atlantic was in the offing. Further apparent evidence that this was the Germans' intention had come in the afternoon, when a RAF reconnaissance aircraft reported an enemy battlecruiser and two cruisers off Trondheim, steaming west. In fact, the ships were the *Hipper* and her accompanying destroyers, covering the Group Two invasion force.

It was not until 1900 hours on 8 April that the Admiralty, following an assessment of further intelligence reports on the movements of German vessels (including one from the submarine HMS *Trident*, which made an unsuccessful torpedo attack on the battleship *Lützow* as the latter headed for Oslo Fjord)

Below: The end of the *Graf Spee*, scuttled off Montevideo on 17 December 1939. Captain Hans Langsdorff shot himself; his crew were interned in Argentina until 1945.

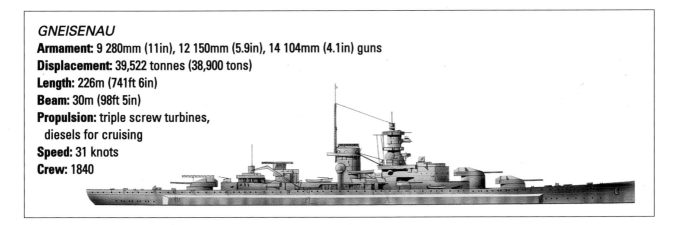

GNEISENAU
Armament: 9 280mm (11in), 12 150mm (5.9in), 14 104mm (4.1in) guns
Displacement: 39,522 tonnes (38,900 tons)
Length: 226m (741ft 6in)
Beam: 30m (98ft 5in)
Propulsion: triple screw turbines, diesels for cruising
Speed: 31 knots
Crew: 1840

Above The battlecruiser *Gneisenau* was damaged by RAF bombs at Kiel in February 1942, and she never saw action again. Her guns were later removed for coastal defence.

decided that an invasion was under way – although the possibility of a simultaneous breakout was not discounted. A signal was flashed to the commander of the northernmost group of British warships, Vice-Admiral William Whitworth, in HMS *Renown*.

'Most immediate. The force under your orders is to concentrate on preventing any German force proceeding to Narvik.' It was too late. Before midnight, the German invasion forces were already entering the fjords that led to their objectives.

At 0337 hours on 9 April, however, *Renown*, positioned 80km (43nm) off the entrance to Vestfjord, sighted the *Scharnhorst* and *Gneisenau*, heading northwest to prevent any British interference with the Narvik assault group. Mistaking one of the enemy ships for the cruiser *Hipper*, the British battlecruiser opened fire at and got three heavy hits on the *Gneisenau*. The German warships returned fire, hitting *Renown* twice but causing little damage, and then turned away to the northeast; the German commander, Admiral Lütjens, had decided not to take unnecessary risks against what he believed to be the battleship *Repulse*. It was perhaps lucky for the *Renown* that one of her shells put the *Gneisenau*'s Seetakt ranging radar and its associated gunnery control system out of action. *Renown* herself, at this stage, was not radar-equipped.

In the afternoon of 9 April, units of the Home Fleet were attacked almost without pause for three hours by 41 Heinkel 111s of KG26 and 47 Junkers 88s of KG30. The battleship *Rodney* received a direct hit from a 500kg (1100lb) bomb which splintered her armoured deck but failed to explode; the cruisers *Devonshire, Southampton* and *Glasgow* were damaged by near misses, and the destroyer, *Gurkha* was sunk west of Stavanger. The Germans lost just four Ju 88s. During this first encounter, the Royal Navy learned to its cost what it meant to operate in range of land-based bombers without any fighter cover. The need for more aircraft carriers had been clearly demonstrated.

One major success was registered by HMS *Spearfish* (Lt Cdr J.G. Forbes). Early on 11 April, she was on the surface recharging her batteries after running the gauntlet of enemy warships when the battleship *Lützow* was sighted, returning to Germany at high speed. Forbes fired a salvo of torpedoes at her and one struck her right aft, wrecking her propellers and rudder and leaving her helpless. Unaware that the battleship had no anti-submarine escort, and with his batteries still not replenished, Forbes broke off the attack, leaving the *Lützow* wallowing in the water. She summoned help and was towed to Kiel in a near-sinking condition. It was to be a year before she was ready for sea again.

THE BISMARCK

In May 1941 the Royal Navy faced the most serious threat so far to the vital convoy routes when the Germans initiated Operation Rhein¸bung, a sortie into the North Atlantic by the new battleship *Bismarck* and the heavy cruiser *Prinz Eugen*. The Germans had originally intended that a simultaneous sortie was to be made by the *Scharnhorst* and *Gneisenau*, but the latter had been badly damaged in a torpedo attack by a Beaufort of RAF Coastal Command at Brest on 6 April 1941.

Nevertheless, the battle group that sailed from Gdynia in the eastern Baltic under the command of Admiral Lütjens, the Fleet Commander, on 18 May was formidable enough. The *Bismarck* (Capt Lindemann) was at that time undoubtedly the most

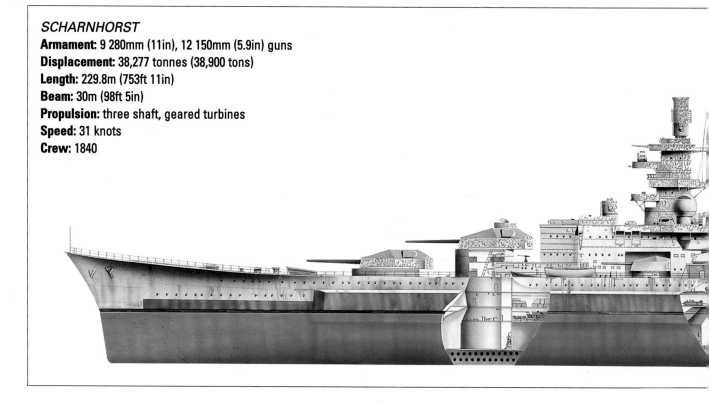

SCHARNHORST
Armament: 9 280mm (11in), 12 150mm (5.9in) guns
Displacement: 38,277 tonnes (38,900 tons)
Length: 229.8m (753ft 11in)
Beam: 30m (98ft 5in)
Propulsion: three shaft, geared turbines
Speed: 31 knots
Crew: 1840

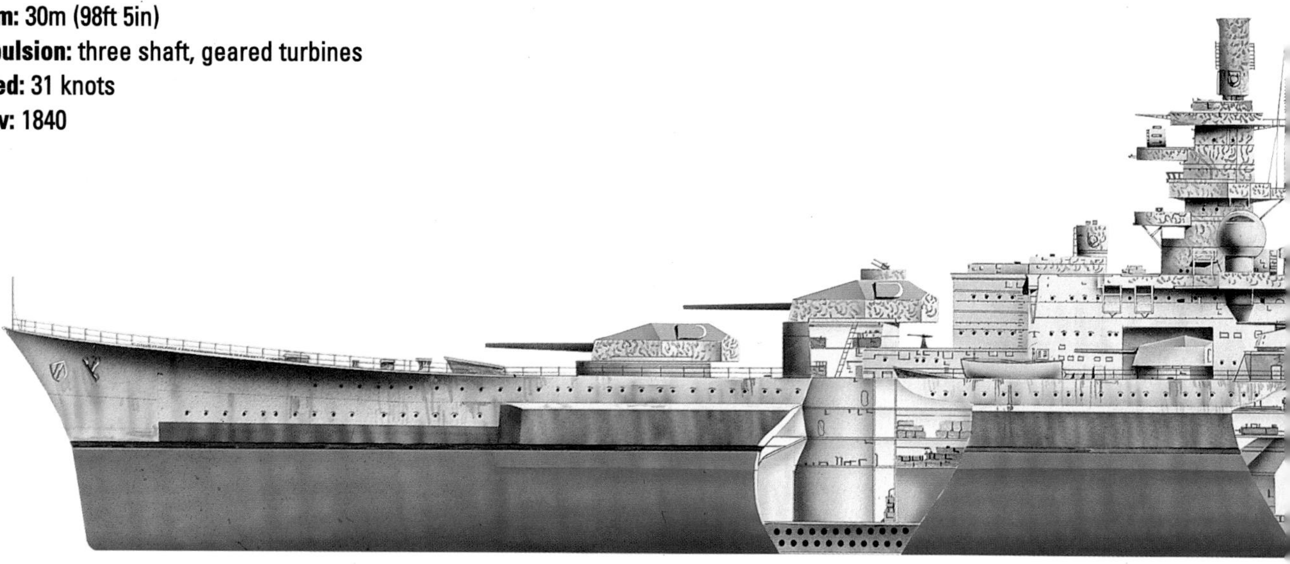

Above: The battlecruiser *Scharnhorst.* With her sister, the *Gneisenau*, she was to remain a constant thorn in Britain's side until she was sunk off North Cape in December 1943.

powerful warship afloat, while the heavy cruiser *Prinz Eugen* (Capt Brinkmann) was also new, having been completed in 1940. The sortie was supported by a supply ship, six tankers, two patrol ships and three weather ships, deployed in the Arctic and Atlantic, while escort during the passage into the Norwegian Sea was provided by three destroyers and three minesweepers.

On 20 May the force was reported in the Kattegat by the Swedish cruiser *Gotland*, and intelligence of the enemy force's northward movement reached the British Admiralty early the next day. Admiral Sir John Tovey, who was now C-in-C, Home Fleet, at once strengthened surveillance of the northern passages into the Atlantic, ordering the battleship *Prince of Wales*, the battlecruiser *Hood* and six destroyers to sail from Scapa Flow under Vice-Admiral L.E. Holland, while reconnaissance aircraft were despatched far and wide to search for the enemy. That same afternoon, the *Bismarck* and her consort were photographed by a PRU Spitfire as they refuelled in Korsfjord, near Bergen. Then, shortly before nightfall on the 22nd, a Martin Maryland reconnaissance aircraft penetrated Korsfjord. Peering through the gloom, the plane's crew discovered that the *Bismarck* and *Prinz Eugen* were gone.

At 2245 hours Admiral Tovey left Scapa Flow with the main body of the Home Fleet, heading for Icelandic waters to reinforce the heavy cruisers *Norfolk* and *Suffolk*, then patrolling the Denmark Strait. Three more cruisers were guarding Lütjens' alternative breakout route, between Iceland and the Faeroes.

First to arrive were the Home Fleet's two fastest ships, the *Prince of Wales* and the *Hood*, which had set out in advance of the main force; behind them came Tovey's Fleet Flagship, the new battleship *King George V*, the aircraft carrier *Victorious*, four cruisers and six destroyers. The carrier was not yet fully worked up, and her air group comprised only nine Swordfish and six Fulmars. She had been earmarked to escort Convoy WS.8B, bound for the Middle East with troops, but had been released on Admiralty orders to take part in the hunt for the *Bismarck*. So had the battlecruiser *Repulse*, which also sailed north accompanied by three destroyers withdrawn from the Western Approaches.

At 1922 hours on 23 May the *Bismarck* and *Prinz Eugen* were sighted by the cruiser *Suffolk* (Capt R.M. Ellis), emerging from a snow squall in the Denmark Strait. About an hour later *Suffolk* was joined by *Norfolk* (Capt A.J.L.Phillips), flying the flag of Rear-

Admiral W.F. Wake-Walker, commanding the 1st Cruiser Squadron. HMS *Norfolk* came under enemy fire at a range of 11,985m (13,000yds) and was straddled by three 380mm (15in) salvoes before retiring under cover of smoke, miraculously undamaged, to radio her enemy sighting report to Admiral Tovey, whose main fleet was still some 1100km (600nm) to the southwest. The two cruisers continued to shadow Lütjens' ships at high speed throughout the night, *Suffolk* maintaining contact with her Type 284 radar.

The *Prince of Wales* and *Hood*, meanwhile, were coming up quickly. Vice-Admiral Holland's ships had been about 408km (220nm) away at the time of the first sighting report, and Holland was anticipating a night action. His plan was to concentrate the fire of his heavy ships on the *Bismarck*, leaving Wake-Walker's cruisers to deal with the *Prinz Eugen*. What he did not know was that the *Bismarck* was no longer in the lead; the blast from her guns had put her own forward radar out of action, so L¸tjens had ordered the *Prinz Eugen* to change position.

As his heavy ships approached, Admiral Holland, conscious of the need for surprise, imposed strict radio and radar silence, relying on *Suffolk*'s reports to keep him informed of the enemy's position. Soon after midnight, however, *Suffolk* lost contact, and did not regain it until 0247 hours. In the meantime Holland had turned his ships south to await full daylight, but when information once again began to come through from *Suffolk* he increased speed to 28 knots and turned on an interception course. It was now 0340 hours, and visibility was 22km (12nm).

HOOD DESTROYED

At 0537 hours the opposing forces sighted each other at a range of 27km (14.5nm), and opened fire at 0553 hours. Both German ships concentrated their fire on the *Hood* and, thanks to their stereoscopic range-finders, straddled her immediately; the *Bismarck*'s second and third salvoes struck the battlecruiser amidships, and those from the *Prinz Eugen* started a fire among her ready-to-use AA ammunition.

At 0600 hours, as the British warships were altering course in order to bring all their guns to bear, the *Hood* was hit again by a salvo which pierced her lightly-armoured decks and detonated in her aft magazines. She blew up with a tremendous explosion and disappeared with a speed that stunned all who witnessed the event. Only three of her crew of 1419 officers and ratings survived. As the *Prince of Wales* altered course sharply to avoid the wreckage she herself came under heavy fire: Within moments she sustained hits by four 380mm (15in) and three 203mm (8in) shells, one of which exploded on the bridge and killed or wounded almost everyone there except her captain, J.C. Leach, who ordered the battleship to turn

Above: The *Gneisenau* in Norway, April 1940. With the *Scharnhorst*, she played an important part as the covering force during the German invasion.

away under cover of smoke. The *Prince of Wales* was so new that she had not yet finished working-up. The contractors were still working on her 355mm (14in) turrets when she sailed and she was therefore not fully battleworthy, a fact of which Captain Leach was obviously conscious. The additional damage had made her even more vulnerable, and Leach's intention now was to use his damaged ship to assist Wake-Walker's cruisers in maintaining contact with the enemy until Admiral Tovey's main force could reach the scene.

What Leach had no means of knowing was that his gunners had obtained three hits on the *Bismarck*, causing two of her fuel tanks to leak oil and contaminating others. Because of this, Lütjens decided it was too risky to continue. He abandoned the sortie and decided to steer southwest for St Nazaire, the only port on the Atlantic coast of France with a dry dock large enough to accommodate his flagship, and wait while repairs were carried out.

Tovey's ships were still 611km (330nm) to the southeast and could not expect to make contact until 0700 hours on 25 May at the earliest. However, other ships were also heading for the scene. Admiral Somerville's Force H had been ordered north from Gibraltar by the Admiralty to intercept the German squadron, and the battleships *Rodney, Revenge* and *Ramillies* and the cruiser *Edinburgh* were also released from escort duties. The main concern now was to reduce the *Bismarck*'s speed, giving the hunters a chance to close in for the kill, and at 1440 hours on 24 May Admiral Tovey ordered the carrier *Victorious* to race ahead to a flying-off point 185km (100nm) from the enemy ships and launch a Swordfish strike against them.

At 2210 hours the carrier flew off nine Swordfish of No 825 Squadron, led by Lt Cdr Eugene Esmonde. Flying through rain and sleet, they obtained radar contact with the enemy at 2337 hours and briefly sighted the *Bismarck*, only to lose her again. Twenty minutes later the shadowing British cruisers re-directed the Swordfish on to their target and they made their attack through heavy defensive fire. One torpedo hit the *Bismarck* without causing significant damage; the other eight missed. The Swordfish crews, all of whom recovered safely to the carrier, reported no sign of the *Prinz Eugen*, which in fact had been detached by Admiral Lütjens to continue on her way alone. She arrived in Brest unmolested on 1 June.

At 0300 hours on 25 May Lütjens altered course to the southeast, and at this critical juncture the shadowing cruisers, which had been following at extreme radar range, lost contact. The problems facing *Bismarck*'s pursuers were compounded by the receipt of some bearings transmitted by the Admiralty which, through a combination of errors, led Admiral Tovey to believe that the battleship was heading northeast, into the Atlantic. As a result, Tovey followed this false trail throughout most of the 25th, until, at about 1800 hours, he decided that the *Bismarck* was probably heading for Brest and changed course. A signal received at 1924 hours indicated that the Admiralty also thought that this was the case. In fact, the Admiralty had earlier already instructed Admiral Somerville's Force H to position itself on a line from which its ships and aircraft could intercept the *Bismarck* should she head for the Bay of Biscay. It turned out to be a fortuitous move.

Although Tovey's warships had lost valuable ground during their false quest to the northeast, the net around *Bismarck* was gradually closing, and at 1030 hours on the 26th *Bismarck* was sighted nearly 1126km (608nm) west of Brest by a Catalina of No 209 Squadron from Castle Archdale in Northern Ireland. Soon afterwards, contact was also made by two Swordfish reconnaissance aircraft from the *Ark Royal*, Force H's aircraft carrier, and Admiral Somerville sent the cruiser *Sheffield* to shadow the battleship with her Type 79Y radar and, when the opportunity arose, to direct a strike by the carrier's Swordfish torpedo-bombers. Fourteen of the latter were flown off at 1450 hours in conditions of high winds, driving rain and rough seas, and some time later their radar revealed a target which their crews assumed was the *Bismarck*. In fact it was the *Sheffield*, whose presence in the area had not been signalled to *Ark Royal*. The Swordfish came down through low cloud and attacked from different directions; several of them released their torpedoes before the mistake was recognised, but fortunately – thanks to a combination of effective evasive manoeuvring by the cruiser and faulty magnetic pistols fitted to the torpedoes – no damage was caused.

THE END OF THE *BISMARCK*

This first strike force returned to the carrier, which at 1910 hours launched a second wave of 15 Swordfish. The aircraft had little chance of making a coordinated attack in the prevailing weather conditions, coupled

Below: The *Scharnhorst* hoisting aboard an Arado Ar196 reconnaissance seaplane. At least one of these was carried by all German capital ships.

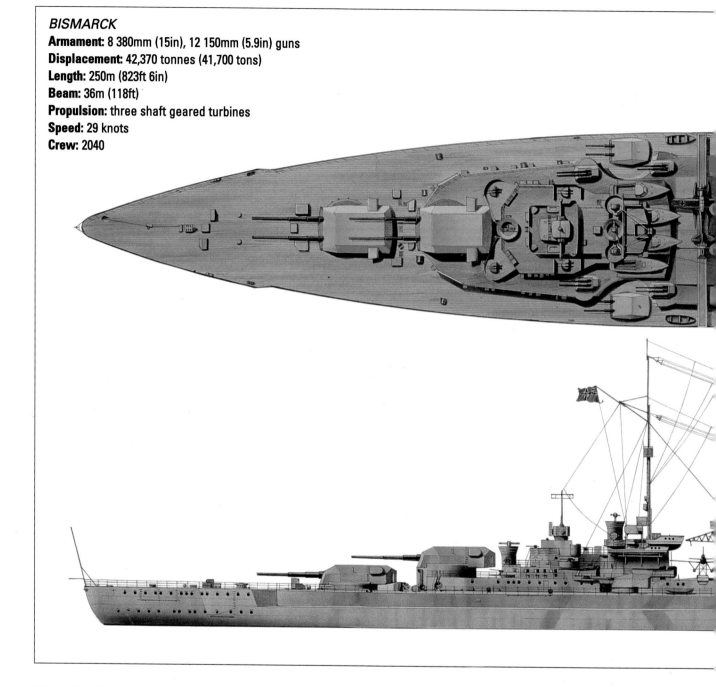

BISMARCK
Armament: 8 380mm (15in), 12 150mm (5.9in) guns
Displacement: 42,370 tonnes (41,700 tons)
Length: 250m (823ft 6in)
Beam: 36m (118ft)
Propulsion: three shaft geared turbines
Speed: 29 knots
Crew: 2040

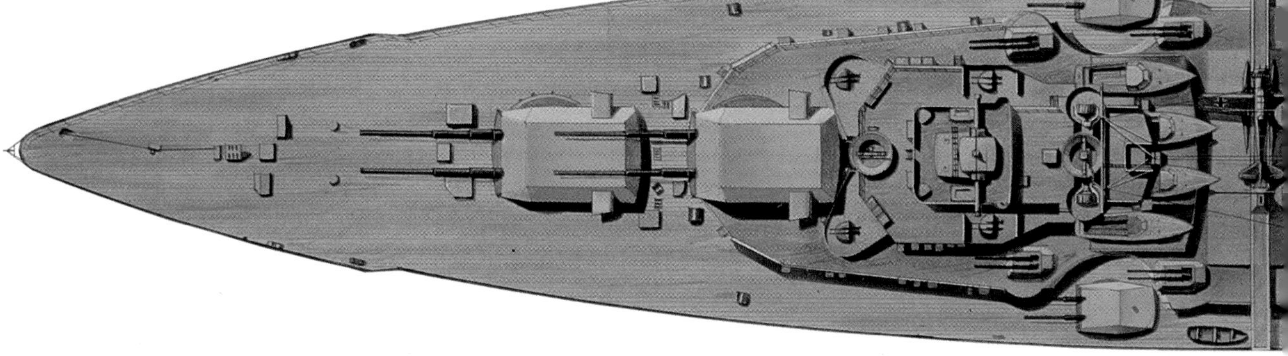

Above: The *Bismarck*, the most powerful German warship afloat in May 1941, and the sister ship of the *Tirpitz*. Six even more powerful vessels were cancelled in 1940.

with fading light and heavy defensive fire. Nevertheless, two torpedoes found their mark; one struck the *Bismarck*'s armoured belt and did little damage, but the other struck her extreme stern, damaging her propellers and jamming her rudders. At 2140 hours Admiral Lütjens signalled Berlin: 'Ship no longer manoeuvrable. We fight to the last shell. Long live the Führer.'

Shortly afterwards, five destroyers, led by the *Cossack*, arrived on the scene. They made contact with the *Bismarck* and shadowed her throughout the night, transmitting regular position reports and making determined torpedo attacks, but these were disrupted by heavy and accurate radar-controlled gunfire. During the night, the battleships *King George V* and *Rodney* came within striking distance of their crippled enemy, but Admiral Tovey, aware of the accuracy of her radar-directed gunnery, decided to wait until daylight before engaging her. She had no means of escaping him now.

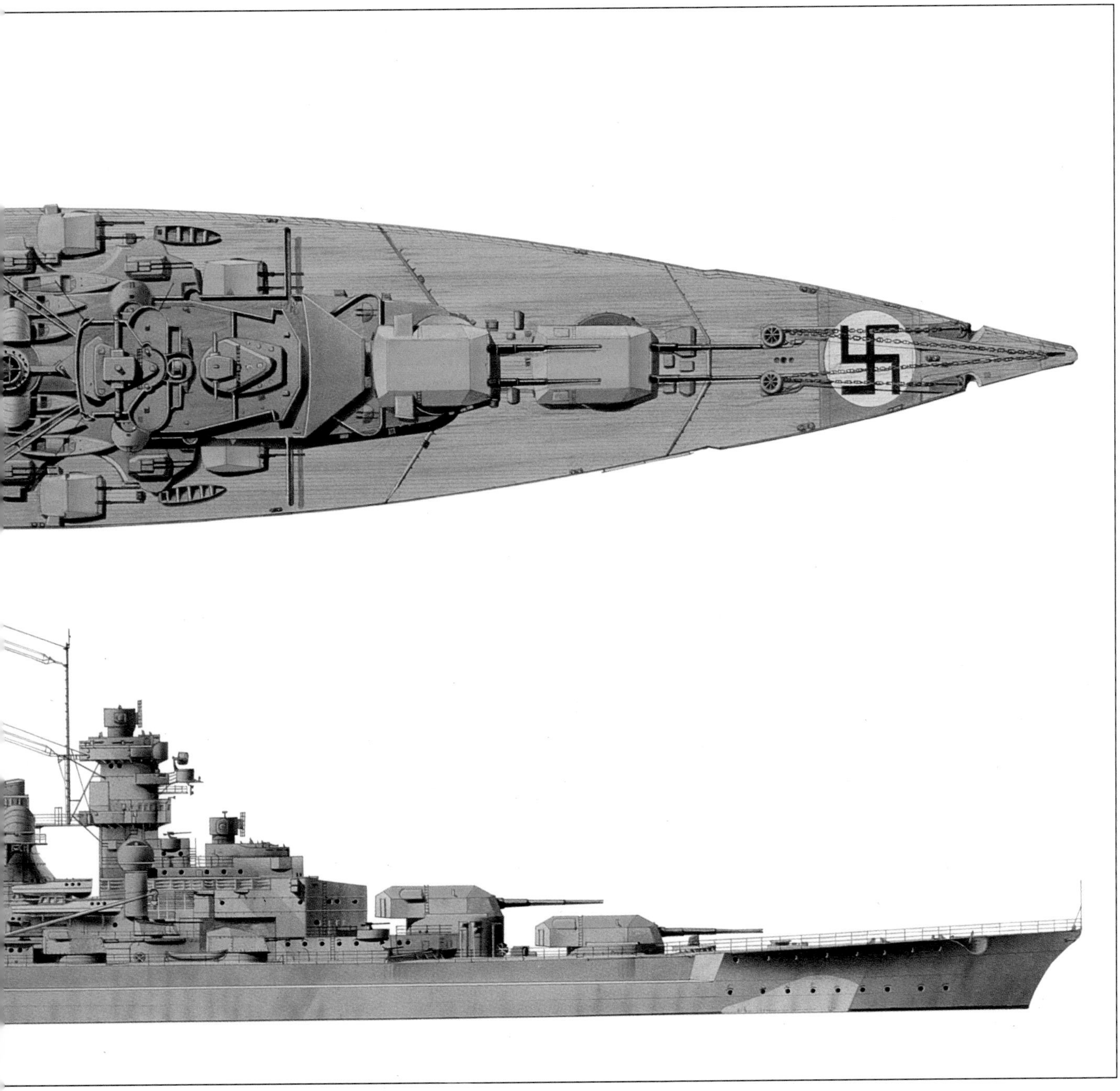

Soon after dawn on 27 May he closed in from the northwest, the battleships *King George V* and *Rodney* opening fire at about 0845 hours from a range of 14,640m (16,000yds). By 1020 hours the *Bismarck* had been reduced to a blazing wreck, with all her guns, even the secondary armament, out of action. Despite the battering she had received, she remained afloat, and it was left to the cruisers *Norfolk* and *Dorsetshire* to close in and finish her off with torpedoes. She sank at 1036 hours, her colours still flying, taking all but 119 of her crew of over 2000 officers and men with her.

ACTION IN THE MEDITERRANEAN

With this major threat removed, the focus now shifted to the Mediterranean, where the Royal Navy had pulled off a stunning coup against the Italian Battle Fleet a few months earlier.

When Italy entered the war on 10 June, 1940, she had at her disposal six battleships (only two of which were ready for operations), seven heavy cruisers, 12 light cruisers, 59 destroyers, 67 torpedo boats and 116 submarines. Against this, the British in the eastern Mediterranean had four battleships, nine light cruisers, 21 destroyers and six submarines, to which could

Above: Adolf Hitler inspecting *Bismarck* in Danzig. Hitler once confessed that although warships fascinated him, he was 'a coward at sea'.

be added one French battleship, three heavy cruisers, one light cruiser, a destroyer and six submarines. Six more British submarines and a destroyer were at Malta. In the western Mediterranean, the combined Anglo-French naval assets were five battleships (four of them French) one aircraft carrier, four heavy cruisers, seven light cruisers (six French), 46 destroyers (37 French) and 36 submarines (all French).

Towards the end of June 1940 a powerful Royal Navy squadron assembled at Gibraltar under the command of Vice-Admiral Sir James Somerville. Known as Force H, it consisted of the aircraft carrier *Ark Royal*, newly arrived from Britain, the battleships *Valiant* and *Resolution*, two cruisers and 11 destroyers, together with the battlecruiser *Hood*.

THE SHELLING OF THE FRENCH FLEET

Force H was only a week old when it was called upon to carry out one of the most tragic and melancholy operations in the history of the Royal Navy; the attempted destruction of the French Fleet at Oran and Mers-el-Kebir (Operation Catapult). Admiral Somerville was ordered to sail with his squadron to Oran and to offer an unpleasant ultimatum to the French commander, Admiral Gensoul. If the latter refused to join forces with the British, to sail to the French West Indies with reduced crews or to scuttle his ships, then Somerville had orders to destroy them. On 3 July Captain C.S. Holland, in command of the *Ark Royal*, was sent to Oran to parley with Gensoul, but the French admiral refused even to consider any of the alternatives.

Shortly before 1800 hours the *Valiant, Resolution* and *Hood* opened fire, directed by Swordfish spotter aircraft from the *Ark Royal*, while another flight of Swordfish laid mines in the entrance of the nearby port of Mers-el-Kebir. The heavy shells hit the magazine of the battleship *Bretagne* and she blew up; the *Dunkerque* and *Provence* were badly damaged, and two destroyers were sunk.

As the sun went down, the battleship *Strasbourg* and five destroyers made a dash for safety. They were attacked by the *Ark Royal*'s Swordfish, but in the face of heavy anti-aircraft fire and the gathering darkness the pilots' aim was poor and the French warships got away to Toulon. The following morning, the *Ark Royal* launched another strike of torpedo-carrying Swordfish to finish off the *Dunkerque*, which was

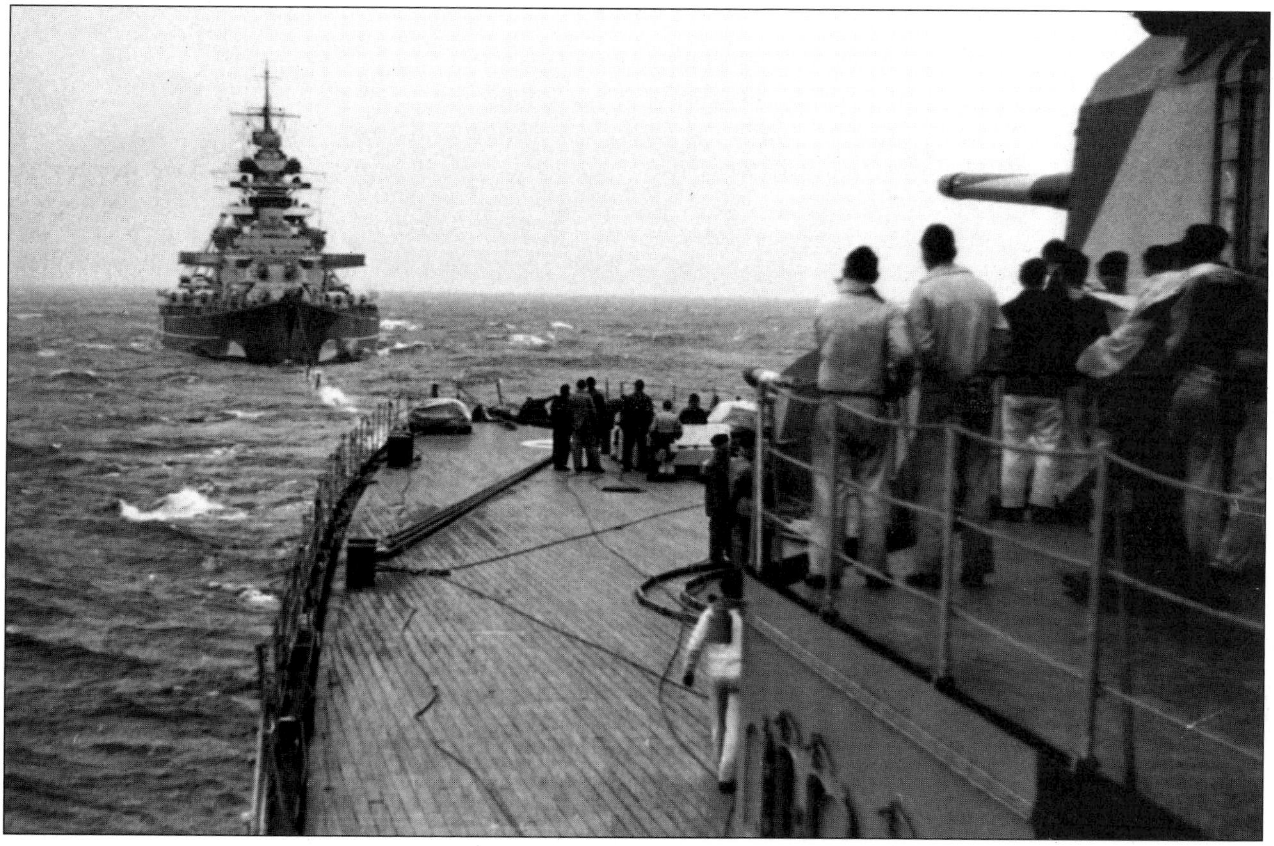

aground in Oran harbour. Four torpedoes hit the auxiliary vessel *Terre Neuve*, which was lying alongside *Dunkerque* with a cargo of depth charges. These exploded and ripped open the battleship's side, putting her out of action.

Another French squadron, comprising the battleship *Lorraine*, four cruisers and a number of smaller warships, was at Alexandria, where it had been operating under Admiral Cunningham before France's collapse. Here Cunningham managed to arrive at a peaceful settlement with his French opposite number, Admiral Godfroy, and the French warships were deactivated safely. However that still left the new battleships *Jean Bart* and *Richelieu* – which had escaped from Brest before the Germans arrived – in the West African ports of Casablanca and Dakar. On 8 July a fast motor boat from the carrier *Hermes* entered Dakar harbour and dropped depth charges under the *Richelieu*'s stern in an attempt to put her rudder and propellers out of action. Unfortunately the depth charges failed to explode. The battleship was later attacked by Swordfish flying from the carrier *Hermes*, but their torpedoes only inflicted light damage. She was attacked again two months later, by the *Ark Royal*'s aircraft, during an abortive British attempted landing in Senegal; but once again the air strikes proved ineffective, and this time nine Swordfish and Skuas were shot down.

Above: The *Bismarck* in line astern, taken from the *Prinz Eugen*. The two warships were worked up in the Baltic prior to their operational foray into the North Atlantic.

HARRYING THE ITALIAN NAVY

On 7 July Admiral Cunningham, having dealt with the French squadron in Alexandria, sailed from that port with the twofold intention of providing protection for two convoys carrying supplies from Malta to Alexandria, and also of throwing down a challenge to the Italian Navy by operating within sight of the southern coast of Italy. Cunningham's force was split into three; the leading unit (Force A) consisted of five cruisers, the centre (Force B) of the battleship *Warspite* and her destroyer screen, and bringing up the rear was Force C, comprising the carrier *Eagle*, accompanied by 10 destroyers and the veteran battleships *Malaya* and *Royal Sovereign*. The British Fleet's air cover consisted of 15 Swordfish of Nos 813 and 824 Squadrons and three Sea Gladiators of a fighter flight, forming *Eagle*'s air group.

Early on 8 July a patrolling submarine reported that a strong enemy force, including two battleships, was steaming southwards between Taranto and Benghazi. Reconnaissance Swordfish were launched, and they in turn reported that the enemy warships were following an easterly course, which led Cunningham to believe that they were covering a convoy en route to Benghazi. Postponing the departure of the British convoy from Malta, he altered course in order to position himself between the enemy and their base at Taranto.

Below: A dreadnought of the 'Bretagne' class, *Provence* was updated in the 1930s. She was badly damaged by the British at Mers-el-Kebir in July 1940.

At dawn on 9 July, his fleet having endured five days of air attacks that inflicted little damage, Cunningham was 97km (52nm) off the southwest tip of Greece, with the enemy force – two battleships, 16 cruisers and 32 destroyers – about 278km (150nm) ahead of him, in the Ionian Sea. By 1145 hours only 167km (90nm) separated the two forces, and the *Eagle* launched a strike force of nine Swordfish in an attempt to slow down the enemy force. They failed to find the main force, which had altered course, but launched their torpedoes through a heavy barrage of fire at an Italian cruiser in the rear, missed, and returned to the *Eagle* to refuel and rearm.

WARSPITE
Armament: 8 380mm (15in), 16 152mm (6in) guns
Displacement: 33,548 tonnes (33,020 tons)
Length: 197m (646ft)
Beam: 28m (90ft 6in)
Propulsion: quadruple screw turbines
Speed: 23 knots
Crew: 951

Above: The British battleship HMS Warspite as she appeared in 1943. Severely damaged by radio-controlled bombs off Salerno, she was only partially repaired.

At 1515 hours Cunningham's advance force of cruisers sighted the enemy, who immediately opened fire on them. Minutes later the *Warspite* arrived and engaged the Italian cruisers until they were forced to withdraw making smoke. At 1545 hours a second Swordfish strike was launched. Three minutes later the *Warspite* made contact with the Italian flagship *Giulio Cesare* and opened fire on her from a range of 23,790m (26,000yds), severely damaging her and slowing her to 18 knots. The Italian commander, Admiral Campioni, at once broke off the action and headed for the Italian coast accompanied by the *Cesare*'s sister ship *Conte di Cavour*, while ordering his destroyer flotillas to attack and lay down smoke.

At 1615 hours the nine Swordfish, led by Lt Cdr Debenham, arrived in the vicinity of the Italian warships, the pilots striving to identify targets in the dense pall of smoke that now hung over the sea. After a few minutes, Debenham spotted two large warships emerging from the smoke and led his aircraft in to the attack. In fact, the two ships were the cruisers *Trento* and *Bolzano*; they immediately turned away into the smoke once more, throwing down a heavy barrage in the path of the attacking Swordfish as they did so. The torpedoes failed to find their mark, and all the aircraft returned safely to the carrier. They landed-on in the middle of yet another high-level attack by Italian bombers. None of the British warships were hit, although both *Eagle* and *Warspite* were shaken by near misses.

Cunningham abandoned the chase at 1730 hours and set course for Malta, where his ships refuelled and rearmed before returning to Alexandria. Without adequate fighter cover, it would have been suicidal to sail any closer to the Italian coast. The 'Action off Calabria', as Cunningham's brush with the Italians came to be known, was the first fleet action in which carrier aircraft took part.

THE ATTACK ON TARANTO

In the autumn of 1940, the Italians began to concentrate their heavy naval units at Taranto naval base, in southern Italy, to counter the threat from the British Mediterranean Fleet. Taranto had long been regarded as a tempting target for the Fleet Air Arm, but with only the old *Eagle* at Admiral Cunningham's disposal, an attack on the Italian base had been considered impracticable. The deployment of the large, modern aircraft carrier HMS *Illustrious* to the Mediterranean at the end of August 1940 changed the picture completely; the plans were revised, and it was decided to mount a strike from the *Illustrious* and *Eagle* on the night of 21 October, the anniversary of the Battle of Trafalgar. Before that date, however, a serious fire swept through *Illustrious*'s hangar; some aircraft were totally destroyed and others put out of action, and the strike had to be postponed.

Air reconnaissance had revealed that five of the six battleships of the Italian battle fleet were at Taranto, as well as a large force of cruisers and destroyers. The battleships and some of the cruisers were moored in the outer harbour, the Mar Grande, a horseshoe-shaped expanse of fairly shallow water, while the other cruisers and destroyers lay in the inner harbour, the Mar Piccolo. The ships in the outer harbour were protected by torpedo nets and lines of barrage balloons, which would present the greatest hazard to the low-flying Swordfish.

The date of the attack (Operation Judgment) was fixed for the night of 11 November. Due to the many near-misses she had suffered in enemy air attacks, the *Eagle* had to be withdrawn from the operation at the last moment; five of her aircraft were transferred to the other carrier. *Illustrious* and the fleet sailed from Alexandria on 6 November. Two days later the warships made rendezvous with several convoys in the Ionian Sea, on their way from Malta to Alexandria and Greece. The concentration of ships was located and attacked by the Regia Aeronautica during the next

Below: The *Duilio* seen partly submerged after being torpedoed by Fleet Air Arm aircraft at Taranto in November 1940. She took no further part in the war.

CAIO DUILIO
Armament: 10 320mm (12.6in) guns
Displacement: 29,861 tonnes (29,391 tons)
Length: 187m (613ft 2in)
Beam: 28m (91ft 10in)
Propulsion: twin screw turbines
Speed: 27 knots
Crew: 1198

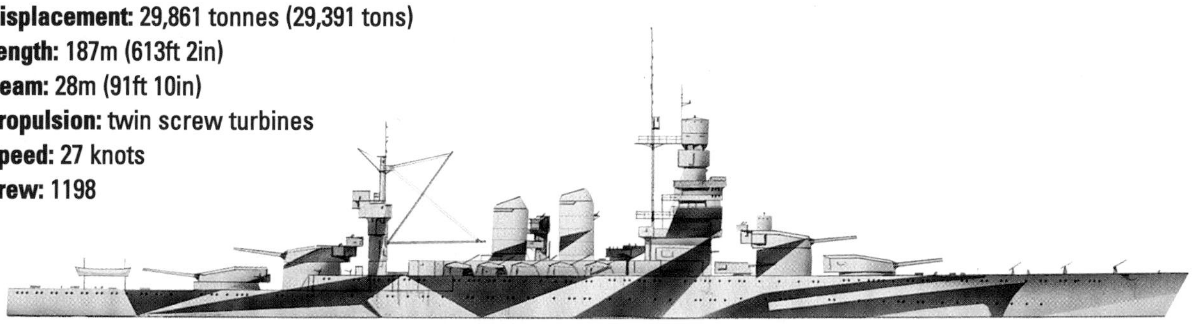

Above: Like other Italian battleships, the *Caio Duilio* was virtually rebuilt between the two world wars, receiving new armour, new guns and a seaplane.

two days, but the attacks were broken up by 806 Squadron's Fulmars, which claimed the destruction of 10 enemy aircraft for no loss.

At 1800 hours on the 11th, with the convoys safely on their way under escort, the *Illustrious*, with a screen of four cruisers and four destroyers, detached herself from the main force and headed for her flying-off position 315km (170nm) from Taranto. Twenty-one aircraft were available for the strike from 815 Squadron, led by Lt Cdr K. Williamson, and No 819 under Lt Cdr J.W. Hale. Due to the restricted space over the target, only six aircraft in each wave were to carry torpedoes; the others were to drop flares to the east of the Mar Grande, silhouetting the warships, or to dive-bomb the vessels in the Mar Piccolo.

The first wave of Swordfish began taking off at 2040 hours and set course in clear weather, climbing to 2440m (8000ft) and reaching the enemy coast at 2220 hours. The Swordfish formation now split in two, the torpedo-carriers making their approach from the west while the flare-droppers headed for a point east of the Mar Grande. At 2300 hours the torpedo aircraft began their attack, diving in line astern. Williamson, descending to 9m (30ft), passed over the stern of the battleship *Diga di Tarantola* and released his torpedo at the destroyer *Fulmine*; it missed but ran on to strike the side of the battleship *Conte di Cavour*. The Swordfish was hit by AA fire and had to ditch; Williamson and his observer, Lt N.J. Scarlett, being taken prisoner. Two torpedoes from the other Swordfish hit the brand-new battleship *Littorio*; the aircraft all got clear of the target area and returned to the carrier. So did the other six aircraft, whose bombs had damaged some oil tanks and started a big fire in the seaplane base beside the Mar Piccolo.

The second wave, which had taken off some 50 minutes after the first, had no difficulty in locating Taranto; the target area was lit up by searchlights and fires. There were only eight aircraft in this wave; one had been forced to return to the carrier with mechanical trouble. This time, the torpedo-carriers came in from the north. Two torpedoes hit the *Littorio* and another the *Caio Duilio*; a fourth narrowly missed the *Vittorio Veneto*. The fifth Swordfish (Lt G.W. Bayley and Lt H.G. Slaughter) was hit and exploded, killing both crew members. By 0300 hours all the surviving Swordfish had been recovered safely. A number of bombs had failed to explode; one had hit the cruiser *Trento* amidships, only to bounce off into the water, and the same had happened to the destroyer *Libeccio*.

The following day, RAF reconnaissance photographs told the full story of the damage inflicted on the Italian Fleet. The mighty *Littorio*, with great gaps torn in her side by three torpedoes, was badly down by the bow; it would take four months to effect repairs. The *Caio Duilio* and the *Conte di Cavour* had taken one hit each; the former had been beached and the latter had sunk on the bottom. The *Duilio* was repaired and returned to service after six months; the *Cavour* was later salvaged and moved to Trieste, where RAF bombers sank her on 17 February 1945.

It was the first time that a formidable battle fleet had been crippled by carrier aircraft, and the effect on the morale of the Italian Navy was shattering. After Taranto, the Italian Fleet was permanently on the defensive, and the superiority of the Royal Navy in the Mediterranean was assured. The Italian warships would never again present a serious threat to the security of the British convoys that were passing through the Mediterranean in increasing numbers.

CHAPTER EIGHT

The Naval War in the West 1942–45

The first years of the war had proven how dangerous German battleships such as the *Bismarck* could be to Allied warships and merchantmen alike. As her sister ship, the *Tirpitz*, prepared to put to sea, the prospect of further disruption to Allied shipping loomed. Now, however, as the tide of the war began to turn, the British were determined to contain or eliminate the threat of the German capital ships once and for all.

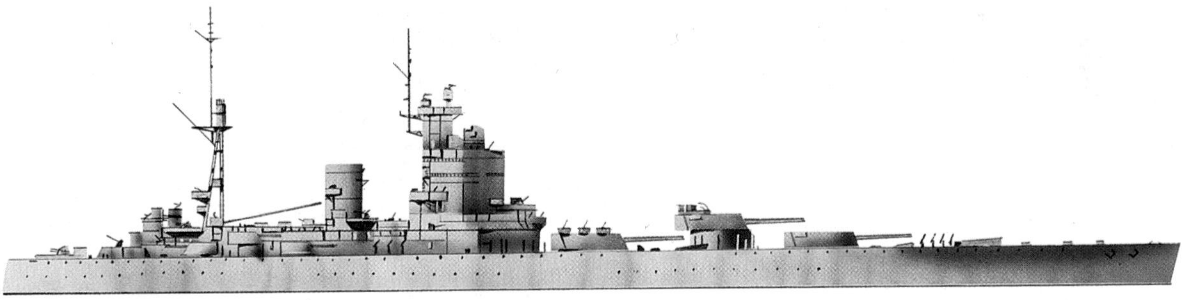

In the Atlantic area, in mid-1941, the threat posed by the *Bismarck* had been removed and the battlecruisers *Scharnhorst* and *Gneisenau*, along with the *Prinz Eugen*, were bottled up in the French Channel ports for the time being. For the British Admiralty, however, there remained the spectre of *Bismarck*'s sister ship, the *Tirpitz*. After completion of her trials in the autumn of 1941 she was designated as flagship of the German Baltic Fleet, which was then commanded by Vice-Admiral Ciliax. In September 1941 she formed part of a battle group that sailed to the mouth of the Gulf of Finland to counter a possible breakout into the Baltic by the Soviet Fleet. In the event this never happened, the Russian warships having been subjected to fierce air attack at Kronstadt, their principal base, which effectively prevented any offensive action for the foreseeable future.

Left: A dancing troupe entertaining the ship's crew of the *Tirpitz* in Norway. Note the camouflage canvas on the ship's 380mm (15in) guns.

Towards the end of October British Naval Intelligence received indications that the *Tirpitz* was about to move into the Atlantic. As an insurance against this, Admiral Tovey positioned units of the Home Fleet – the battleship *King George V*, the air-

Above: Crewmen cleaning the main armament of the *Admiral Hipper.* One of the most active and effective of Germany's warships, the *Hipper* was scuttled in May 1945.

craft carrier *Victorious*, three heavy and two light cruisers – and an American battle squadron (the battleships *Idaho* and *Mississippi* and two cruisers) south of Iceland and in the Denmark Strait. Although not yet at war with Germany – the US entered the conflict in December 1941 – the US Navy had been involved in Atlantic convoy escort work since August 1941, following a vital meeting between Winston Churchill and US President Franklin D. Roosevelt.

THE *TIRPITZ* SAILS

It was not until 16 January 1942, however, that the *Tirpitz* left her home port of Wilhelmshaven for ever, flying the flag of Admiral Ciliax and under the command of Captain Topp. Her destination was Trondheim, in Norway. Hitler himself has decided on her destinationat a meeting with Admiral Raeder in November 1941. It was based on two considerations; the first was Hitler's concern that the British might attempt a landing in Norway, and the second was a shortage of fuel oil, greatly reducing her radius of action and stopping her from being sent out into the Atlantic. From now on the Arctic would be her

hunting-ground, and the frequent Allied convoys supplying the Russian war effort her quarry.

On 6 March, the *Tirpitz*, accompanied by three destroyers, set out to intercept convoys PQ12 and QP8, the first bound for Murmansk, the second on its way home. PQ12 had been detected by a FW 200 the day before 130km (70nm) south of Jan Mayen Island, and the submarines *U.134*, *U.377*, *U.403* and *U.584* were also deployed to intercept it. Meanwhile *Tirpitz* was being shadowed by the submarine *Seawolf* (Lt Raikes), and units of the Home Fleet, comprising the battleships *King George V*, *Duke of York* and *Renown*, the carrier *Victorious*, the cruiser *Kenya* and 12 destroyers placed themselves between the threat and the convoys, which passed one another off Bear Island on 7 March. Ciliax detached some of his destroyers to search for the convoys and they sank one straggling Russian freighter, but apart from that no contact was made and the Germans turned southwards again.

Thanks to intercepted radio signals, Admiral Tovey knew of the Germans' intentions and tried to cut them off. At daybreak on the 9th, a reconnaissance Albacore from the *Victorious* spotted the *Tirpitz*, and 12 torpedo-carrying Fairey Albacores took off soon afterwards to attack the warship. The attack, however, was carried out in line astern, which gave the *Tirpitz* room to avoid all the torpedoes, although one passed within 6m (30ft) of her. Two Albacores were shot down. The failure of this attack was a bitter pill for the Royal Navy, but it did have one result: on Hitler's orders, the *Tirpitz* never put to sea again if carrier-based aircraft were known to be nearby.

Below: The USS *Washington* was the second ship in the North Carolina class. They were superior in speed, armament and protection to any battleship except *Yamato*.

WASHINGTON
Armament: 9 400mm (16in), 20 127mm (5in) guns
Displacement: 47,518 tonnes (46,770 tons)
Length: 222m (728ft 9in)
Beam: 33m (108ft 4in)
Propulsion: quadruple screw turbines
Speed: 28 knots
Crew: 1880

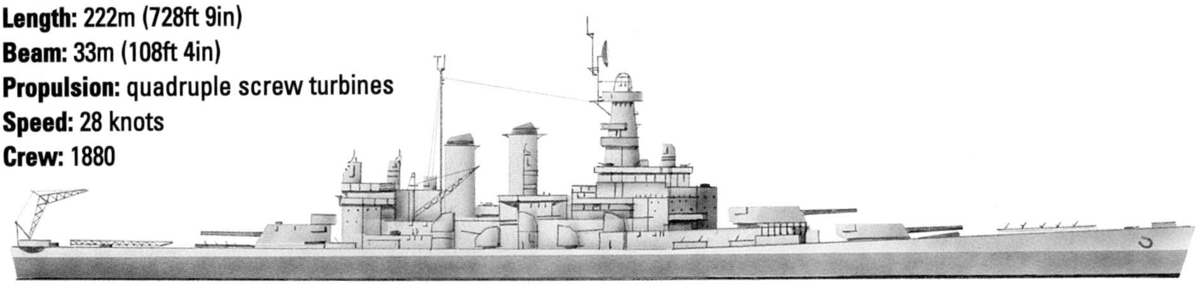

Above: A 'pom-pom' mounting aboard a British battleship. This 40mm gun was used on many British ships and proved a very effective close-range anti-aircraft weapon.

On 11 March the battleship entered Narvik, and on the following day she sailed for Trondheim, evading a force of British destroyers which tried to intercept her off Bodo. On 27 June 1942 the Russia-bound convoy PQ17 sailed from Iceland with 36 freighters, protected by a close support force and a cover group of four cruisers and three destroyers. Additional long-range support was provided by a cover force from the Home Fleet, consisting of the battleships HMS *Duke of York* and USS *Washington*, the latter attached to Admiral Tovey's command, the carrier *Victorious*, two cruisers and 14 destroyers. As soon as they learned of PQ17's departure, the German Navy initiated Operation Rösselsprung (Knight's Move), its aim the total destruction of the convoy. In the afternoon of 2 July, Force I under Admiral Schniewind, comprising the battleship *Tirpitz* and the cruiser *Admiral Hipper*, with four destroyers and two torpedo boats, set out from Trondheim, and the next day Vice-Admiral Kummetz's Force II, comprising the heavy cruisers *Lützow* and *Admiral Scheer*, with five destroyers, sailed from Narvik and headed north to join Force I at Altenfjord. There they waited, the German commanders unwilling to risk their ships until they had more information about the strength of the enemy's covering forces.

Tirpitz did not sortie from Altenfjord until 5 July. She made no contact with the enemy, although she had a narrow escape when a Soviet submarine, the *K.21* (Capt 2nd Class Lunin) fired a salvo of torpedoes at her, which missed.

MIDGET SUBMARINES

Although the *Tirpitz* remained inactive during the remainder of 1942 and the spring of 1943, the presence of the battleship and other heavy units, strategically placed in northern Norway, persuaded the Allies to suspend convoys to Russia during the Arctic summer, when the cover of darkness was stripped away. Desperate measures to eliminate the *Tirpitz* were called for. In August 1943 plans were laid to attack her with four-man midget submarines known as 'X-craft'. These would be towed across the North Sea by specially-modified submarines, make the final run to the battleship under their own power, and lay explosive charges under her.

The final preparations were well under way when reconnaissance revealed that the *Tirpitz* had left Altenfjord on 6 September. She had sailed at the head of a task force, comprising the *Scharnhorst* and nine destroyers, to bombard Allied bases on Spitzbergen. While the warships destroyed coastal batteries, the destroyers landed a battalion of the 349th Grenadier Regiment, the troops blowing up coal and supply dumps, water and electricity stations before withdrawing. It was the only occasion on which *Tirpitz*'s main guns were fired in anger against a surface target.

The midget submarine attack, Operation Source, finally got underway on 21 September 1943, after it was confirmed that the enemy warships had returned to Altenfjord. Two of the small craft, *X.8* and *X.9*, were lost in passage; *X.5* was never heard from again, probably destroyed while passing through a minefield; and *X.10* had to abandon the sortie after breaking down. Only *X.6* (Lt D. Cameron RNR) and *X.7* (Lt B.G.C. Place RN) succeeded in penetrating into the anchorage to lay their charges under the Tirpitz. Cameron then scuttled his craft, he and his crew being picked up and taken on board the battleship. Place tried to force his way back through the torpedo nets surrounding the *Tirpitz*, but was still entangled when the charges detonated, sending *X.7* out of control. Place and one other crew member got clear, but the other two were lost when the craft sank.

The charges exploded at 0812 hours on 22 September, the *Tirpitz*'s log recording 'Two heavy consecutive detonations to port at a tenth of a second interval. Ship vibrates strongly in vertical direction, and sways slightly between the anchors.' The ship seemed to rise several feet out of the water and fell back with a slight list. All lights went out, watertight doors jammed, stores broke loose, and uproar ensued. The damage was substantial. A turbine had been shaken from its bed, and 'C' turret, which weighed about 2032 tonnes (2000 tons), had been lifted by the explosion, which had occurred directly underneath it, off the roller path of ball bearings on which it rested, then dropped down again and jammed. All the rangefinders and fire control gear had been put out of action. Everything but the turret could be repaired on the spot, but it would take a long time.

For her repairs *Tirpitz* retreated into Kaafjord, a narrow body of water off Altenfjord. The berth had been selected earlier, as the high, steep mountains on both sides of the fjord made air attack very difficult, especially for torpedo-bombers. On the night of 10/11 February 1944, however, 15 Ilyushin Il-4 bombers of the Soviet Naval Air Arm, each carrying a 1000kg (2250lb) bomb, set out to attack the battleship. Four of the Russian crews found their target, and one bomb registered a near miss, causing slight damage.

AIR ATTACKS

In a bid to knock the *Tirpitz* out once and for all, before she could be made fully seaworthy, the C-in-C Home Fleet (now Admiral Sir Bruce Fraser) planned a massive Fleet Air Arm strike against her. To simulate her anchorage in Altenfjord, a dummy range was built on Loch Eriboll in Scotland, and during March this was the scene of intense activity as aircraft from the *Victorious* and *Furious* rehearsed the attack plan.

The strike was to be carried out by the 8th and 52nd TBR (Torpedo-Bomber Reconnaissance) Wings, operating the Fairey Barracuda, a type that

Below: The 43,588-tonne (42,900-ton) battleship *Tirpitz*, pictured surrounded by anti-torpedo nets in a Norwegian fjord. She only fired her guns in anger once.

TIRPITZ
Armament: 8 380mm (15in), 12 150mm (5.9in) guns
Displacement: 53,444 tonnes (52,600 tons)
Length: 248m (813ft 1in)
Beam: 36m (118ft Xin)
Propulsion: three shaft geared turbines
Speed: 29 knots
Crew: 2608

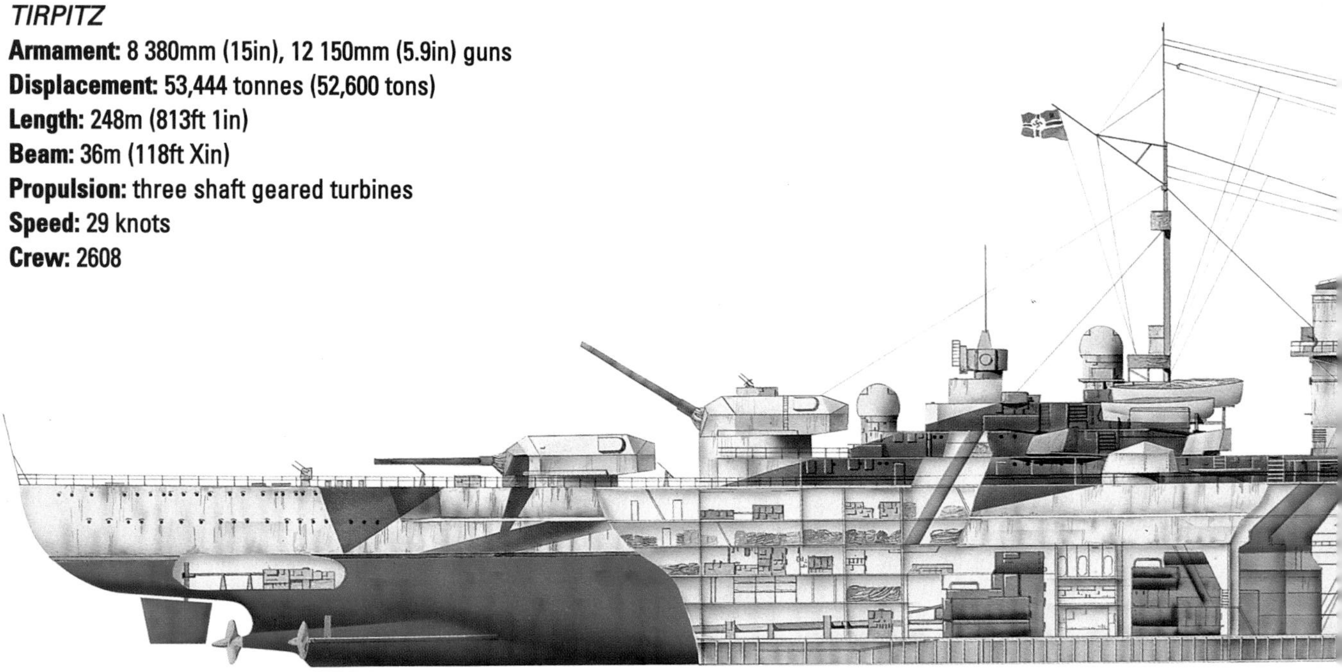

Above: The battleship *Tirpitz* might have caused much destruction had she operated aggressively against the Arctic convoys; but she never did.

had first seen action during the Salerno landings in Italy eight months earlier. In addition to their TBR Wings, the *Victorious* and *Furious* also carried Nos 1834 and 1836 Squadrons, equipped with American-built Vought Corsair fighters, and Nos 801 and 880 Squadrons with Seafires. More fighter cover was to be provided by the Hellcats of Nos 800 and 804 Squadrons (HMS *Emperor*) and the Martlet Vs of Nos 861, 896, 882 and 898 Squadrons (HMS *Pursuer* and *Searcher*), while anti-submarine patrols were to be flown by the Swordfish of 842 Squadron on board HMS *Fencer*. The carrier group was to be covered by warships of the Home Fleet, consisting of the battleships *Duke of York* and *Anson,* the cruisers *Belfast, Jamaica, Royalist* and *Sheffield* and 14 destroyers. The strike was timed to coincide with the passage of a Russian convoy, JW58.

On 30 March 1944, with the convoy well on its way, the Home Fleet units sailed from Scapa Flow in two forces, the first comprising the two battleships, the *Victorious*, one cruiser and five destroyers, and the second of the *Furious*, the four escort carriers and three cruisers. The actual attack on the *Tirpitz*, codenamed Operation Tungsten, was to be conducted by Vice-Admiral Sir Henry Moore, second-in-command of the Home Fleet, flying his flag in the *Anson*.

The forces assembled in the afternoon of 2 April about 350km (220nm) to the northwest of Altenfjord and from there moved to the flying-off position, 222km (120nm) northwest of Kaafjord, reaching it during the early hours of the following morning. At 0430 hours, 21 Barracudas of No 8 TBR Wing, escorted by 21 Corsairs and 20 Hellcats, took off from the *Victorious* and set course for the target. Eighty kilometres (50 miles) from their objective, the Barracudas, which had been flying low to avoid radar detection, went up to 2440m (8000ft) and began their final approach, preceded by the fighters which went in at low level to suppress flak. The Germans were taken by surprise and the *Tirpitz*, lying naked under the beginnings of a smoke screen, was hit by nine armour-piercing or semi-armour-piercing bombs.

An hour later, a second attack was made by 19 Barracudas of No 52 TBR Wing, escorted by 39 fighters. By this time the smoke screen was fully developed, but it hindered the German gunners far more than it did the Barracuda crews, who had no difficulty in locating their target. In all, the battleship was hit by 14 bombs, 122 of her crew being killed and 316 wounded. Although the bombs failed to penetrate her heavy armour, they caused extensive damage to her superstructure and fire control systems and put her out

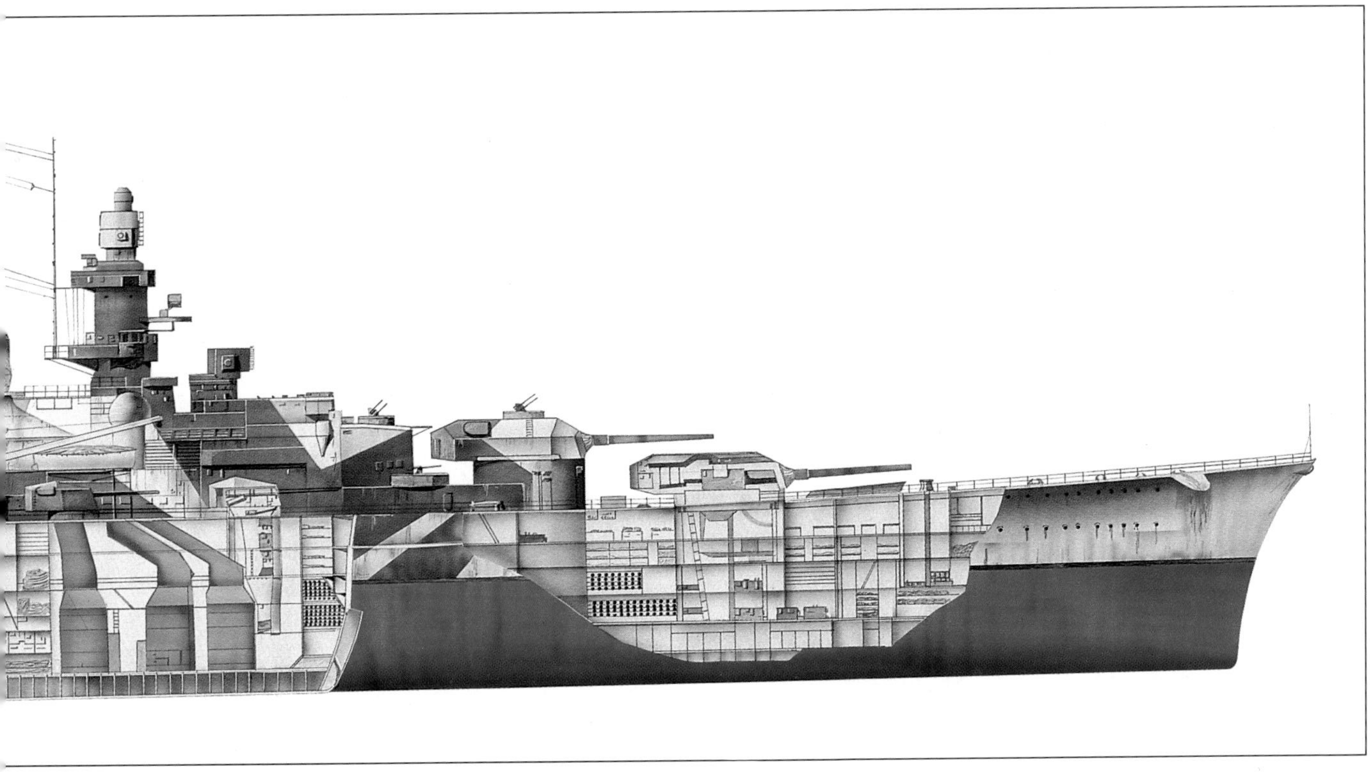

of action for a further three months. The British lost two Barracudas and a Hellcat.

Further attempts to attack the *Tirpitz* in May were frustrated by bad weather. It was not until 17 July 1944 that another raid was carried out, this time by aircraft from the *Formidable*, *Furious* and *Indefatigable* under the command of Rear-Admiral R.R. McGrigor. The covering force of the battleship *Duke of York*, the cruisers *Bellona*, *Devonshire*, *Jamaica* and *Kent*, was commanded by Admiral Sir Henry Moore, now C-in-C Home Fleet in place of Admiral Sir Bruce Fraser. Forty-five Barracudas of Nos 820 and 826 Squadrons (*Indefatigable*) and 827 and 830 Squadrons (*Formidable*) set out to make the attack. The 50-strong fighter escort included the Fairey Fireflies of No 1770 Squadron, making their appearance in combat for the first time. However, the enemy had plenty of warning: the smoke screen obscured the warship, the AA defences were fully alerted, and the raid was unsuccessful.

The next attack, carried out on 22 August, was a disaster; the incoming aircraft were detected and intercepted by Me 109s of JG5, the Luftwaffe's 'Arctic Wing', which shot down 11 of them, mostly Barracudas. The escort carrier *Nabob* was torpedoed off North Cape by the *U.534* and damaged beyond repair; the *U.534* was herself sunk by aircraft from the escort carrier *Vindex* three days later. Two minor bomb hits were obtained on the *Tirpitz* in an attack on 24 August, the Barracuda crews bombing blind through the smoke, and a further attack, on the 29th, was unsuccessful. Counting a mission that had to be aborted due to the weather on 20 August, the Fleet Air Arm flew 247 sorties in this series of attacks.

The *Tirpitz* was moved to Tromso for repairs; and it was there, on 12 November 1944, that she was finally destroyed by 5443kg (12,000lb) 'Tallboy' deep-penetration bombs dropped by Lancasters of Nos 9 and 617 Squadrons, RAF Bomber Command.

A NEW THREAT

By this time another major threat to the Allied Atlantic convoys, the battlecruiser *Scharnhorst*, had also been removed. In February 1942, together with her sister ship *Gneisenau* and the *Prinz Eugen*, she had broken out from Brest and made an epic dash through the English Channel, bound for the north German ports. Damaged by mines en route, the *Scharnhorst* was pronounced battleworthy again in October 1942, and on 11 January 1943, together with the *Prinz Eugen* and three destroyers, she attempted a move to Norway. West of the Skagerrak, however, the ships were sighted by British reconnaissance aircraft, and ordered to return to Germany.

A second transfer attempt, in stormy weather on 8 March 1943 (without the *Prinz Eugen*) proved successful, and on the 11th the *Scharnhorst* and *Tirpitz*, accompanied by destroyers and torpedo boats, moved up from Trondheim to join the heavy cruiser *Lützow* near Narvik. On 22 March the heavy units moved again, this time to Altenfjord.

On 6 September 1943 the *Scharnhorst* accompanied the *Tirpitz* on Operation Sicily, the landing of troops and bombardment of shore stations on Spitzbergen, described earlier. She did not put to sea again until December, and this time it was to engage the Arctic convoys. After an interval of several months, when no convoys had passed to Russia because of the dangers involved, they had resumed in November when Convoy RA54A sailed from Archangel to the UK without incident. Two more outward-bound convoys, JW54A and JW54B, also made the journey to Russia unmolested. The next two, however, were both reported by the Luftwaffe, and Admiral Dönitz issued orders that they were to be attacked not only by the 24 U-boats based on Bergen and Trondheim, but by available surface units, including the *Scharnhorst*.

Below: British personnel inspecting the upturned hulk of the *Tirpitz* after the war. She was despatched by the RAF's six-ton 'Tallboy' armour-piercing bombs.

At 1400 hours on Christmas Day, the *Scharnhorst* – now under the command of Captain F. Hintze and flying the flag of Admiral Bey, recently appointed to command the Northern Battle Group – sailed from Norway accompanied by five destroyers to intercept convoy JW55B, which had been located by air reconnaissance on 22 December. The convoy had already been attacked by Ju 88s and by U-boats, but without success. On 26 December, Admiral Bey ordered his destroyers to form a patrol line to search for the convoy in heavy seas. He knew that a British cruiser covering force comprising the *Belfast*, *Norfolk* and *Sheffield* was operating in the Barents Sea; he did not know that there was also a distant covering force commanded by the C-in-C, Home Fleet, Admiral Sir Bruce Fraser, and comprising the battleship *Duke of York*, the cruiser *Jamaica* and four destroyers.

Fraser, aware that JW55B had been located by enemy aircraft, was convinced that the *Scharnhorst* would make a sortie against it, and detached four destroyers from Convoy RA55A, which he did not consider to be under immediate threat, to reinforce JW55B's close escort. His hope was that this strengthened destroyer force would drive off the *Scharnhorst*, and might perhaps damage her enough for the *Duke of York* to finish her off. At this point

Above: The 'Channel Dash' by the *Scharnhorst, Gneisenau* and *Prinz Eugen* in February 1942 was a considerable humiliation for the British.

Fraser's ships were 370km (200nm) southwest of North Cape and the cruiser force, under Admiral Burnett, 278km (150nm) to the east.

Admiral Bey's five destroyers, meanwhile, had failed to locate the convoy, and, due to a signalling error, lost touch with the flagship. Subsequently ordered to return to base, they took no part in the coming events. At 0840 hours on the 26th the cruisers *Norfolk* and *Belfast* obtained radar contact with the *Scharnhorst*, and at 0921 hours the *Sheffield* glimpsed her in the stormy darkness at 11,895m (13,000yds). A few minutes later all three destroyers opened fire on the battlecruiser and obtained three hits, one of which put her port fire control system out of action. The *Scharnhorst* replied with a few harmless 280mm (11in) salvoes, then Bey turned away to the southeast while Burnett placed his cruisers between the threat and the convoy, screened by four destroyers.

At 1221 hours the three cruisers again sighted the *Scharnhorst* and opened fire with full broadsides at 10,065m (11,000yds), while the destroyers fanned out to attack with torpedoes. However the battlecruiser retired to the north-east, her gunfire having put one of *Norfolk*'s turrets and all her radar out of action. *Sheffield* also suffered some splinter damage but the *Scharnhorst* had taken punishment too, including a hit abreast 'A' turret and one on her quarterdeck.

At 1617 hours the *Duke of York*, only 37km (20nm) away to the north, obtained a radar echo from the *Scharnhorst*, and at 1650 hours Fraser ordered *Belfast* to illuminate her, and *Duke of York* opened fire with her 355mm (14in) armament. Admiral Bey was now trapped between Burnett's cruisers to the north and Fraser's warships to the south – he had no choice but

Above: The German Navy's Commander Battleships, Admiral Ciliax, inspecting the crew of the *Scharnhorst*, accompanied by Captain Hoffman (right).

to fight it out. Once *Scharnhorst's* gunners had recovered from their surprise their fire was accurate, but although they straddled the British battleship many times they failed to register a serious hit on her. The *Duke of York*'s gunnery was excellent; she scored 31 straddles out of 52 broadsides, with enough hits to put the battlescruiser's 'A' and 'B' turrets out of action and to rupture some steam pipes, reducing her speed so that Bey had no chance of escape.

With a third of *Scharnhorst*'s turrets out of action, Fraser, realising that the *Duke of York*'s 355mm (14in) shells were unlikely to pierce the enemy's armour, turned away to let the destroyers finish the job. Two of them, the *Savage* and *Saumarez*, approached from the northwest under heavy fire, firing starshell, while *Scorpion* and *Stord* attacked from the southeast. As Hintze turned his ship to port to engage them, one of *Scorpion*'s torpedoes struck home, closely followed by three more from the first two destroyers. As the small ships retired under cover of smoke, the *Duke of York* and the cruisers closed in to batter the enemy warship. Lieutenant B.B. Ramsden, an officer of Royal Marines on HMS *Jamaica*, later wrote that the *Scharnhorst* 'must have been a hell on earth. The 14-inch from the flagship were hitting or rocketing off from a ricochet on the sea. Great flashes rent the night, and the sound of gunfire was continuous, and yet she replied, but only occasionally now with what armament she had left.'

By 1930 hours the battlecruiser was a blazing wreck, her hull glowing red-hot, and the destroyers closed in to finish her off with torpedoes. Fifteen minutes later she blew up, and only 36 of her crew of 1968 officers and men were rescued. Like their comrades of the *Bismarck*, they had fought gallantly. Now, pulled from the oil-soaked waters, they were transferred to the *Duke of York* for the voyage to England, and captivity. So ended the Battle of North Cape, and the last attempt by a German capital ship to challenge the supremacy of the Royal Navy.

In addition to their normal task of convoy protection, Allied capital ships in the Atlantic and Mediterranean theatres were being increasingly used for shore bombardment. In November 1942, American battleships *Massachusetts* and *Texas* joined the British warships of Force H – the battleships *Duke of York, Nelson* and *Rodney*, and the battlecruiser *Renown* – in supporting the Allied landings in North Africa (Operation Torch). In July 1943 British and American cruisers and destroyers provided close bombardment support for the Allied landings in Sicily. The British battleships *Nelson, Rodney, Warspite and Valiant* were a powerful covering force, backed up by the *King George V* and *Howe*, the last two having been relieved of Home Fleet duty by the US battleships *Alabama* and *South Dakota.*

THE ITALIANS SURRENDER

On 8 September 1943 the Italian government accepted armistice terms tabled by the Allies, and this decision was publicly announced that evening. The Royal Navy C-in-C, Admiral Cunningham, at once ordered a powerful naval force to Taranto, where it landed the 1st Airborne Division (Operation Slapstick) and instructed the Italian fleet, whose transfer to the Allies had been agreed in the armistice terms, to sail south from Spezia by a special route. The fleet, comprising the battleships *Roma*, *Vittorio Veneto* and *Italia* (formerly the *Littorio*), six cruisers and eight destroyers, put to sea in the early hours of the 9th, but that afternoon the ships were attacked by six Dornier 217s of KG100 carrying FX radio-controlled guided missiles. The *Roma*, hit by two of these weapons, sank with the loss of 1255 lives; the *Italia* was also hit, but reached Malta safely. The destroyers *Da Noli* and *Vivaldi,* sailing to join the Allies from Castellamare, were shelled by German-manned coastal batteries in the Straits of Bonifacio and the latter was sunk; the *Da Noli* fell victim to a mine. At Taranto, meanwhile, the occupying British forces had taken over other Italian ships, including the battleships *Andrea Doria*, *Caio Duilio* and *Giulio Cesare*.

On 9 September Allied forces went ashore at Salerno, on the 'toe' of the Italian mainland. The initial landing was successful against strong German opposition, but the troops at first failed to reach their objectives despite heavy naval fire support. On 13 September the Germans launched a strong counterattack, and for a time the Allied position was precarious. Reinforcements were requested, and the battleships *Warspite* and *Valiant* were brought up from Malta to lend additional fire support. By nightfall on the 16th the enemy had been stopped, although not without significant cost to the naval forces involved. On the 11th, Dornier 217s of KG100 attacked with FX1400 radio-controlled missiles and Hs 293 glider bombs, badly damaging the cruisers USS *Savannah* and HMS *Uganda*, sinking the hospital ship *Newfoundland* and a supply ship and damaging several other vessels. Then, on the 16th, HMS *Warspite* took two Hs 293 hits and was so badly damaged that she had to be towed to Malta. She was partially repaired, and transferred back to Britain in time to take part in the offshore bombardment force that lent its firepower to the Allied invasion on the Normandy beaches on 6 June 1944.

In all, seven battleships, two monitors, 23 cruisers, three gunboats, 105 destroyers and 1073 smaller vessels were involved in that momentous operation. The battleships involved were the USS *Nevada, Texas* and *Arkansas,* along with HMS *Nelson, Ramillies, Rodney* and *Warspite,* all covering their respective landing beaches and providing direct fire support for the troops as they moved inland. It was the mightiest concentration of naval firepower the world had ever seen, designed by its sheer volume to cow the German defenders of the Normandy coast. It would be matched only by events that were to unfold half a world away in the months to come, as Allied naval task forces battled their way towards Japan.

Below: Laid down in 1922 and completed in 1927, the battleship HMS *Nelson* was Fleet Flagship until 1941. The war took her from the Arctic to the East Indies.

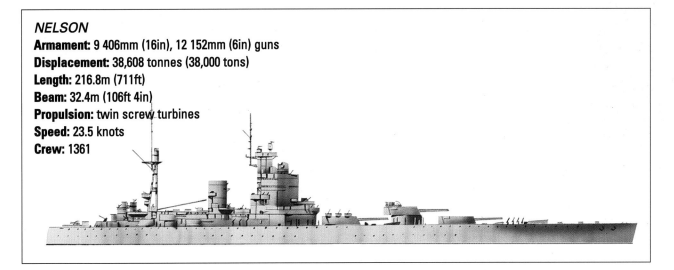

NELSON
Armament: 9 406mm (16in), 12 152mm (6in) guns
Displacement: 38,608 tonnes (38,000 tons)
Length: 216.8m (711ft)
Beam: 32.4m (106ft 4in)
Propulsion: twin screw turbines
Speed: 23.5 knots
Crew: 1361

CHAPTER NINE

The Naval War in the Far East 1941–45

Pearl Harbor sounded the death knell for the battleship, as the new force at sea – air power – demonstrated its might. The naval battles of the Far East were conducted at long distance between carrier groups. Battleships such as the *Yamato* showed that they could still be formidable opponents, and useful for bombardment purposes, but without air cover they were easy prey for torpedo bombers.

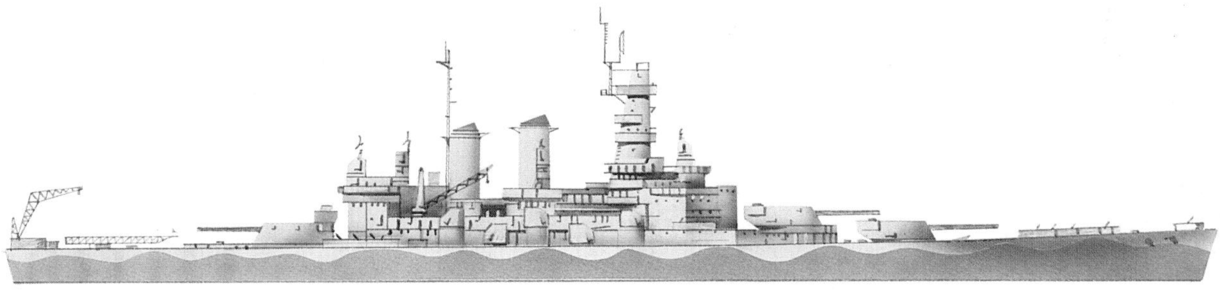

On 26 November 1941, a Japanese striking force, comprising six aircraft carriers and a strong escort that included the former 'Kongo' class battlecruisers *Hiei* and *Kirishima*, now reclassified as battleships following reconstruction in the late 1930s, left its assembly area at Hittokappu Bay and headed out into the Pacific. Eleven days later, on 7 December, nearly 300 bombers, dive-bombers and torpedo-bombers from the carriers, attacking in two waves, swept down on Pearl Harbor, Hawaiian base of the United States Pacific Fleet.

Left: The battleship USS *Arizona* ablaze at Pearl Harbor, 7 December 1941. She was one of four US battleships sunk – a fifth was beached and three more damaged.

Among the casualties was the battleship *Arizona*, pride of the Pacific Fleet and flagship of Rear-Admiral Isaac C. Kidd, which was hit by a torpedo and eight bombs, and sank with the loss of 1404 lives. Also hit was the *California*. Severely damaged by bombs and with 98 of her crew dead, she sank three days later. A similar fate befell the *Nevada, Oklahoma, West Virginia, Maryland, Pennsylvania* and *Tennessee,* all of which were either sunk, beached or, at the very least, heavily damaged, leaving the Pacific Fleet crippled in the space of a few hours.

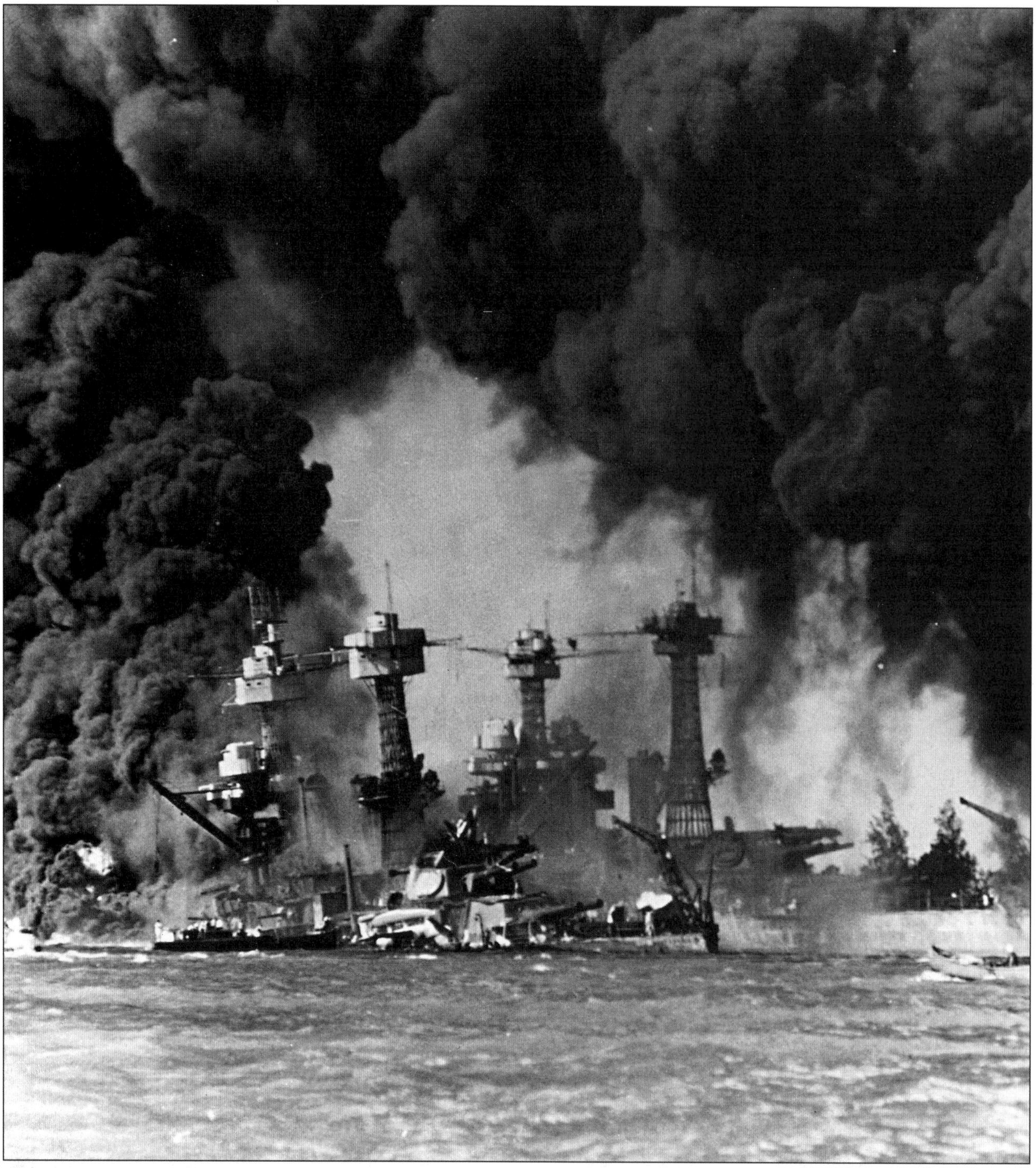

Above: The battleships USS *West Virginia* and *Tennessee* ablaze after the Japanese attack on Pearl Harbor. Both ships were rebuilt and went on to serve in the Pacific.

Pearl Harbor, a 'day of infamy' for the Americans, was a masterstroke of planning and execution. Its architect was Admiral Isoroku Yamamoto, C-in-C of the Japanese Navy, one of the ablest naval commanders of all time, and one on whom the lesson of the British air attack on the Italian Fleet at Taranto just over a year earlier had not been lost.

The destruction of the American capital ships left the way open for rapid Japanese conquest of the various islands in the Pacific, surprise and a lack of support hindering any significant opposition to the Japanese advance. There remained, however, the Indian Ocean and the Java Sea, the respective preserves of Great Britain and the Netherlands.

SINGAPORE AND JAPANESE EXPANSION

The Admiralty's plan to reinforce the Indian Ocean theatre with warships drawn from the Mediterranean Fleet, leaving the French Navy to concentrate on the Mediterranean, was dislocated by the collapse of France in 1940. In August 1941, another Admiralty plan envisaged reinforcing the Far East with six capital ships, a modern aircraft carrier and supporting light forces by the spring of 1942. In the meantime, the best that could be done was to send out the new battleship *Prince of Wales*, supported by the old battlecruiser *Repulse* and the aircraft carrier *Indomitable*, which was to provide the essential air component. Even this plan was disrupted when the *Indomitable* ran aground off Jamaica while she was working up there. It was another fortnight before she was ready to sail.

The *Prince of Wales*, meanwhile, flagship of Rear-Admiral Sir Tom Phillips, had sailed from the Clyde on 25 October accompanied by the destroyers *Electra* and *Express*, under orders to proceed to Singapore via Freetown, Simonstown and Ceylon, where they were joined on 28 November by the *Repulse* from the Atlantic and the destroyers *Encounter* and *Jupiter* from the Mediterranean. The force reached Singapore on 2 December.

The Admiralty had always been reluctant to concentrate its warships on Singapore, preferring to base them further back on Ceylon; the fact that they were there at all was at the insistence of Winston Churchill, whose view – supported by the Foreign Office – was that their presence would be enough to deter the Japanese from taking aggressive action. There were justifiable fears, in view of the *Indomitable*'s absence, of the force's vulnerability to enemy air attack, as the RAF's air defences on Singapore and the Malay peninsula were woefully weak. Anxiety over the exposed position of Phillips' ships led the Admiralty

Below: The attack on Pearl Harbor, with 'Battleship Row' in the foreground. The loss of its battleships forced the Pacific Fleet to rely heavily on aircraft carrier task groups.

to urge him to take them away from Singapore, and on 5 December 1941 the *Repulse* (Capt Tennant) sailed for Port Darwin in north Australia. The next day, however, a Japanese convoy was reported off Indo-China, and Tennant was ordered back to Singapore to rejoin the flagship. Only hours later came the news of the Japanese attack at Pearl Harbor, with simultaneous amphibious assaults elsewhere, including Malaya and Siam, and on the evening of 8 December Admiral Phillips took the *Prince of Wales, Repulse* and four destroyers, collectively known as Force Z, to attack Japanese amphibious forces which had landed at Singora on the northeast coast of Malaya.

Early the next morning Singapore advised him that no fighter cover would be available and that strong Japanese bomber forces were reported to be assembling in Siam, and this, together with the knowledge that his warships had been sighted by enemy reconnaissance aircraft, persuaded Phillips to abandon his sortie at 2015 hours on 9 December, reversing course for Singapore. (In fact Force Z had also been sighted by the submarine *I.65*, but the position it transmitted was inaccurate, and other enemy submarines failed to detect the ships at this time.)

Just before midnight, Phillips received a signal that the Japanese were landing at Kuantan and he turned towards the coast, intending to intercept this new invasion force. The report was false, but in the early hours of 10 December Force Z was sighted by the submarine *I.58* (Lt Cdr Kitamura). He made an unsuccessful torpedo attack, then shadowed the British ships for five and a half hours, sending regular position reports that enabled reconnaissance aircraft of the 22nd Naval Air Flotilla to sight them and maintain contact. Already airborne from airfields in Indo-China were 27 bombers and 61 torpedo aircraft, the flotilla's attack element, flying steadily south. They passed to the east of Force Z and flew on for a considerable distance before turning, and at about 1100 hours they sighted the ships.

The air attacks were executed with great skill and coordination, the high-level bombers – Mitsubishi G4M1 Bettys – running in at 3660m (12,000ft) to distract the attention of the warships' AA gunners while the torpedo-bombers, G3M2 Nells, initiated their runs from different directions. Two torpedo hits were quickly registered on the *Prince of Wales,* severely damaging her propellers and steering gear and putting many of her AA guns out of action. For some time the *Repulse*, by skilful evasive action, managed to avoid the attackers; but there were too many aircraft, and eventually she was hit by four torpedoes. At 1233 hours she rolled over and sank, and 50 minutes later the same fate overtook the flagship, which had meanwhile sustained two more torpedo hits. The accompanying destroyers picked up 2081 officers and men; 840 were lost, among them Admiral Phillips and Captain Leach of the *Prince of Wales.* Captain Tennant of the *Repulse* survived, having been literally pushed off the bridge by his officers at the last moment.

The Japanese were now able to land at points on the Malayan coast virtually unopposed and advance on Singapore, which fell early in 1942. Allied naval resistance to the enemy landing in Java and Sumatra was quickly crushed, the old Dutch battleship

Below: The *North Carolina* was transferred to the Pacific from the Atlantic after Pearl Harbor. She survived being torpedoed by the Japanese submarine I19 in 1942.

NORTH CAROLINA
Armament: 9 400mm (16in), 20 127mm (5in) guns
Displacement: 47,518 tonnes (46,770 tons)
Length: 222m (728ft 9in)
Beam: 33m (108ft 3in)
Propulsion: quadruple screw turbines
Speed: 28 knots
Crew: 1880

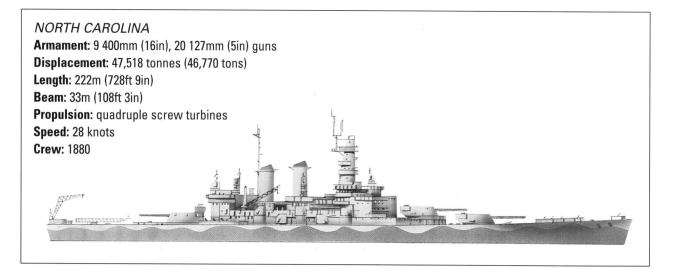

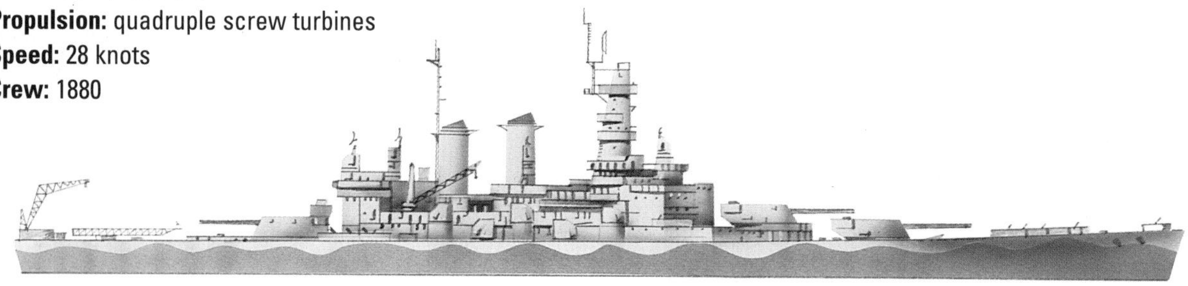

Soerabaja (formerly *De Zeven Provincien*, the Dutch Navy's last battleship) falling victim to air attack on 18 February.

Above: Japan's naval might at anchor: from front to rear, the battleship *Nagato*, the battlecruiser *Kirishima*, the battleship *Ise* and the battlecruiser *Hiei.*

THE THREAT TO INDIA

In the spring of 1942, while the victorious Japanese consolidated their lightning conquests in South East Asia and the Pacific, the British Admiralty focused its attention on constructing a new Eastern Fleet to operate from Ceylon, the base the Admiralty had recommended in the first place. By the end of March the new Eastern Fleet comprised two large aircraft carriers, the *Indomitable* and *Formidable*, the latter operational once more after a 10-month break following the damage she had sustained off Crete in May 1941, and a small one, the *Hermes*. Also included were five battleships, the *Ramillies, Resolution, Revenge, Royal Sovereign* and *Warspite,* all of World War I vintage; seven cruisers, 16 destroyers and seven submarines. The Fleet was commanded, from 27 March, by Admiral Sir James Somerville, the able and experienced former commander of Gibraltar's Force H.

Somerville faced an immediate crisis on his appointment. On 4 April, a Catalina flying boat sighted a Japanese task force approaching Ceylon from the south and radioed its position minutes before it was shot down. The enemy force was Admiral Nagumo's 1st Carrier Striking Force, comprising five aircraft carriers accompanied by four battleships, three cruisers and nine destroyers.

The Japanese intention was clearly to achieve total naval domination in the east by destroying the British Eastern Fleet. For the British this was a most dangerous move; for all they knew, the Japanese might try to seize Ceylon, from where not only India but also the ocean supply routes to the Middle East could be threatened with relative ease. To compound British worries, this was at a time when all supplies had to be routed around the Cape; Rommel was driving the Eighth Army back towards Egypt, threatening the Suez Canal, and a new German offensive was building in Russia. The possibility of a German–Japanese link-up in the Middle East may seem far-fetched with hindsight, but it was of very real concern to Churchill and his colleagues. Later, and with good reason, he was to call it the most dangerous moment of the war.

As soon as the news of the approaching Japanese task force was received, Admiral Layton, the naval commander in Ceylon, ordered every ship that could do so to sail from Colombo harbour. The cruisers *Cornwall* and *Dorsetshire*, which had been detached earlier on Somerville's instructions, were also ordered to rejoin Force A, the fast group of the Eastern Fleet which included the aircraft carriers and the *Warspite*.

Early on 5 April – Easter Sunday – the Japanese fleet was sighted by a second Catalina. Soon afterwards it launched a strike of 53 Nakajima B5N Kate high-level bombers and 38 Aichi D3A Val dive-bombers, escorted by 36 Zero fighters, to attack Colombo. The attack caused heavy damage to built-up areas but the damage to shipping and the port installations was relatively light, although the auxiliary cruiser *Hector* and the destroyer *Tenedos* were sunk.

At about noon, the cruisers *Cornwall* and *Dorsetshire* were sighted by a reconnaissance aircraft from the heavy cruiser *Tone* and 53 Val dive-bombers

Left: The *Alabama* was one of America's most modern battleships at the outbreak of war. She served on Arctic convoy duty in 1942 before transferring to the Pacific.

Above: The *Indiana* fought throughout the Pacific war, being successively damaged in a collision, by a Japanese kamikaze aircraft, and finally by a typhoon off Okinawa.

were immediately sent out to attack them. The bombing was devastatingly accurate and both ships were sunk, 1112 men (of a total of 1546) being rescued later by the cruiser HMS *Enterprise* and two destroyers. Albacores from the *Indomitable* later made a night radar search for the enemy force, but it had withdrawn to the southeast to refuel before heading back north to strike at Trincomalee naval base. At this time Admiral Somerville's Force A was steaming towards Ceylon from Addu Atoll, with his slow division (Force B) a long way behind. His ships were at times only 370km (200nm) from Nagumo's task force, but neither side made contact with the other. Addu Atoll had been set up as the Eastern Fleet's secret base, and Somerville, unable to locate the enemy, turned back towards it to safeguard it against a possible surprise attack.

On 8 April a Catalina once again established contact with the Japanese carrier force 740km (400nm) to the east of Ceylon and the ships at Trincomalee were ordered to put to sea. All units – including the light

QUEEN ELIZABETH
Armament: 8 380mm (15in), 16 152mm (6in) guns
Displacement: 33,548 tonnes (33,020 tons)
Length: 197m (646ft)
Beam: 28m (90ft 6in)
Propulsion: quadruple screw turbines
Speed: 23 knots
Crew: 951

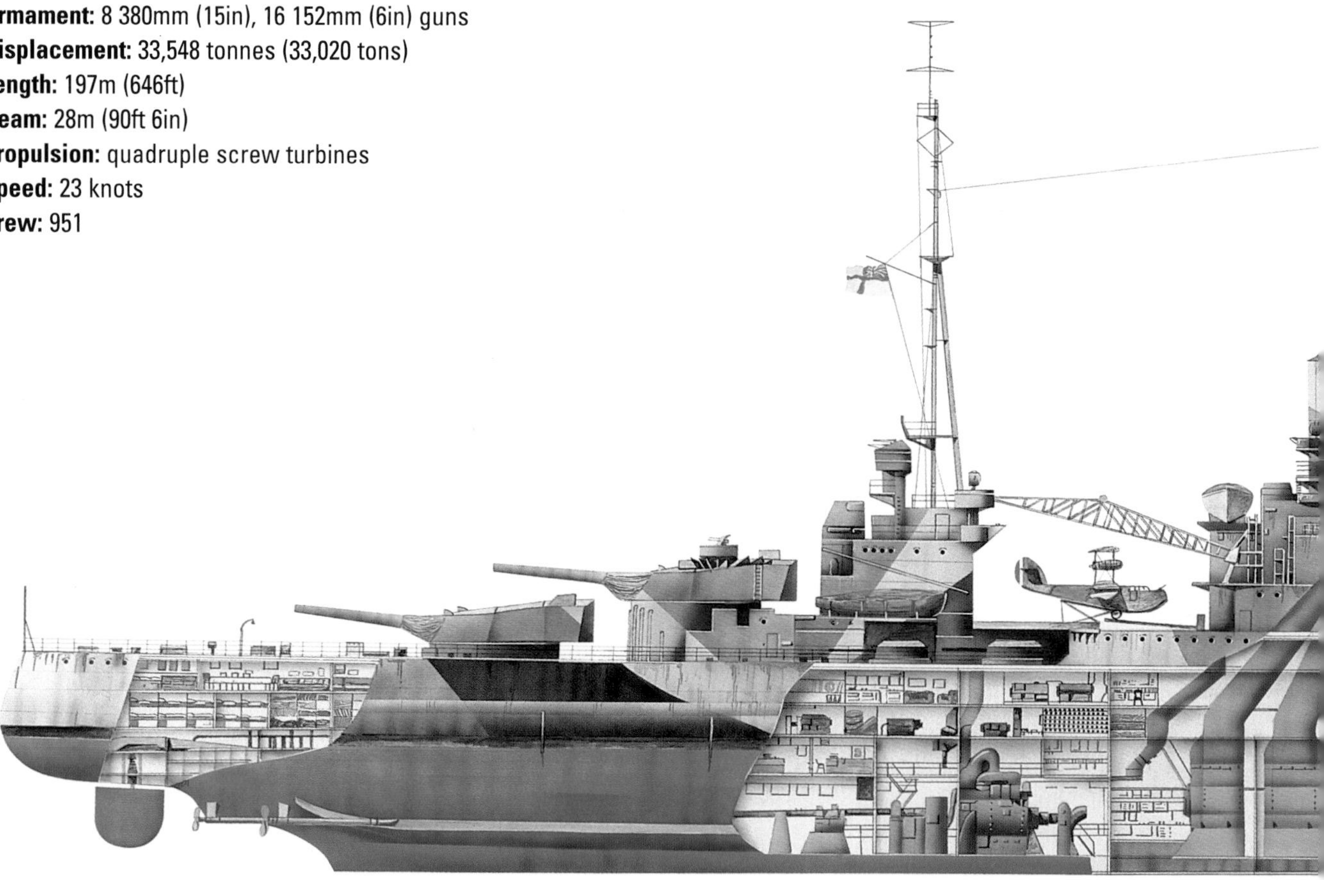

Above: The battleship HMS *Queen Elizabeth* was severely damaged by Italian frogmen at Alexandria in 1941. After repair, she served in the Indian Ocean in 1944–45.

carrier *Hermes* – were able to get clear before the expected attack by 91 high-level and dive-bombers, escorted by 38 fighters, developed early on the 9th. On the way back to their ships the Japanese aircrews sighted several ships, including the *Hermes*, the Australian destroyer *Vampire*, the corvette *Hollyhock* and two tankers. Three hours later, 80 dive-bombers arrived on the scene and sank all three warships and the tankers about 104km (56nm) from Trincomalee. The *Hermes*, which had no aircraft on board, radioed desperately for help, but the surviving fighters at Trincomalee were in no position to offer it.

Meanwhile, part of Nagumo's force – a light carrier and six cruisers under Admiral Ozawa – had been detached to operate against shipping in the Bay of Bengal. In a five-day spree beginning on 7 April Ozawa destroyed 23 merchant ships. Fortunately perhaps for the Eastern Fleet (whose Force A deployed to Bombay immediately after the attacks on Ceylon, and Force B to East Africa to protect the convoy route) a Japanese task force never again made an appearance in the Indian Ocean.

MIDWAY AND GUADALCANAL

Instead, Admiral Nagumo withdrew to the Pacific in readiness for the next big venture: the occupation of Midway Island. In the event it proved to be a costly exercise, for during the Battle of Midway on 4/5 June 1942 the carriers *Akagi, Kaga, Hiryu* and *Soryu* were all sunk by US naval aircraft.

Midway was decided by naval air power alone, without the opposing surface fleets making contact with one another. The seven battleships at Admiral Yamamoto's disposal had been irrelevant to the outcome. After Midway, both sides decided that carrier task forces would decide the outcome of future sea battles, and design work on future battleships was suspended to concentrate on carriers.

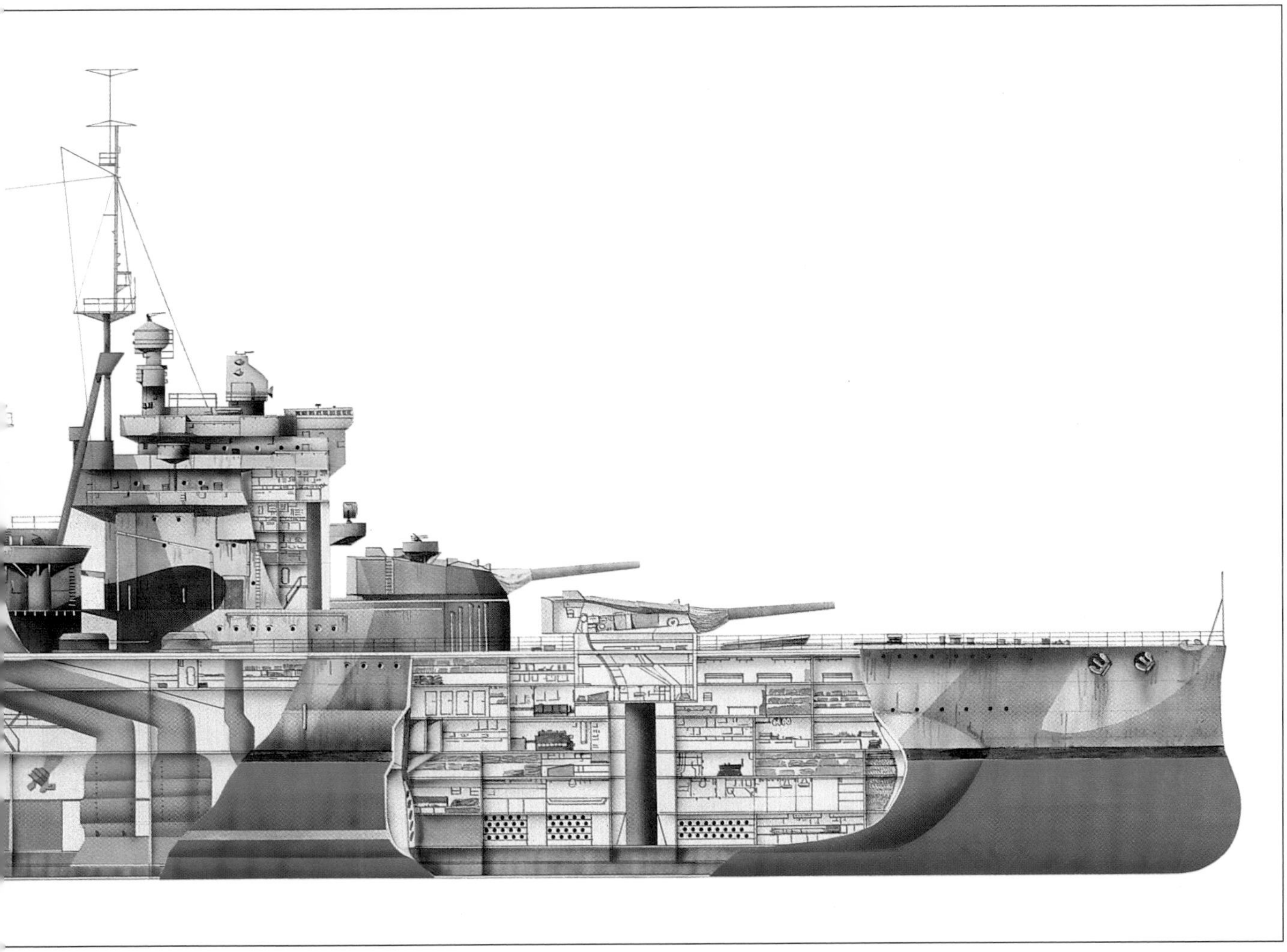

By this time, the US battleships conceived in 1937 – *North Carolina* and *Washington* – were commissioned and operating with the Atlantic Fleet on convoy escort duty, but the 'South Dakota' class ships of 1938 were only just coming into service. The US Navy was making tremendous efforts to repair the casualties of Pearl Harbor, with the exception of the *Arizona* and *Oklahoma*. The *California* was raised and refloated in March 1942, to be reconstructed over the next 10 months or so; *Nevada* underwent a similar programme, and would serve off the Normandy beachhead in June 1944 before returning to the Pacific; *West Virginia* and *Pennsylvania* would also see active service during the final assault on Japan, while *Tennessee* would be recommissioned as early as May 1943.

The first real test of battleship firepower in the Pacific conflict came during the battle for Guadalcanal, in the Solomon Islands, when powerful Japanese surface forces were committed in an attempt to dislodge American forces that had landed there. On the night of 11/12 November 1942, the fast battleships *Hiei* and *Kirishima* attempted to bombard the vital Henderson Field airstrip, but were surprised by US cruisers and destroyers and forced to withdraw after sustaining damage. The next day, the *Hiei* was located and attacked off Savo Island by aircraft from the USS *Enterprise* and set on fire. With 300 of her crew dead, she was abandoned and sunk by Japanese destroyers to avoid her capture.

The *Kirishima* attempted another bombardment on the following night, but this time the US battleships *Washington* and *South Dakota*, the former redeployed from her Atlantic duties, were in support. The battle opened with a series of actions between the Japanese battle group and US destroyers, three of which were sunk and a fourth damaged. Shortly afterwards, the *South Dakota*, with her radar out of action and manoeuvring to avoid the burning destroyers, came up against the *Kirishima* and the heavy cruisers *Atago* and *Takao*, which opened fire, scoring 42 shell hits on her superstructure. Luckily for the *South Dakota*, the

Above: The French battleship *Richelieu*, one of the best to see service in the war. After being damaged by British aircraft at Dakar, she later joined the British Eastern Fleet.

Washington, unseen by the Japanese, approached to within 7686m (8400yds) with radar assistance, and in seven minutes she hit the enemy battleship with nine 406mm (16in) shells. Abandoned and ablaze, the *Kirishima* was finished off by destroyers.

By mid-1943 the US Navy had a substantial battleship force in the Pacific. The US landings on New Georgia in June and July, for example, were supported by the *Massachusetts*, *Indiana*, *North Carolina* and two older vessels, the *Maryland* and *Colorado*. But the aircraft carrier and its air groups continued to be the primary weapon in the Pacific, as indeed it did in the Indian Ocean from 1944, following the strengthening of British naval resources there.

THE EASTERN FLEET

At the end of 1943, the British Eastern Fleet – apart from the small escort carrier HMS *Battler* – was reduced to the battleship *Ramillies*, eight cruisers, two auxiliary cruisers, 11 destroyers, 13 frigates, sloops and corvettes and six submarines. It therefore came as a welcome event when, on 30 January 1944, the British naval presence in the Indian Ocean was strengthened by the arrival at Colombo of the battleships *Queen Elizabeth* and *Valiant*, the battlecruiser *Renown*, the carriers *Illustrious* and *Unicorn*, two cruisers and seven destroyers, the whole force having made a fast passage through the Mediterranean after leaving Scapa Flow and the Clyde a month earlier.

Between 22 and 27 July 1944 the Eastern Fleet, following a series of smaller operations, mounted Operation Crimson, a major attack on Sabang by air and surface forces. While Corsairs from the two carriers strafed airfields and Barracudas attacked fuel facilities, the battleships *Queen Elizabeth*, *Valiant*, *Renown* and *Richelieu* – the latter having arrived in the theatre in April from operations in the North Atlantic – supported by five cruisers and five destroyers, fired 294 380mm (15in), 134 203mm (8in), 324 152mm (6in), 500 127mm (5in) and 123 100mm (4in) shells into Sabang. In the wake of this bombardment, the Dutch cruiser *Tromp* and the Australian destroyers *Quilliam*, *Quality* and *Quickmatch* penetrated the harbour and attacked shipping with torpedoes and close-range shellfire. The cruiser and two of the destroyers sustained damage, but got clear.

At the end of August 1944, the Eastern Fleet comprised the battleships *Howe*, *Richelieu*, *Queen Elizabeth*, the battlecruiser *Renown*, the carriers *Indomitable* and *Victorious*, 11 cruisers and 32 destroyers. The *Howe* had joined the fleet on 8 August; ironically, on the same day the *Valiant* was badly damaged in the collapse of the floating dock at Trincomalee. For the time being, then, the Eastern Fleet still had three battleships at its disposal instead of the planned four.

Three months later the Eastern Fleet was reorganised, part of it becoming the British East Indies Fleet under Vice-Admiral Sir Arthur Power. It comprised the battleship *Queen Elizabeth*, the battlecruiser *Renown*, five escort carriers, eight cruisers and 24 destroyers. The more modern warships were assigned to the British Pacific Fleet under Admiral Sir Bruce Fraser and included the battleships *King George V* and *Howe*, the carriers *Indefatigable*, *Illustrious*, *Indomitable* and *Victorious*, the cruisers *Swiftsure*, *Argonaut*, *Black Prince*, *Ceylon*, *Newfoundland*, *Gambia* and *Achilles*, and three destroyer flotillas.

On 16 January 1945, under the mantle of Operation Meridian, the British Pacific Fleet, as Task Force 63, sailed from Trincomalee for Sydney in the first stage of its planned deployment to the Pacific. It comprised the battleship *King George V*, the carriers *Illustrious*, *Indefatigable*, *Indomitable* and *Victorious*, three cruisers and nine destroyers.

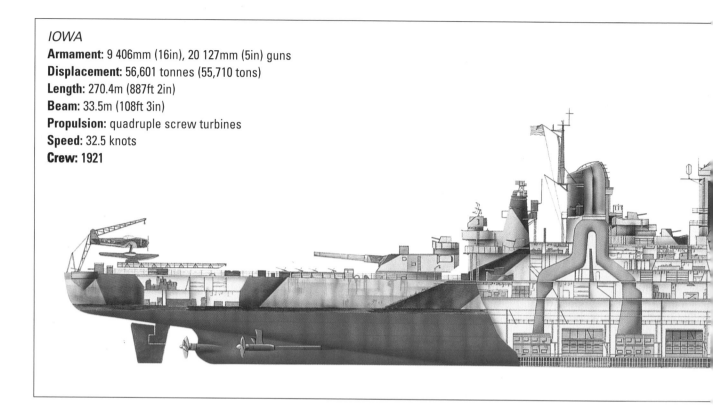

IOWA
Armament: 9 406mm (16in), 20 127mm (5in) guns
Displacement: 56,601 tonnes (55,710 tons)
Length: 270.4m (887ft 2in)
Beam: 33.5m (108ft 3in)
Propulsion: quadruple screw turbines
Speed: 32.5 knots
Crew: 1921

Above: The battleship USS *Iowa* took part in the final stages of the Pacific war and remained with the Pacific Fleet until 1948. She later served in the Korean War.

Below: The mighty *Yamato* at speed. On 7 April 1945, she was sunk by US aircraft on a mission against US naval forces off Okinawa, with the loss of 2498 lives.

The warships of the East Indies Fleet continued to pound Japanese targets around the periphery of the Indian Ocean. Between 8 and 18 April 1945, for example, the Fleet carried out Operation Sunfish: this involved a sortie by the battleships *Queen Elizabeth* and *Richelieu*, the heavy cruisers *London* and *Cumberland*, and the destroyers *Saumarez, Vigilant, Verulam, Virago* and *Venus* against targets on the north coast of Sumatra, in the course of which Sabang was heavily shelled.

RECONQUEST OF THE PHILIPPINES

Meanwhile, the last great naval battles of the Pacific war had been fought. In the Battle of the Philippine Sea, which took place in June 1944 as US naval forces operated in support of landings on the Marianas, the battleships were deployed in a battle line 24km (13nm) to the east of the US carriers, their task to put up a powerful AA barrage against any Japanese aircraft that tried to break through. This they did very effectively, contributing to many of the 242 Japanese aircraft lost in what became known as the 'Marianas Turkey Shoot' on 19 June.

In October 1944 the reconquest of the Philippines began with American landings at Leyte. On learning of the invasion, the C-in-C, Japanese Combined Fleet, Admiral Toyoda, ordered Vice-Admiral Kurita's Centre Force to sail from Brunei in Borneo on 22 October with the battleships *Yamato, Musashi, Nagato, Kongo* and *Haruna,* two cruisers and 15 destroyers. This was followed by Vice-Admiral Nishimura's Southern Force, with the battleships *Fuso, Yamashiro*, one cruiser and four destroyers.

On 24 October the Centre Force was attacked by four waves of American carrier aircraft. During these attacks the *Musashi* was hit by 10 bombs and six torpedoes and sank in about eight hours, with the loss of 1039 of her crew. The *Yamato* was also hit by two bombs but these had little effect on her. In the Southern Force, the *Fuso* was sunk by gunfire and torpedoes in Surigao Strait. This force was then engaged by the battleships *West Virginia, California, Tennessee, Maryland* and *Mississippi,* as well as US and Australian cruisers. The *Yamashiro* sank, hit by numerous shells and three torpedoes – Vice-Admiral Nishimura went down with her.

At this juncture, with the US and Australian naval forces in pursuit of the surviving Japanese warships, Admiral Kurita might have been justified in ordering an all-out attack on the invasion fleet, which was left virtually undefended. Instead, doubtless shocked by the loss of the *Musashi* and four heavy cruisers, he ordered a withdrawal.

The Japanese were to suffer yet more losses. At dawn on 25 October, Task Force 34 was formed from the US battleships *Iowa, New Jersey, Washington,*

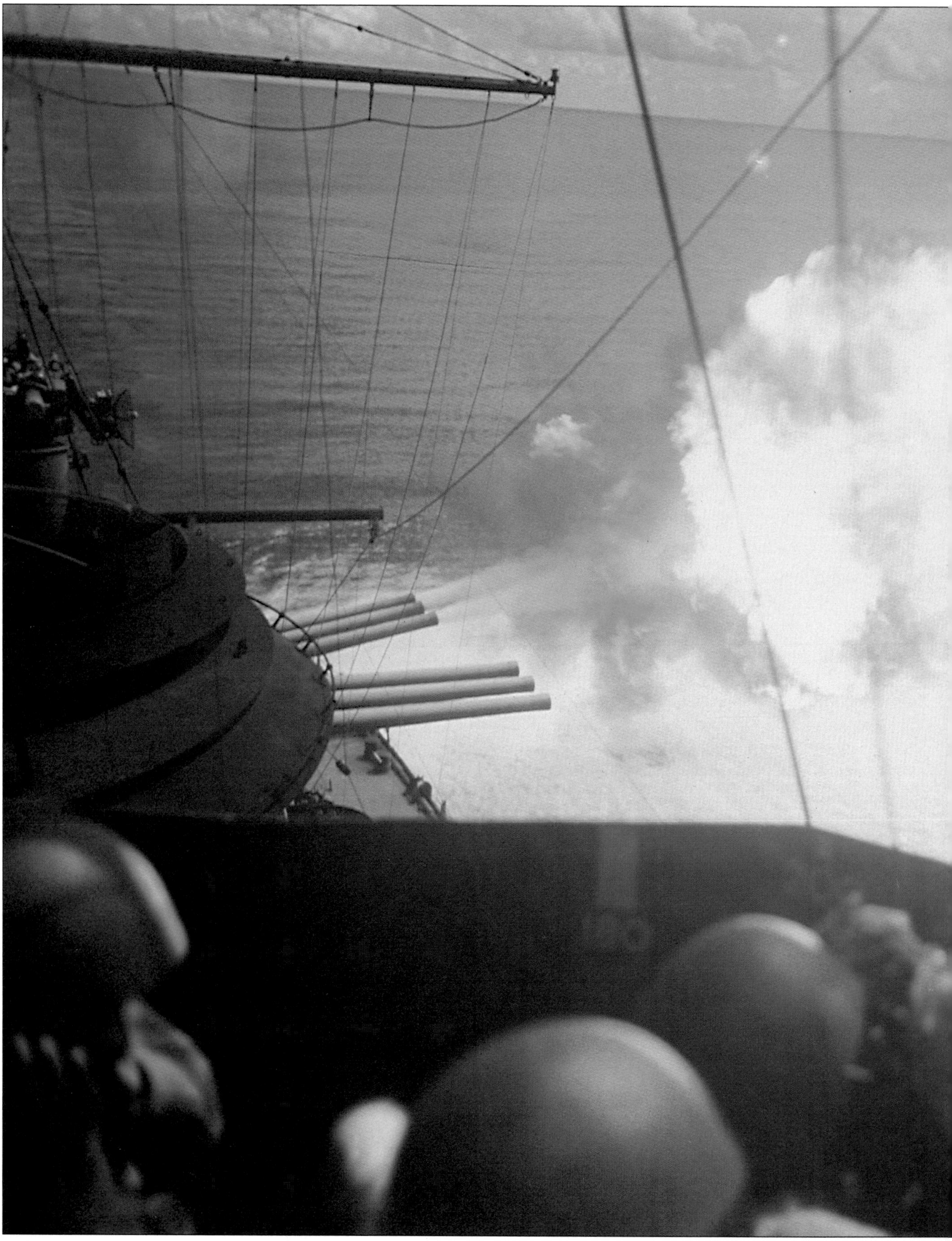

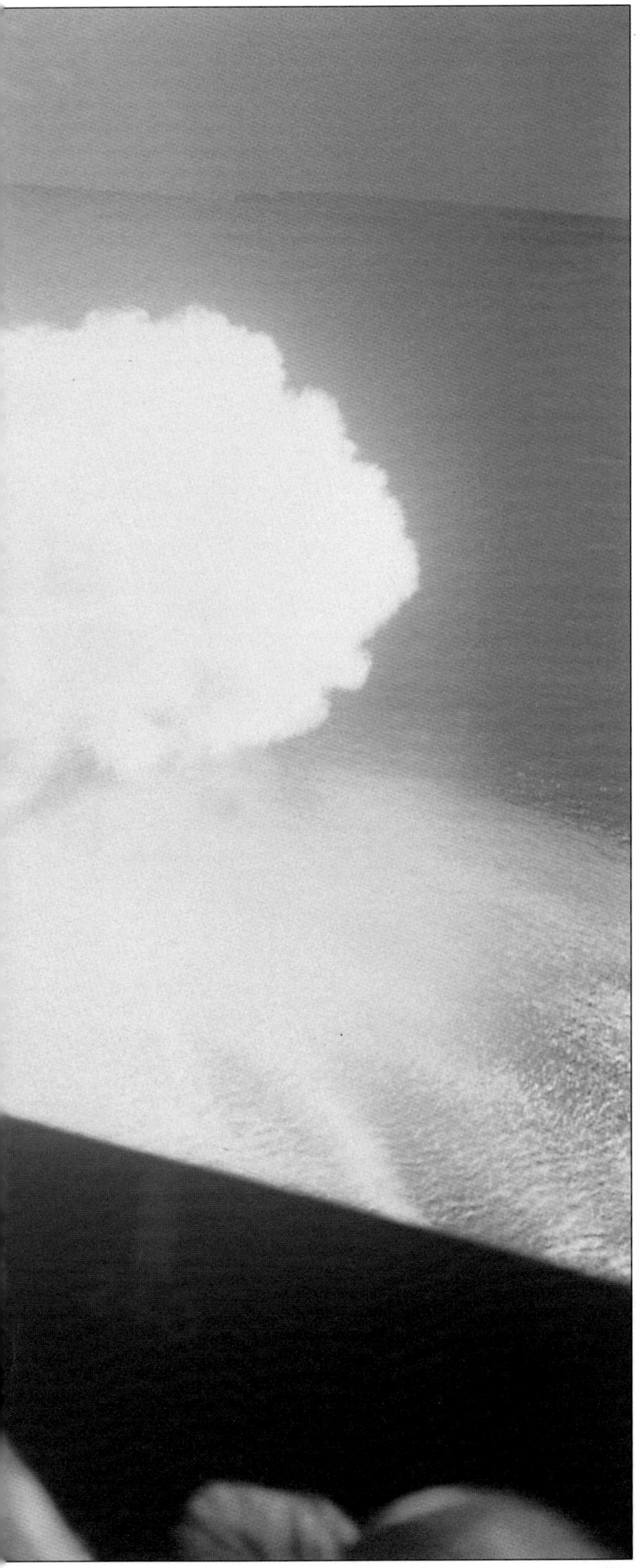

Alabama, Massachusetts and *Indiana,* four cruisers and 10 destroyers with the object of destroying a diversionary force, approaching from the north under Vice-Admiral Ozawa. Instead, Admiral Halsey, flying his flag in *New Jersey*, took his ships south to hunt down what remained of Kurita's force, leaving carrier aircraft to deal with Ozawa. This tactic proved successful and the carriers *Chitose, Zuikaku, Zuiho* and *Chiyoda,* as well as a destroyer were all sunk.

The Battle of Leyte Gulf spelled ruin for the Japanese Navy. Its carriers were gone and though it still had surface warships, most were confined to harbour through lack of fuel. Losses at sea continued, too. On 21 November 1944 the battleship *Kongo* was torpedoed and sunk by the US submarine *Sealion* northwest of Keelung. Even so, the Americans knew that the assault on the last Pacific islands before Japan itself would be fraught with peril, for at Leyte US warships had been subjected to the first planned attacks by Japanese suicide pilots – the kamikaze.

KAMIKAZE

The Allied naval forces felt the full weight of the kamikaze attacks during the assault on Okinawa in April 1945. Ten US battleships lent their weight to the Fire Support Group in this operation: they were the USS *Texas* and *Maryland* (Group 1, with one cruiser and four destroyers); *Arkansas* and *Colorado* (Group 2, with two cruisers and five destroyers); *Tennessee* and *Nevada* (Group 3, with two cruisers and six destroyers); *Idaho* and *West Virginia* (Group 4, with three cruisers and six destroyers); and *New Mexico* and *New York* (Group 5, with two cruisers and seven destroyers). In addition, the battleships *New Jersey, Wisconsin, Missouri, Massachusetts* and *Indiana* participated in softening-up bombardments prior to the invasion. Two British battleships, *King George V* and *Howe*, also operated in support of the Okinawa landings, joining aircraft from four Royal Navy carriers in bombarding enemy airfields in the Sakishima Gunto island group southwest of Okinawa. The British Pacific Fleet formed Task Force 57, which in turn was part of the US Fifth Fleet; the Fleet flagship was the battleship USS *Indianapolis* (Adm Spruance).

The *Indianapolis, West Virginia, Nevada* and *Maryland* were all damaged during the intense series of kamikaze attacks that accompanied the preliminary

Left: The USS *New Mexico* bombarding the Japanese-held island of Guam. An attack on the battleship by a Kamikaze at Lingayen on 6 January 1945 left 31 dead.

bombardment of Okinawa and the landing phase itself, which took place between 1 and 5 April 1945. But. in desperation at the approach of the seemingly unstoppable American forces, the Japanese Navy also had notions of a suicide mission.

THE LAST THROW OF THE DICE

On 6 April, a Japanese Task Force under Vice-Admiral Ito sailed from Tokuyama on Japan's inland sea. At its heart was the mighty *Yamato*, flying the flag of Rear-Admiral Ariaga. The battleship was accompanied by the cruiser *Yahagi* (Capt Hara, with the Commander of the 2nd Destroyer Flotilla, Rear-Admiral Komura, on board); and eight destroyers. The battle group's destination was Okinawa. Its purpose: to inflict as much damage as possible on the US invasion fleet. It would be a one-way mission; a critical shortage of fuel ensured that there could be no return to port.

It was unfortunate for the Japanese that their progress was reported by the crew of a B-29 bomber and then by two US submarines. Early on 7 April, the warships were sighted by reconnaissance aircraft, and at 1000 hours the American carriers off Okinawa launched a strike of 280 aircraft. In the first attack, the cruiser *Yahagi* and the destroyer *Hamakaze* were sunk; the battleship was hit by two bombs and a torpedo.

A second strike of 100 aircraft was launched at 1400 hours. Its first victims were the destroyers *Isokaze, Asashimo* and *Kasumi;* then, after taking nine more torpedo and three bomb hits, the *Yamato* began to flood uncontrollably and develop a serious list. Finally, after the order to abandon ship had been given, she rolled over and blew up in a tremendous explosion, probably caused when internal fires reached her magazines. The loss of life was enormous: 3665 Japanese sailors perished, 2498 of them on the *Yamato* herself. Of the 386 American aircraft that took part in the attacks, only 10 failed to return.

Below: The USS *Tennessee* bombarding Okinawa prior to the initial assault by US Marines. Amphibious landing craft (AMTRACS) are already heading for the beaches.

BATTLESHIP AND BATTLECRUISER LOSSES 1939–45

Listed below in date order are the battleship losses of the major combatant nations during World War II.

France

3 July 1940
BRETAGNE
BATTLESHIP
Sunk by British naval gunfire, Mers-el-Kebir

27 November 1942
DUNKERQUE
BATTLESHIP
Scuttled at Toulon.

27 November 1942
PROVENCE
BATTLESHIP
Scuttled at Toulon.

27 November 1942
STRASBOURG
BATTLESHIP
Scuttled at Toulon.

9 June 1944
COURBET
BATTLESHIP
Scuttled as breakwater, Normandy.

Germany

17 December 1939
ADMIRAL GRAF SPEE
'POCKET BATTLESHIP'
Scuttled at Montevideo.

27 May 1941
BISMARCK
'POCKET BATTLESHIP'
Sunk by gunfire and torpedoes, North Atlantic.

26 December 1943
SCHARNHORST
BATTLECRUISER
Sunk by gunfire and torpedoes off North Cape, Norway.

28 March 1945
GNEISENAU
BATTLECRUISER
Scuttled at Gdynia.

9 April 1945
ADMIRAL SCHEER
'POCKET BATTLESHIP'
Sunk by air attack, Kiel.

4 May 1945
LUTZOW
'POCKET BATTLESHIP'
Scuttled after air attack, Swinemünde.

Great Britain

14 October 1939
ROYAL OAK
BATTLESHIP
Sunk by *U.47* in Scapa Flow.

24 May 1941
HOOD
BATTLECRUISER
Sunk by *Bismarck*,

25 November 1941
BARHAM
BATTLESHIP
Sunk by *U.331*, Mediterranean.

10 December 1941
PRINCE OF WALES
BATTLESHIP
Sunk by Japanese air attack off Malaya.

10 December 1941
REPULSE
BATTLECRUISER
Sunk by Japanese air attack off Malaya

Greece

23 April 1941
KILKIS
BATTLESHIP
Sunk by air attack, Piraeus.

23 April 1941
LEMNOS
BATTLESHIP
Sunk by air attack, Piraeus.

Italy

9 September 1943
ROMA
BATTLESHIP
Sunk by German glider bombs, Mediterranean.

12 November 1940
CONTE DI CAVOUR
BATTLESHIP
Sunk by air attack, Trieste

Japan

13 November 1942
HIEI
BATTLECRUISER
Sunk by air attack off Guadalcanal.

15 November 1942
KIRISHIMA
BATTLECRUISER
Sunk by gunfire and torpedoes off Guadalcanal.

8 June 1943
MUTSU
BATTLESHIP
Blew up, Hiroshima Bay.

24 October 1944
MUSASHI
BATTLESHIP
Sunk by air attack, Sibuyan Sea.

25 October 1944
FUSO
BATTLESHIP
Sunk by gunfire and torpedoes, Surigao Strait.

25 October 1944
YAMASHIRO
BATTLESHIP
Sunk by gunfire and torpedoes, Surigao Strait.

21 November 1944
KONGO
BATTLESHIP
Sunk by US submarine *Sealion* off Keelung, Formosa (Taiwan).

7 April 1945
YAMATO
BATTLESHIP
Sunk by air attack southwest of Kyushu.

24 July 1945
HYUGA
BATTLESHIP
Sunk by air attack, Kure.

27 July 1945
HARUNA
BATTLECRUISER
Sunk by air attack, Kure.

28 July 1945
ISE
BATTLESHIP
Sunk by air attack, Kure.

United States

7 December 1941
ARIZONA
BATTLESHIP
Sunk by Japanese air attack, Pearl Harbor.

7 December 1941
OKLAHOMA
BATTLESHIP
Sunk by Japanese air attack, Pearl Harbor.

USSR

23 September 1941
MARAT
BATTLESHIP
Sunk by air attack, Kronstadt.

CHAPTER TEN

Sovereigns of the Sea No More

World War II demonstrated the limitations of the battleship in modern naval warfare. The aircraft carrier was now the flagship of any fleet, and the battleship's roles had been usurped. Aircraft and, later, missiles could strike land and sea targets far beyond the range of the largest guns. Size was a handicap, not a benefit. Yet some battleships survived to see service in the Gulf War, a final flourish for these magnificent vessels.

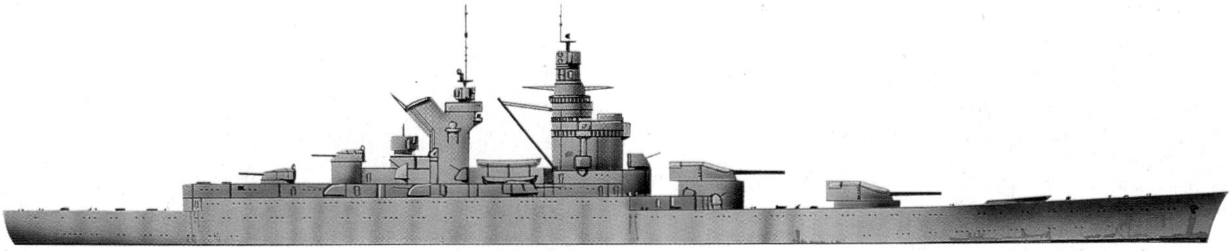

At the end of World War II, it was abundantly clear to the world's navies that the aircraft carrier, with its long-range striking power and its own air defence, would be the capital ship of the future. The war had shown that the battleship, bereft of air cover, was a vulnerable target to air attack, especially when stand-off missiles were used against it. The sinking of the Italian battleship *Roma* in September 1943 was a case in point.

Left: The USS *Iowa* at sunset. From 1952 to 1958 she served with the US Atlantic Fleet, forming an important component of NATO's naval forces.

The Royal Navy was quick to dispose of its battleships once hostilities were over. The *Nelson* and *Rodney* both went to the breaker's yard in 1948. Of the 'King George V' class, the *Anson* returned from Far Eastern waters in 1946 to be placed in reserve and was eventually broken up in 1957; the *Duke of York*, having deployed to the Pacific too late to take part in the final battles against the Japanese, was also laid up in reserve in 1951 and broken up in 1958. The *Howe*, veteran of battles from the Atlantic to Okinawa, suffered a similar fate, as did the *King George V*, the class leader having been decommissioned in September 1949.

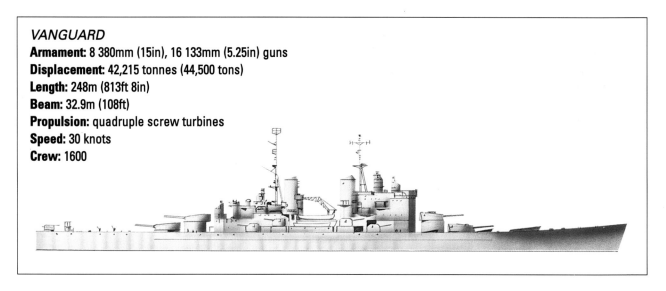

VANGUARD
Armament: 8 380mm (15in), 16 133mm (5.25in) guns
Displacement: 42,215 tonnes (44,500 tons)
Length: 248m (813ft 8in)
Beam: 32.9m (108ft)
Propulsion: quadruple screw turbines
Speed: 30 knots
Crew: 1600

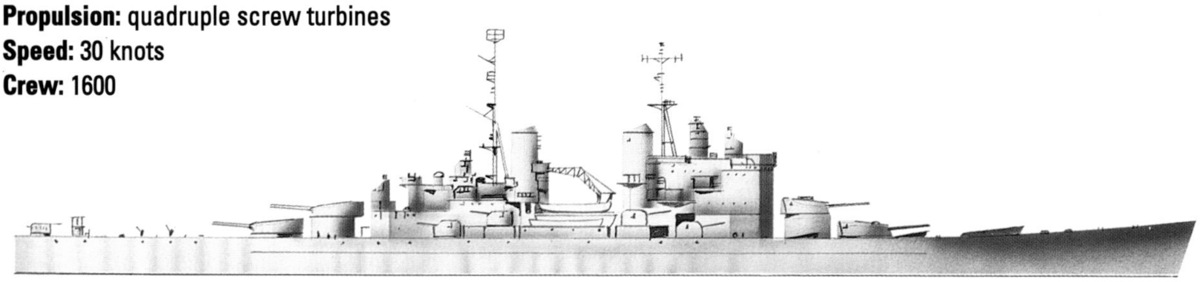

Above: HMS *Vanguard*, Britain's last battleship. She took the British Royal Family to South America in 1947, served briefly in the Mediterranean, and was scrapped in 1960.

Of the old 'Queen Elizabeth' class, HMS *Warspite*, as though in final protest, ran aground and was wrecked in Mounts Bay, Cornwall, while under tow to the breaker's yard in April 1947. Her sisters, the *Valiant* and *Queen Elizabeth*, were both broken up in 1948. The survivors of the even older 'Royal Sovereign' class, the *Ramillies*, *Resolution* and *Revenge*, had all ended the war as training ships. They were also broken up in 1948.

The 'Lion' class of 1938–9, enlarged'King George V' types with 406mm (16in) guns, which were to have been named *Conqueror*, *Lion*, *Thunderer* and *Temeraire*, were never built. Only one British battleship was laid down during the war, in 1941; she was HMS *Vanguard*, also an enlarged 'King George V' type battleship of 45,215 tonnes (44,500 tons). Launched in 1944, she was commissioned too late to see service in World War II. Her four twin turrets mounted 380mm (15in) guns originally used in the light battlecruisers *Courageous* and *Glorious* before their conversion to aircraft carriers; she also carried 16 133mm (5.25in) guns and a very heavy AA armament of 71 40mm (1.6in) Bofors guns. She carried a complement of 1600. In 1947 she made a royal tour to South Africa and in 1949 served briefly in the Mediterranean before being placed on the reserve in 1956. She was decommissioned and sent to the breaker's yard at Faslane in 1960, the last battleship to serve in the Royal Navy. At one point in her short career, in 1953, *Vanguard* exercised with the American battleships *Iowa* and *Wisconsin* in the Atlantic. It was the last time that an Anglo-American battleship force put to sea together.

EUROPEAN DECOMMISSIONING

France continued to operate her two battleships, the *Richelieu* and the *Jean Bart*, for some years after the war. The former was used for fire support duty during French operations in Indo-China in 1945–6; she was placed in reserve in 1956 and broken up in 1960. The *Jean Bart*, damaged at Casablanca by gunfire from the USS *Massachusetts* and air attack in November 1942, was towed to Cherbourg after the war and completed at Brest. In 1956 she operated in support of ground forces and in an anti-aircraft role during the Anglo-French operations in the Suez Canal zone. From 1961 she was used as a gunnery training ship, being broken up in 1970.

Of the Italian battleships that had surrendered to the Allies in 1943, two, the *Littorio* and *Vittorio Veneto*, were interned until February 1946, when they were returned to Italy. Both were stricken in 1948 and broken up in 1960. The *Andria Doria*, after internment at Malta, was briefly used as a training ship by the Italian Co-Belligerent Navy in 1944 before being inactivated. Reactivated in 1949, she was once again used for training until 1956, when she was stricken. She was broken up at La Spezia in 1961, where the *Caio Duilio*, also interned at Malta and subsequently used for training, had been broken up in 1957. Italy's other battleship, the *Giulio Cesare*, was transferred to the Soviet Union under peace treaty terms in 1948 and renamed *Novorossisk*. Assigned to the Black Sea Fleet, she blew up and sank in Sevastopol harbour on 4 November 1955. The next Soviet warship to bear the name was a 'Kiev' class aircraft carrier.

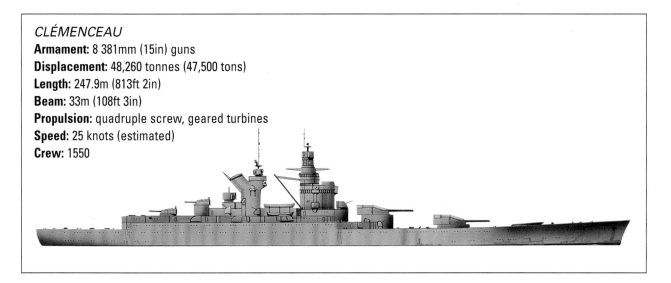

CLÉMENCEAU
Armament: 8 381mm (15in) guns
Displacement: 48,260 tonnes (47,500 tons)
Length: 247.9m (813ft 2in)
Beam: 33m (108ft 3in)
Propulsion: quadruple screw, geared turbines
Speed: 25 knots (estimated)
Crew: 1550

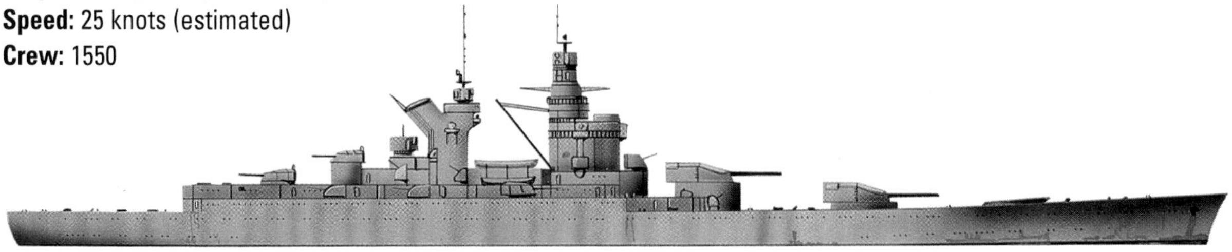

Above: The French battleship *Clémenceau* was only 10 per cent completed when the Germans occupied Brest in June 1940. The hull was simply designated 'R'.

Below: The *Richelieu*'s sister ships were the *Jean Bart* and *Clémenceau.* Though launched, the latter was never completed and her hull sunk by British aircraft in 1944.

ADMIRAL USHAKOV (EX-KIROV)
Armament: 20 SS-N-19 SSM
Displacement: 24,385 tonnes (24,000 tons)
Length: 248m (813ft 8in)
Beam: 28m (91ft 10in)
Propulsion: twin shaft, two nuclear reactors with combined superheating boilers
Speed: 30 knots
Crew: 800

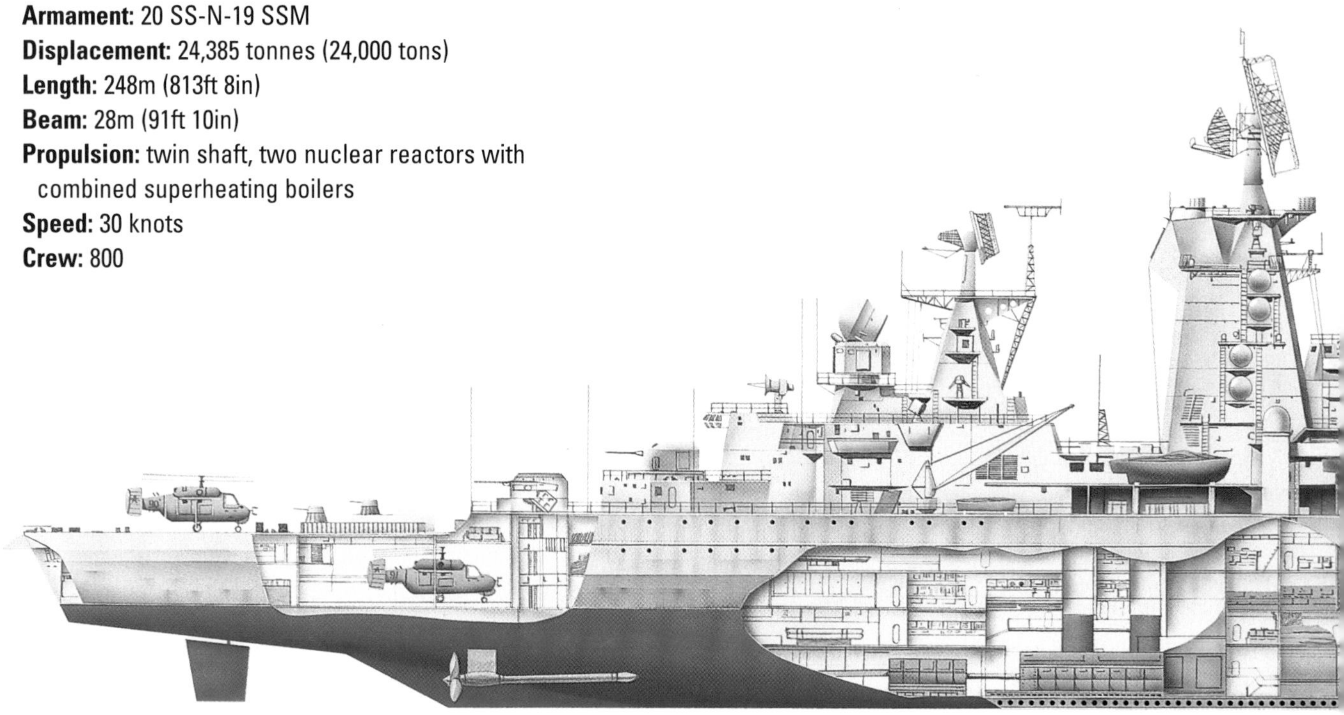

Above: The Russian nuclear-powered guided missile cruiser *Kirov* (as she then was) came as a considerable surprise to NATO when she first appeared in 1981.

SOVIET BATTLESHIPS

The Russians laid down four new battleships in 1937; they were the *Sovietski Soyuz, Sovietskaya Bielorossia, Sovietskaya Rossia,* and *Sovietskaya Ukraina.* Difficulties in obtaining construction materials, seriously delayed the building programme, and two were abandoned in 1940. The *Sovietski Soyuz* was ready for launching when the German invasion of June 1941 brought a halt to further work on her, and she was broken up on the slip in 1948–50. The *Sovietskaya Ukraina* was 75 per cent complete when she was captured by the Germans at Nikolayev; they destroyed the slip to prevent her being launched after their retreat from the Crimea and she was broken up between 1944–7.

The Soviet Navy consequently had only three indigenous battleships in commission during World War II, all belonging to the 'Gangut' class of 1908 dreadnoughts. One of these, the *Marat* (formerly the *Petropavlovsk*) was severely damaged on 23 September 1941 during an attack on Kronstadt harbour by Ju 87 Stuka dive-bombers, her bow and 'A' turret being destroyed and resting on the bottom. Refloated in 1943, she became a training ship, renamed *Volkhov*, and was broken up in 1953.

The second battleship, the *Oktyabrskaya Revolutsia*, was the original *Gangut*, having been renamed in 1925. She was used for bombardment duty during the brief winter war with Finland in 1939–40, and later in the defence of Leningrad. During the 23 September 1941 air attack on Kronstadt she was hit by six bombs and severely damaged, and on 4 April 1942 she was hit by another four bombs. She was broken up at Kronstadt in 1956–9.

That left the *Sevastopol*, which was named the *Parizhskaya Kummuna* from 1921–43, when she reverted to her original nomenclature. Serving with the Black Sea Fleet, she was used in the defence of Sevastopol in 1941–2. Damaged by German air attack in September 1942, she was not repaired until 1946, being broken up in 1957.

In May 1944 the British battleship *Royal Sovereign* was loaned to the Soviet Navy and renamed *Archangelsk*. In service with the Arctic Fleet, she went aground and was damaged in the Barents Sea in 1947. In February 1949 she was returned to Great Britain and broken up. The Russians also planned to build two 39,036-tonne (38,420-ton) battlecruisers,

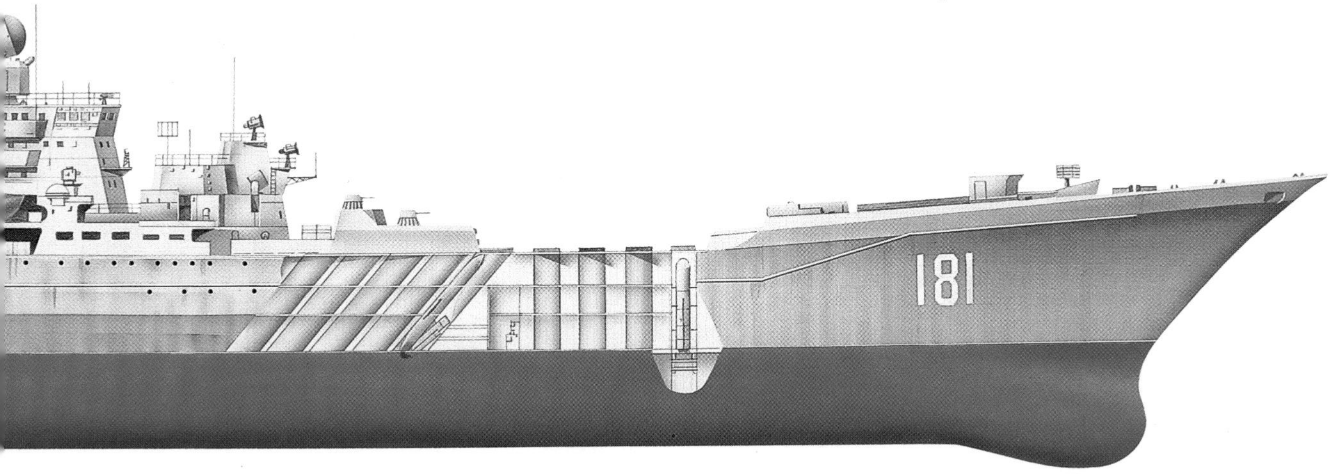

the *Moskva* and *Stalingrad*, during World War II, but construction only began after the war and was abandoned following a change in policy. The *Moskva* was broken up on the stocks in 1954 and the *Stalingrad*, launched in 1953 when 60 per cent complete, was used for weapons trials before being grounded off the Crimea in 1954 to end her days as a target ship.

The Russians, however, still had a surprise up their sleeve. In December 1977, the Soviet Navy – which by then had expanded its operations worldwide to become a true 'blue water' fleet, launched the *Kirov*, the largest warship built by any nation since World War II apart from aircraft carriers. Designated *Raketnyy Kreyser*, or missile cruiser, the 24,385-tonne (24,000-ton) vessel was more akin, in terms of appearance and firepower, to the obsolete battlecruis-

Below: The Italian *Littorio*, damaged at Taranto, was damaged twice more by air attack in 1942. In 1943 she was renamed the *Italia*, and surrendered to the Allies.

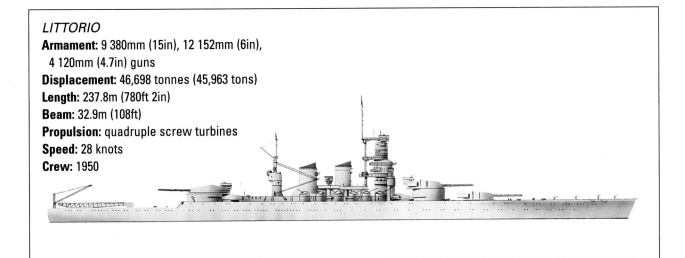

LITTORIO
Armament: 9 380mm (15in), 12 152mm (6in), 4 120mm (4.7in) guns
Displacement: 46,698 tonnes (45,963 tons)
Length: 237.8m (780ft 2in)
Beam: 32.9m (108ft)
Propulsion: quadruple screw turbines
Speed: 28 knots
Crew: 1950

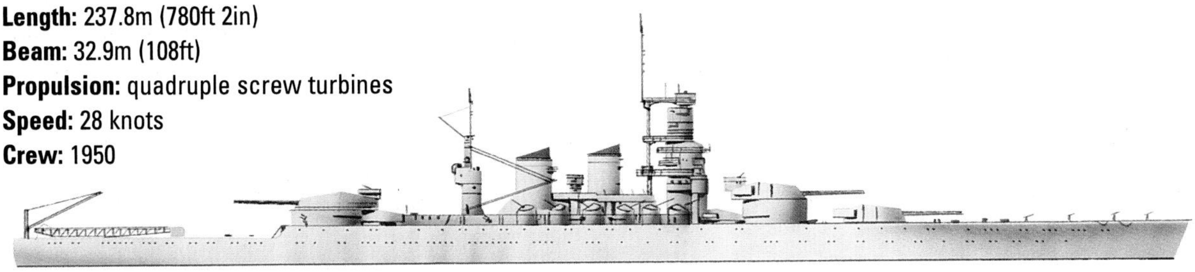

er category. *Kirov* and her sister ships, *Frunze, Kalinin,* and *Yuri Andropov* are unique in that their powerplant is a combined nuclear and steam propulsion system, with two reactors coupled to oil-fired boilers that superheat the steam produced in the reactor plant to increase the power output available during high-speed running. The *Kirov* carries the heaviest armament of any Russian warship. She was renamed the *Admiral Ushakov* in May 1992, after the collapse of the Soviet Union.

THE POST-WAR US NAVY

Of the US Navy's old reconstructed dreadnoughts, the USS *Nevada, Pennsylvania, New York* and *Arkansas* were used as target ships in the American nuclear tests at Bikini. The *Arkansas* was sunk in the second test on 25 July 1946; the *Nevada, Pennsylvania* and *New York* all survived, to be decommissioned in 1946 and finally sunk as targets by aircraft and gunfire off Hawaii and Kwajalein in July 1948. (As a matter of interest, the German heavy cruiser *Prinz Eugen*, consort of the ill-fated *Bismarck*, also survived the nuclear blasts and was sunk as a target off Kwajalein in November 1947.)

Of the two 'New Mexico' class battleships, *Idaho* was decommissioned in 1946 and broken up in the following year. *Mississippi* served on for some years after the war as a training and experimental gunnery ship before being deactivated and broken up in 1956.

Tennessee and *California* were both decommissioned in 1947 and broken up in 1959, as were *Colorado, Maryland* and *West Virginia. North Carolina* had a better fate; in 1961 she was transferred to the care of the State after which she was named and preserved as a memorial at Wilmington. There was no such happy outcome for the USS *Washington*, which was broken up in 1961.

THE 'IOWA' CLASS

The *Alabama* was also preserved at Mobile by her State, and *Massachusetts* became a memorial at Fall River, but *South Dakota* went to the breaker's yard in 1962 and *Indiana* followed her a year later. Now only the four powerful 'Iowa' class remained. Their careers, however, were far from over, and they were to be given the chance to see active service again in several conflicts around the world.

Right: Still bearing her original name *Kirov*, the *Admiral Ushakov* is seen moored across the jetty from the 'Slava' class cruiser *Marshal Ustinov* in July 1992.

КИРОВ
1513

All but the *Missouri* had been deactivated in 1948–9. The *Missouri*, the ship on which Japan's surrender had been accepted by General Douglas MacArthur on behalf of the Allies in Tokyo Bay on 2 September 1945, served with the Atlantic Fleet until 1950. She suffered a mishap in January of that year when she went aground on Thimble Shoal, Chesapeake Bay. She was refloated a fortnight later and deployed to Korean waters for bombardment duty. In 1951–2 she served once again with the Atlantic Fleet, before returning to Korea for another tour of duty. She was then decommissioned in 1955.

THE KOREAN WAR

The Korean War also brought about the reactivation of the other three battleships. On 15 March 1952 the *Wisconsin* was damaged by a shell from North Korean shore batteries. Returning to the Atlantic Fleet, she was badly damaged in a collision with the destroyer USS *Eaton* and was repaired with the bow section of another 'Iowa' class vessel, the *Kentucky*. The *Kentucky* had been laid down in 1944, and had been scheduled to commission in September 1946, but work on her was suspended when she was 69 per cent complete. She was launched in January 1950, simply to clear the slipway, and in 1954 she went aground in James River during a hurricane. She was broken up in 1958 after being used as a target. The *Wisconsin* was also decommissioned in 1958.

VIETNAM

The *Iowa* and *New Jersey* came through their tours of duty in Korean waters unscathed, and both warships subsequently served with the Atlantic Fleet before being decommissioned in 1957–8. The *New Jersey*, however, was not destined to remain in mothballs for long. On 6 April 1967 she began her second reactivation refit for active service off Vietnam as a fire support ship. During this deployment she spent 120 days on the 'gun line', firing 5688 406mm (16in) rounds and 14,891 127mm (5in) rounds at various targets. The Mk7 Mod 0 guns, mounted in the *New Jersey*'s three 1735-tonne (1708-ton) triple turrets were the largest-calibre naval guns in existence, each gun weighing 108,479kg (239,156lb) without its breech block. A crew of 77 men was needed to serve each gun mount, plus an additional 30–36 men in the magazines. The ammunition fired was either High-Capacity High Explosive (HCHE) or Armour-Piercing (AP), the latter being capable of penetrating up to 9m (29ft 5in) of reinforced concrete or 559mm (22in) of armour plate. The battleship had a magazine load of 1220 projectiles. The guns proved highly accurate, capable of hitting targets in direct support of ground troops and others which were heavily defended and inland. Maximum range with HCHE was 38km (23.6 miles) and 36.7km (22.8 miles) with AP.

REBIRTH OF THE 'IOWA' CLASS

In 1969 *New Jersey* fell foul of economy measures and was once more deactivated and mothballed along with the other three ships. By the 1970s the four battleships were considered to be little more than relics from a past age, but in 1980 the need to augment the US surface combat fleet and match new classes of Soviet warships resulted in Congress approving funds

Left: The USS *Iowa* firing her 406mm (16in) guns in a broadside. Her main gun turrets were protected by 241-432mm (9.5-17in) of armour plating.

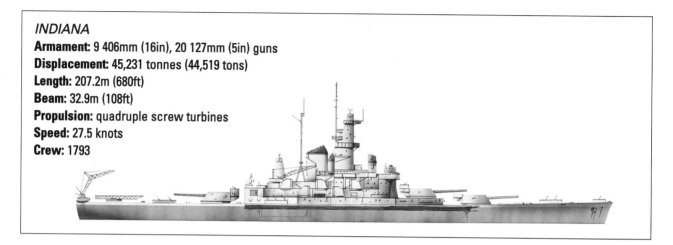

INDIANA
Armament: 9 406mm (16in), 20 127mm (5in) guns
Displacement: 45,231 tonnes (44,519 tons)
Length: 207.2m (680ft)
Beam: 32.9m (108ft)
Propulsion: quadruple screw turbines
Speed: 27.5 knots
Crew: 1793

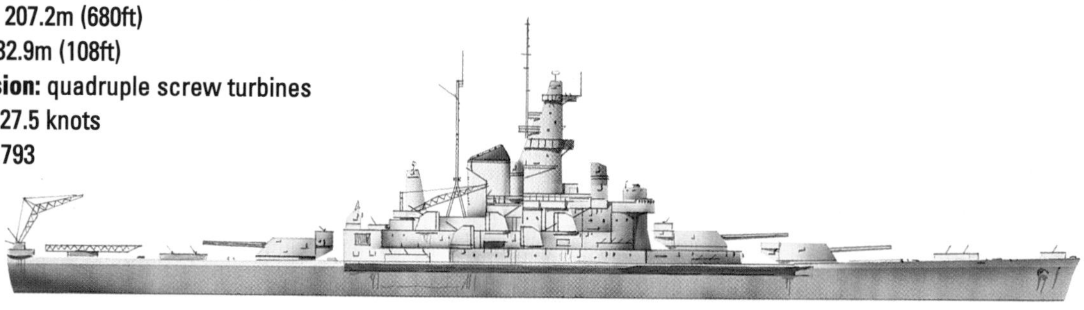

Above: The 'South Dakota' class *Indiana* was completed in April 1942 and subsequently took part in all the Pacific naval campaigns. She was decommissioned in 1947.

to reactivate the battleship force. After much heated debate, the New Jersey was modernised and recommissioned on 27 December 1982, beginning her first operational deployment with the Pacific Fleet in March 1983. By the end of that year she had served as part of the task forces deployed off the Nicaraguan coasts in response to a crisis, and in December off the Lebanon, where she used her formidable armament to bombard Syrian anti-aircraft positions that had fired on US Navy reconnaissance aircraft supporting US Marine Corps units operating ashore.

Starting with *New Jersey*, all four of the 'Iowa' class underwent a modernisation programme costing nearly $1500 million in the mid-1980s. The vessels received new fire control and multi-functional radar systems; Tomahawk and Harpoon cruise missiles; and upgraded communications gear, including WSC-3 SATCOM equipment. In 1989, an explosion in one of

Below: The USS *New Jersey* launching a Tomahawk cruise missile. She was the first US battleship to be fitted with the system.

Above: The USS Missouri, nicknamed 'Mighty Mo', seen here during the Korean War, bombarding Chinese communist lines of communication at Chong Jin.

Below: USS *Iowa* in passage through the Panama Canal. The photograph well illustrates the battleship's size, and her helipad is clearly visible at the stern.

Above: All four 'North Carolina' class battleships carried the Israeli-built Pioneer remotely-piloted vehicle, seen here aboard the USS *Missouri* during the Gulf War.

Iowa's 406mm (16in) gun turrets killed 47 officers and men. Although the accident's cause was never established for certain, an investigation showed that the most likely cause was that a detonating device had been placed between powder bags in the gun magazine. Plans to repair the turret were deferred when it was decided that *Iowa* and *New Jersey* would be mothballed in 1991. In fact, *Iowa* was paid off in October 1990 and *New Jersey* in February 1991.

A FINAL HURRAH

Missouri and *Wisconsin*, however, remained active, and both were deployed in support of Coalition operations in the Gulf during the Desert Shield/Desert Storm in 1990–1, firing their cruise missiles at targets in Iraq. From her station in the Red Sea, the *Wisconsin* fired dozens of BGM-109 cruise missiles during the opening phase of Desert Storm, while *Missouri* sailed into the Gulf to join other Coalition warships shelling Iraqi positions in Kuwait. Initially, the ships fired from a range of 30km (18.6 miles), but with the threat from Iraqi Silkworm anti-ship missiles removed by air attack they closed in to 20km (12.4 miles), at which range their gunnery was immensely effective. On the night of 25 February 1991, the Iraqis launched two Silkworms at the *Missouri* from an undetected site, but these were destroyed by Sea Dart missiles fired by one of the Royal Navy's Type 42 'goalkeeper' destroyers, HMS *London*.

FITTING MEMORIALS

So the era of the battleship came to an end; but for the 'Iowa' class there was not to be the final indignity of the breaker's yard. Under the US Navy's 'homeporting' programme, *Iowa*'s final resting place is at Staten Island, New York, together with other ships. *Wisconsin* lies at Corpus Christi, Texas, and *New Jersey* at Long Beach, California. As for *Missouri*, fittingly she is a permanent memorial to a lost generation of warships – at Pearl Harbor.

Index

Page references in *italics* refer to illustrations.